D0732748

SAINTLY
MEN
OF
MODERN TIMES

SAINTLY MEN OF MODERN TIMES

JOAN CARROLL CRUZ

OUR SUNDAY VISITOR PUBLISHING DIVISION
OUR SUNDAY VISITOR, INC.
HUNTINGTON, INDIANA 46750

Our Sunday Visitor Publishing Division
Our Sunday Visitor, Inc.
200 Noll Plaza
Huntington, IN 46750

ISBN: 1-931709-77-7 (Inventory No. T43)
LCCN: 2002115705

Cover design by Troy Lefevra
Interior photos are used with permission
Interior design by Robert L. Hoffman

PRINTED IN THE UNITED STATES OF AMERICA

"Would that at the present day there were many more who cultivated the virtues as did the saints of former times, who by their humility, their obedience, their self-restraint, were mighty in work and word to the great benefit not only of religion,
but also of public and civil life."

Pope Leo XIII

Table of Contents

Martyrs of the Spanish Persecution

Acknowledgments

With heartfelt gratitude, I must first thank the Rev. Bozidar Nagy, S.J., in Rome for his many kindnesses, his generosity, his helpfulness, and his friendship that means so much to me. I am deeply grateful.

Also to the Rev. Redemptus Valabek, O. Carm.; Rev. Paola Molinari, S.J. of Rome; Rev. Joel Francis Victorino of the Philippines; Ms. Vera Valcic-Belic and Vlasta Molinar; Archbishop Gabriel Montalvo; Msgr. Michal Jagosz, P.A.; Msgr. James A. Kelly; Msgr. Anthony Chirayath; Msgr. Tommaso Giussani; Msgr. Flavio Capucci; Rev. Hernan Arboleda, C.SS.R.; Rev. Armando Oberti; Fr. John Gueguen, O.M.I.; Rev. Tito M. Sartori; Rev. Lucio Migliaccio, O.M.D.; Rev. Antonius Saez de Albeniz, O.SS.T.; Rev. Lucio De Stefano, M.S.C.; Rdo. Ricardo Aviao; Rev. Jose Vogt; Rev. A. Oberti; General Curia for Alcide de Gasperi; Rev. Armandi; Rev. Giovanni Zubiani, C.P.; Rev. Paul Lombardo, O.F.M.; Rev. Ambrose Sanna; Rev. Simeon of the Holy Family; Rev. Antonio S. Sospedra y Buye, C.P.C.R.; Rev. DiRaimondo, M.Sp.S.; Rev. Giovanni Zubiani, C.P.; Rev. Pasquale Liberatore; Rev. Lopez Quintas; Rev. Andres Wildhaber; Rev. Alfonso Bielza; Rev. Mario Mesa; Dele S. Aguilo; Rev. Luca M. De Rosa, O.F.M.; Rev. Antonio Ascenzi; Rev. Fernando Rojo Martinez, O.S.A.; Rev. Giovannino Tolu; Rev. Cristoforo Zambelli, O.F.M.Conv.; Rev. Jose Maria Salaverri; Rev. Pasquale Liberatore, and Rev. Antonio Sospedra.

Ann Ball, Francesca Rugglero; Marco Lora of Ufficio Famiglia; Andre Tambi; Dominique Stolz; Maria Chiara e le Ancelle, M.M.; Maria Bertoni of the Instituto Secolare Ancelle Mater Misericordiae; Chris Meadows; the Beatification Committee of Luigi Rocchi; the Circulo Carlos M. Rodriguez; Sr. M. Agnes and Mrs. Marie Walsh of County Cork, Ireland; Mr. John Gavin of the Concilium Legionis Mariae in Ireland and the Prelatura del Opus Dei.

May God bless and reward all of them for their kindness and helpfulness.

Foreword

The Church has been graced with a bountiful array of saints but, as we know, the majority are nuns and priests. By comparison, we have only a small fraction of lay men and women who were declared by the Church as having merited the honors of the altar. Since we are encouraged to imitate the virtues of the saints, wouldn't it seem more appropriate if we had models of holiness who lived outside the cloister in the secular world, saints who endured the struggles and difficulties of every day life as we are encountering in secular surroundings? As St. Teresa of Ávila has written, "We need to cultivate and think upon, and seek the companionship of those saints who, though living on earth like ourselves, have accomplished such great deeds for God."

In my book, *Secular Saints,* examples were given of almost 250 lay men and women who, if not already canonized, were on their way to canonization. They came from the early days of the Church, through the ages, to the present day. In this volume we have only twentieth century saints, many of whom drove cars and used telephones. Some even had television sets as well as many other modern conveniences. All lived and died in the last century with the exception of the following who died in the latter part of the nineteenth century: Frederic Ozanam, founder of the St. Vincent de Paul Society; Leo DuPont, who promoted the Holy Face Devotion; and Pierre Toussaint, a former slave. Their stories are too inspiring to be omitted.

It is hoped that the reader will examine the Appendix, which gives the occupations and the difficulties of life and health encountered by these holy people. By making use of the appendix, the reader may find saints with whom to relate, saints who had a similar occupation or those who experienced the same difficulties or illnesses as the reader is now enduring.

We have here biographies of laymen representing many countries worldwide who are on their way to canonization. They are from such diverse occupations as a horse trader, a prime minister, a ship designer, two fireworks technicians, a judge, and a surveyor, among many other professions. All knew that sanctity could be achieved in the ordinary events of daily life.

An explanation should be given about the various titles.

Servant of God: After five years have elapsed since death, and after the bishop of the diocese officially opens the Cause of beatification, the candidate may be called a Servant of God.

Venerable: After the Congregation for the Causes of Saints receives the case, examines it, and determines that the case has merit, a number of preliminary steps are taken. When completed, a *Decree super Virtutibus* is issued which gives the Servant of God the title of Venerable.

Blessed: Once a miracle, worked through the intercession of the Venerable, has been canonically investigated and approved, this, together with the Decree of Heroic Virtues, is passed to the Holy Father who decides on beatification. After the ceremony of beatification has been held, the Venerable is now given the title of Blessed.

Saint: For canonization, another miracle performed *after* the beatification ceremony is required. After the miracle has been canonically investigated and approved, the pope may perform a canonization ceremony, after which the Blessed is now given the title of Saint.

NOTE: Those without a title are holy persons whose cases are still on the diocesan level, but whose Causes are expected to be officially opened in the near future.

This is the first book in a series of three. The second volume will focus on saintly women and the third on saintly children. The sole purpose in writing these books was to demonstrate to people in every walk of life the virtues practiced and the cares and sufferings endured by laypeople who are now on their way to canonization. Those who have difficulties, and those who are suffering, have examples here of holy people who have had the same struggles and difficulties, and that it was because of these hardships, endured with prayer and confidence in God, that they attained holiness.

How did they do it? Here then, are their stories.

JOAN CARROLL CRUZ

Venerable Albert Marvelli
1918 – 1946
Engineer
Italy

Albert Marvelli was born in Ferrara at the end of the First World War to Alfred Luigi, the manager of a bank in Rovigno and Maria Marvelli, a woman of a high social situation. Of their five sons and one daughter, Albert was the second born. The Marvellis were financially secure and of high social standing. Because of the father's work, the family transferred to various cities in Italy, finally settling in Rimini, where they lived in a villa that had been built by the mother's brother.

Albert's father, Alfred, left a deep impression on his young son. A decent and honest man, Alfred was busy in Catholic movements and served as parish president of the Society of St. Vincent de Paul. When the facist regime closed Alfred's bank, he returned all the money the depositors lost by subtracting the lost amount from his own savings and the money he inherited. Albert wrote in his diary: "I will never forget the exemplary life of my father who lived calmly and piously during the painful moments of his life. He was a complete Christian without half measures, without ostentation, sincere, smiling, always in grace."

Alfred was often absent because of his work, so the care of the children fell primarily to their mother, Maria. She, too, was a heroic example to her children; she was a deeply devout woman who put charity into action by working in the women's division of Catholic Action and the Society of St. Vincent de Paul. After the death of her husband, Maria was an inexhaustible source of love, and she raised her six children in the love and practice of their Catholic faith. She also saw to it that each child received a university education.

As a child, Albert was described as a dynamo, full of energy and always prepared to defend the defenseless. He got along well with his friends and loved every type of sport, especially bicycling. His passion and skill in this sport was to serve him well during the Second World War.

The well-known film director Federico Fellini was a schoolmate of Albert's: "I remember well Marvelli. He was a blonde child with a sweet personality. We had been classmates since the elementary grades. My mother pointed him out as a good child and a model pupil."

Albert was not yet fifteen years old when his father died of meningitis. Because his oldest brother was in the military, Albert became the head of the family, a designation he accepted with concern and scrupulous care. Albert began to keep a diary of his thoughts, his complaints, and his prayers in a school notebook. It began with the words, "God is great! Infinitely great and infinitely good." After his father's death, Albert showed a substantial increase in spirituality, which affected every part of his life.

Albert completed high school in 1936, graduating second in a class of sixty. He set a daily plan for himself that included a morning meditation and another in the evening, a daily Rosary, the daily reception of the Eucharist and a nightly examination of conscience. He also included in his routine plans "to inflict on myself some physical pain," meaning the practice of penance.

At university, Albert applied himself with great dedication, often studying to the early morning hours. When he could, he worked in the

Catholic Action. His fellow workers "were stricken with his purity, affability, and availability." His friends always remembered him as being calm with a strong personality that imposed respect. One professor wrote that he often saw Albert entering the church of St. Bartholomew in Bologna to attend Mass and receive the Holy Eucharist. In his diary that was published after his death, Albert once wrote: "This morning after Holy Communion I consecrated my heart to the Immaculate Madonna praying that she will maintain me in purity and virtue. Please help me to be good, compliant, patient, benevolent."

After reading the life of St. Domenic Savio, Albert adopted the motto: "Death but not sin." He added, "Jesus, rather to die than to sin. Help me to keep this promise."

While at the university, Albert performed in a play "The Passion of Christ" in which he played the part of a Roman soldier. Albert's part called for him to kneel in front of the flagellated Christ and ask, "What have they done to you?" Albert, who was a very handsome young man in his beautiful uniform costume, so impressed the audience with his realistic performance that many began to cry. Albert admitted: "I am not ashamed to say that I also cried." He finished his university courses in 1941, earning a degree in industrial engineering. After graduation, he began working for the Fiat Company in Turin.

Albert also joined the Salesian Order as a secular member and began working with boys, teaching them catechism and showing particular attention to those youngsters who were not as athletic in games as the others were. Albert loved the Salesians and they loved him for his witticism and his ability to impress the youngsters with his deep spirituality. When he could, Albert returned to his work with the Catholic Action. He proved himself a good organizer, and he was soon elected vice-president of his group. He worked intensely in evangelizing nearby parishes through evening and Sunday meetings that received the respect of the priests and the fervor of the young. The apostolate was his primary concern. His friends exhorted him not to work so hard, but he replied, "The time employed in the apostolate helps me to pray and it lightens my family and professional duties."

Albert also served in the military. A fellow soldier tells that during their training the men had to carry heavy devices on their shoulders while they climbed a difficult path up a mountain. Albert saw a fellow soldier struggling under the heavy load, and drew near to the man. In an inconspicuous way, Albert helped the soldier carry his heavy load. When they reached the end of the path, as the soldier turned to thank him, he found Albert had already moved away. During training, Albert was known to sacrifice sleep to be able to attend early Mass almost every day.

During World War II, an atheistic colonel, noting the Christian climate that Albert inspired among the soldiers, said: "The life of Alberto is an action of the love of God." One of Albert's main objectives at the time was to save as many young people as he could who otherwise would have been on their way to the concentration camps. He is known to have helped a group of young people escape from a train bound for such a camp.

Albert's mother's maiden name was German, and since he knew a good deal of the language, he got along well with the Germans. Albert took advantage of the situation, and in a bold move, secured false documents for some of the young men who worked as slaves building roads and shelters for the Germans. Many of the young men escaped, but Albert's efforts were discovered. He was seized and thrown in prison. He managed to escape, and worked to help others do the same. In particular, Albert helped several nuns who were housing forty homeless boys. He brought them all to safety and carried provisions to them on his overly burdened bicycle.

On January 28, 1944, the Cathedral of Rimini was bombed, and neighboring houses were reduced to rubble. Albert helped the injured, encouraged the survivors, and assisted the dying. At the end of the day he went home, covered with the blood of those he had helped, and took his family to safety in the Republic of San Marino. Albert went back to Rimini. A priest tells that once, during another bombardment, a bomb again struck the cathedral and the house of the nuns. After the bombardment, Albert went about on his bicycle, seeking survivors in the damaged buildings. When he discovered the tabernacle of the church, which contained the consecrated hosts, lying in the mud, he crawled under the collapsing timbers of the church to rescue it. Albert took the tabernacle to a room of the Salesian Institute for safekeeping. The priest who related this event pointed out how dangerous a thing this was for Albert to do, and yet Albert bravely rescued the Eucharist that he so dearly loved.

Eventually Albert became known as the mayor of charity. He traveled about on his bicycle, distributing bread and clothing to those who implored his help.

A Franciscan nun reported, "During the war I saw Marvelli arrive at midday, poorly dressed, with wood clogs on his feet pushing a wheelbarrow. He stopped by me and tried to repair some ropes I was working with. I told him that it was dangerous to go around during the frequent aerial raids, but he answered, 'When there is necessity the risk is needed.' "

One day, two undernourished soldiers, having escaped the Germans, arrived in Rimini. Albert noticed that one of them was barefoot. Shoes were not available — except those on Albert's feet. Without hesitation, Albert removed his shoes and gave them to the awestruck soldier.

Through a local hotel Albert organized the distribution of warm soup to the children and the suffering. He distributed mattresses to those who had been sleeping on the ground, and he administered medicines to the sick. In the evenings, he went to the railroad station where crowds were coming and going and asked many to join him in reciting the Rosary. At night, he slept in a room at the Franciscan convent. Every morning he would rise early to participate in the Mass, deriving his energies from the Holy Eucharist. The acts of charity he performed during the war are many, and a good number have been recorded.

When the Germans withdrew from Italy and the Allies entered, the people who had been in hiding returned to their homes. Rimini suffered an estimated 300 bombardments, and since Rimini is located on the northeastern part of Italy on the Adriatic Sea, both the town and the surrounding areas were subjected to fifteen naval attacks. The devastation was extensive. Albert found his family's villa badly damaged, but with the help of others, he eventually repaired it.

The Allied troops instigated an offensive near Rimini on September 20, 1944. With a few friends and a white flag in his hand, Albert went to the Allied forces' camp. He convinced the troops that the Germans had left, and in so doing, he avoided further artillery fire that would have caused greater death and destruction in Rimini.

After the war came the difficulty of reconstruction. Albert, as an industrial engineer, was placed in various positions of responsibility to help organize the rebuilding of the city. He was assigned to the city council, and was one of the first to join the Christian Democratic Party. He served other civil institutions as well, and he performed his duties with scrupulous generosity and competence. For this reason he is sometimes called the "Constructor of the City of God."

During this time Albert's brother Charles stayed with him. Charles relates: "I slept in the same room with him. Sometimes, waking up in the middle of the night, I usually found him toward three in the morning, kneeling close to the bed where he had fallen asleep on his knees. I would call to him to get into bed . . . he never neglected to recite the Rosary."

One day, a lady who had received a great assistance from Albert during the war approached him, asking how she could thank him for all he had done to relieve her suffering. Albert replied, "Pray that God will make me a saint. That is the greatest gift that you can do for me."

Albert was invited by the local bishop to take the presidency of the Catholic Graduates. Albert answered, "My graduates are the poor. This is my daily bread. I believe in this apostolate." In refusing the position, Albert wrote to the bishop asking his blessing to be able to be a "docile tool in your hands." Eventually, Albert accepted the position and organized lectures and functions in which many participated.

On October 5, 1946, the eve of the administrative elections, Albert was on his bicycle going to an electioneering meeting. He had eaten his dinner and had spent time in adoration before the Eucharist. He was traveling along the avenue Regina Elena when a speeding truck passed a trolley bus and then turned right, violently striking the rear wheel of Albert's bicycle. Albert was flung against a wall. The driver immediately disappeared into the night. Critically injured, Albert was transported to the Contarini House for medical care. "My children are so healthy that the Lord, when he calls them to Himself, will have to inflict a violent death," Albert's mother had said when Albert was just a child. With Albert, it was exactly that way. That night he received the last sacraments and died in his mother's arms. He was only twenty-eight years old.

One of the glowing tributes awarded Albert Marvelli came from the Servant of God George La Pira (whose biography is included in this book), who noted, "It is said that the church in Rimini can tell the new generations, 'Here, I show you what an authentic Christian life is in the world.' "

Because his reputation for holiness became so well known, the bishop of Rimini signed the decree in 1968 that began the first actions of the Cause of beatification. The decision was made to transfer the body, which is said to have been found incorrupt, from the city cemetery to the parish church of St. Augustine.

In the diocese of Rimini there is an organization, founded in memory of Albert, known as The Institute of Religious Sciences, Alberto Marvelli. The organization seeks to acquaint the laity "with a theological formation in order to promote the encounter between faith and the culture of our time."

The Holy Father, Pope John Paul II, gave Albert Marvelli the title of Venerable on March 22, 1986.

Venerable Alberto Capellan Zuazo
1888 – 1965
Farmer, Father of Eight
Spain

All of central Spain rejoiced when native son Alberto Capellan Zuazo's Cause was introduced. This pious farmer and father of eight would finally receive recognition for his quiet sanctity, his many charities, and for his devotion to Nocturnal Eucharistic Adoration.

Alberto was born in Santo Domingo de la Calzada. In medieval times, St. Dominic visited the town and built a hospital in the area for the countless pilgrims who passed through on their way to Compostella, the shrine where the relics of St. James the Apostle were kept. This area that bears the saint's name remains primarily farm country.

As a young boy, Alberto liked to serve Mass in the neighboring church of St. Francisco. He claimed to be a poor student, but he excelled at one thing: dancing. At the age of twelve, he joined a group of folk dancers and danced at the festival commemorating the beatification of Jeronimo de Hermosilla. He danced with the folk group for the last time in 1906, at the age of eighteen.

Alberto was definitely a normal teenager, sometimes full of mischief. For example, once, after accompanying his date to her home, he met his friends and, as young people will do, they made a great deal of noise. They made so much noise the entire group of boys went to jail for the night. Another time, when his allowance did not meet the expenses of his little adventures, he "lifted" a sack of wheat from the family barn. His mother saw him leave with it and ordered it back where it belonged.

One of his transgressions troubled his conscience for a long time. On his way to work in the field, the mules pulling his rickety cart became frightened, and in their excitement overturned everything. Alberto found himself under the cart, unhurt, but furious. As he looked into the sky, he blasphemed against God, the Blessed Virgin, and all the saints. He later deeply regretted his words, especially since it was Holy Thursday.

When three dance halls opened in Santo Domingo, Alberto soon became well known as one of their most devoted patrons. The places especially fascinated the local youth because they were so colorful and brightly illuminated. Alberto admitted he liked to dance with pretty girls, especially those that danced well. Alberto also enjoyed the bull-fights: "I liked everything, even the amateur bullfights which I attended with many of my friends."

Alberto became something of a Romeo. Tall with blue eyes, a lean body, and a proud walk, he attracted the attention of the local girls. When he was sixteen years old, he began to court the love of his life, Isabel Mahave. One night, in true Shakespearean fashion, he climbed a ladder to her window and spoke a few words to her. She was not amused, but to show his affection for her, he left a rose on the windowsill.

When Isabel decided to attend a dance with another boy, Alberto experienced what he called "criminal jealousy" when he found out that he had been spurned in favor of another. "I lost my reason and I left in search of a store where they sold weapons. I didn't discuss the price. I bought a big knife and retired to a dark solitary place waiting for them to leave the dance. In those unfortunate moments there was not in my head the thought of a crime or a rival's death." When Alberto saw Isabel and the other boy leave the dance, he stepped out of his hiding place. Two steps later he stopped, and realized his mistake. "I believe the hand of God stopped me."

By the time Alberto was twenty-one he had become more mature in his thinking and behavior, and he won out over his rivals. He and Isabel were married, and while married life calmed him for a time, within six months Alberto grew restless. He had consolidated his land with that of his father-in-law, and he found his work oppressive. He was subject to bad moods, "and discharged against my wife words and treatments that she did not deserve." There were also problems with the father-in-law in the payment of bills that added to the confusion. In spite of everything, Alberto became prosperous, "and every year it increased my small capital."

Alberto remarked that, in spite of his great income, "I lacked something to be happy. What? Simply, God was with me, but I was not with Him. My heart looked at the earth and little to the sky. That was the secret."

Almost all of what is known about Alberto comes from two school notebooks, which he started writing in 1943. He titled them modestly, "Notebook of notes for use of Alberto Capellan." A change in his soul occurred when a neighbor gave him a copy of the Catechism. This became obvious through his writings in his notes. The Catechism fascinated him, and when the finger of God touched his heart, he began to have "an abundance of spiritual comforts." God and the Blessed Virgin made him feel their presence in an intense way, and with the gift of their grace, his heart began to see the world in its proper perspective.

Alberto was a changed man. Now when he was plowing or returning from the fields, he thanked God for his goodness. Instead of his former compulsion to obtain more property and livestock, he sold the part of his land and livestock he thought unnecessary. Even though he had eight children, what remained was enough to support them and his wife. Forty years later, he admitted that he never regretted what he had done.

He wrote in his notebook, "Thanks to God I always maintained enough in the administration of the property and in the execution of my duties to care for my children and to provide them with humble careers and the means to live so that they never lacked bread for a single day." This grace he attributed to the goodness of God.

Alberto's first born, Gloria, became a renowned teacher; son Gerardo became a diocesan priest and worked as a missionary in Burundi; son Pablo works in the Bank of Biscay; and daughter Teresa became a Dominican nun in Peru. The others continued to work the country property. Despite the deaths of various family members and a financial setback as the result of a fire that destroyed his barn — with the entire harvest and many of his animals inside — Alberto held to his belief that God was with him. He continued to attend Mass at 5:30 every morning, before going into his fields to work.

Alberto gradually developed two great interests: night adoration and the love of the poor. He was impressed that other nighttime adorers were giving up part of their rest after a hard day's work to spend an hour in loving adoration before the Eucharist. He decided to do the same. The thirty-seven-year-old Alberto was soon elected president of the Nocturnal Adoration Society in his area, and he was re-elected president for eleven consecutive terms.

As for God's poor, Alberto became keenly aware of the many transients who gathered in front of the Claretian convent waiting to be fed. He wondered where they slept at night, especially in the winter, and he began offering his barn as a shelter. Some of the homeless declined, so Albert provided firewood to those who remained outside. Eventually Alberto constructed a building that he called the *Recogimiento*, meaning "the Collection" or "the Gathering." When bad weather destroyed the building, Alberto built a large two-story structure that stands today. Furnished with beds, blankets, and all that was needed, it became a hotel of charity for the needy. Alberto also opened his home to shepherd boys during the winter, and at night taught them the basics of reading, writing, and the first notions of arithmetic.

Alberto was often called to the homes of the poor. He is said to have responded immediately, and to have gone without complaint or hesitation. He wrote in his notebook, "How many times I have had the happiness, in certain circumstances, of taking Christ on my back, in the person of the poor." He was known to have carried the poor through mud and snow to his home or to the Collection to be properly cared for. Eventually, the city council voted a thank you "to the neighboring Alberto Capellan who unselfishly and without obligation picks up and aids the transient poor." For his part, Alberto said he "did not pay attention either to those who praise or to those who criticize, but only to God."

Alberto Capellan, a farmer without a complete education or any particular religious formation, experienced a life of deep spirituality and lived heroically in the home, church, and the fields. In his notebooks, Alberto kept a record of all the deceased and their dates of death. He once noted, "When I open the notebook, I look for those dates whose memories speak but to my soul: the parents, the friends and the pals of our youth's happiness."

When Alberto reached retirement age, he told his confessor that at eleven o'clock:

> . . . I usually reach for some book and I leave for two hours to walk to the mount, a place where no one usually passes. This satisfies me. Then such thoughts as these enter my mind: My God, what have I done to deserve your friendship? To deserve so many extraordinary attentions that make me feel the happiness of a premature heaven? What have I done for such a happiness of receiving you in my heart during Holy Communion and my visits? All is from God and without Him I am nothing . . . I am already old and my only illusion is the solitude where I sit down closely to God. I look at Him, and he looks at me.

Alberto experienced his first bout with angina, chest pains, when he was seventy-three. He said this was the beginning of his Purgatory. Eventually, he experienced a heart attack. He died quietly on February 24, 1965, at the age of seventy-seven, leaving one desire unfulfilled: to live with the poor. Alberto once said, "If Isabel dies before me, I will live with the poor."

Alberto's son Gerardo, who spent nine years as a missionary priest in Burundi, gave a glowing testimony of his father's life.

> We, all the children, were influenced mutually by the climate of faith that my father transmitted to the home. It influenced us a lot and maybe set in motion my vocation. . . . My father liked very much to walk alone in the fields and I believe in those moments of solitude and silence he experienced the life and love of God. . . . In those days we were given the impression that God was severe, but my father knew that God was merciful, understanding and a friend, and this greatly impressed us. . . .
>
> When a poor person arrived in Santo Domingo, they sent the person to my father, not to the parish, neither to the convents of the city. And the poor knew where to go, to the one who gave them security, assistance, and welcome. They knew that he would assist them and solve their problems. My father knew well that love of the needy summarizes the Gospel teachings. . . . From the time of his conversion he was faithful to his devotions, to the Angelus and the recitation of the daily Rosary.

Based on the entries in Alberto's notebooks, from the time of his conversion, he spent 660 vigils of adoration before the Blessed Sacrament. His zeal for this practice inspired many cities in Spain to adopt Nocturnal Adoration.

Alberto's Cause for beatification was introduced with the Congregation for the Causes of Saints issuing the *Decree super Virtutibus* in 1998.

Servant of God Alcide De Gasperi
1881 – 1954
Prime Minister of Italy
Austria/Italy

Alcide De Gasperi's interest in politics began early in the town of Pieve Tesino where he was born. When Alcide was eleven years old, the Reverend Vittorio Merler, a very active and sensitive priest who held an interest in the Agricultural Society of Catholic Workers, addressed his flock and described the Socialist Party as "deadly." Alcide's father Amedeo, who was an officer in the Austrian police, was present for the reverend's sermon, and was accused by his superiors of being unable to maintain the public peace. To defend himself, Amedeo had to apply to the local magistrate. The unfairness of the workings of the government system left a deep impression on Alcide.

Alcide attended the Episcopal school in Trento from age eleven to sixteen. While there, he entertained the possibility of entering the seminary, and he sought to regulate his life according to the canons of the most severe discipline. He engaged in personal and community prayer, went to confession weekly, and took Communion daily. He read spiritual works, withdrew periodically in religious retreat, and engaged in daily meditation. His interest in a priestly calling faded when he returned to his family.

After college, and because of his political interests, Alcide was offered the position of editor of the diocesan newspaper, *The Catholic Voice*, in which he would defend Italian culture and the economic interests of his own region. He considered his assignment on this newspaper not as a job, but as a vocation.

In 1911, when he was thirty, Alcide was elected to the Austrian parliament as an Italian representative, joining other Italian deputies who sought the annexation of Trentino to Italy. When the annexation of Trentino took place in 1921, Alcide was elected deputy to the Italian parliament as one of the founders of the Popular Italian Party, which represented the liberal Christian Democratic tradition.

The following year Alcide, now forty-one, took time from his political responsibilities to marry Francesca Romani on June 14, 1922. In 1923, the couple's first daughter, Maria Romana, was born, and she was followed by Lucy in 1925, Cecilia in 1930, and Paola in 1934.

Always hostile to the fascists and the dictatorship of Benito Mussolini, Alcide was arrested in 1926 and sentenced to four years imprisonment. In his cell in the Regina Coeli prison in Rome, he learned that his wife was confined in the women's prison, where she remained for twenty days with prostitutes and criminals. This grieved him deeply, since he was helpless to relieve the situation. Repeatedly in his letters, he mentioned the many times he pictured his weary wife before the judge in the courtroom with a broken rosary between her fingers.

During his imprisonment, Alcide considered himself a hermit, and he devoted his time to his spiritual advancement. His letters to his wife reveal his interior struggles, and they confirm the fact that he depended entirely on the mercy and help of God. Mercifully, Pope Pius XI intervened on Alcide's behalf, and he was released after serving sixteen months of his four-year sentence. Alcide was given asylum in the Vatican where he worked in the library.

During the Second World War, with the support of Roman Catholic organizations, Alcide established the Christian Democratic Party, a moderately conservative group that based its platform on the social teachings of the Roman Catholic Church. In December 1945, Alcide De Gasperi became Prime Minister of Italy, an office he held for eight years. As the prime minister, Alcide became the main architect of Italy's postwar, post-fascist recovery. Italian politics took a decisive turn in May 1947, when he excluded the socialist and communist parties from his government, and again in 1948 when he enacted a new constitution.

Prime Minister De Gasperi instituted long-term land reform programs in southern and central Italy and sought to increase utilization of Italy's natural resources by constructing new power plants fueled by natural gas or natural steam of volcanic origin. In foreign affairs, he worked to restore Italy's influential role in international politics by seeking closer ties with the West. Italy entered the North Atlantic Treaty Organization (NATO) in 1951 and began rearming shortly thereafter. He worked for the realization of the Marshall Plan and sought close economic ties with other European countries. He also supported the Schumann Plan for the foundation of a European coal and steel community and helped develop the idea of a common European defense policy.

One day, after debating in parliament, a colleague drew near and asked Alcide the secret of his successes. Alcide, while arranging his papers and without lifting his eyes responded, "The matter is the will of the Lord." This man who held such high offices in government still maintained a spirit of humility, knowing the need of always looking for and doing the will of God in all things. In a letter to his daughter Lucy he mentioned that he prayed always for a clearer understanding of God's wishes — he wanted none to be his own.

After the fall of his government in 1952, Alcide became secretary general of the Christian Democratic Party, which named him its president in May 1954. Alcide was in this post for only a few months when he became seriously ill. In Sella di Valsugana, with his family at his bedside, he repeated the name of Jesus three times and died peacefully. He was seventy-three.

Alcide left an indelible mark on the history of Italy. Sometime after his death, an organization was formed which bears the title, *The Foundation for Peace, An International Cooperation Alcide De Gasperi*. Pope John Paul II addressed this group on February 13, 1999, remarking: " . . . your Foundation, inspires itself to the thought and to the work of the great Italian statesman, Alcide De Gasperi, who engaged himself in promoting peace and cooperation between people, through the study of the problems of the international society and the connection with analogous present institutions in Europe and the world."

The Cause for the beatification of Alcide De Gasperi was introduced shortly after his death. The last action taken on his case was in 1993.

Servant of God Alphonsus "Alfie" Lambe
1932 – 1959
Legion of Mary Envoy
Ireland/South America

Alphonsus "Alfie" Lambe was barely twenty years old when he received permission from the Legion of Mary to emigrate to South America to establish Legion of Mary communities, called "praesidia," throughout South America. During the next six years, his zeal would set fire to a whole continent.

Alfie was born on June 24, 1932 into a farming family living in the town of Tullamore, Ireland. Alfie was blessed to be part of a family of genuine Christian devotion, and this devotion drew Alfie to all things religious. Although a sickly child, Alfie was always ready for fun. He loved to go rabbit hunting with his father and to roam through the fields of the Tullamore countryside.

When he was thirteen, Alfie declared his intention to become a Christian Brother and was received with forty-nine companions into the Christian Brothers' novitiate. He was an ideal novice, greatly attracted to the Blessed Mother, but shy and reserved about making friends. The year following his reception he was sent to St. Mary's Training College where he was diligent in his studies, participated in games despite his frailty, and read a great many books about the Mother of God. One thing alone was troubling: he suffered from fainting attacks. One day when he was delivering a lecture, he fainted. The doctor who was called declared that Alfie would never be able to endure the rigors of religious life and would certainly become seriously ill if he continued. Alfie was told to go back to his family, get well, and come back at another time.

The return to his home left him deeply depressed. Instead of working for God in the religious life, he now had to find satisfaction as an office worker in the secular world.

Alfie wanted to work for the Lord. He learned there was a praesidium, a group of the Legion of Mary, in Tullamore, and sought them out. Alfie investigated and then joined the Legion, realizing that this association meant salvation for many and holiness for him. Now an eighteen-year-old, Alfie plunged wholeheartedly into making home and hospital visitations, serving the parish by encouraging tepid or lapsed Catholics, and ministering to the Gypsies who often stopped in Tullamore. Bolstered by his great love of the Blessed Mother and a spirituality based on the teachings of St. Louis-Marie Grignion de Montfort, Alfie became a proud and contented member of the Legion. After a time he was known to have said to his mother, "I believe I can do more good in the world than I could do in a religious order."

When the concilium (the governing body of several praesidia) needed a volunteer to supervise some very isolated Legion branches, nineteen-year-old Alfie volunteered. He performed his duties in an exceptional manner.

When the mill for which he worked closed, Alfie saw a providential opportunity. He would offer all his time and energies to the Legion. Alfie and another Legion member named Seamus Grace were accepted as envoys, and were sent to Venezuela, South America. The appointment became official in April 1953. Alfie took Spanish lessons in preparation for his assignment, and he and Seamus made plans to go to South America by way of New York City. With a letter of introduction to the South American Episcopate from the Cardinal Primate of Ireland in hand, the two young men began their journey.

Once in South America, Alfie discovered that, due to a lack of priests, the Catholic population was poorly trained in the faith, which made them easy prey for the Protestant evangelists and the propaganda of local communist agents. Adding to Alfie's distress was his lack of skill with the Spanish language — his speaking skills were somewhat better than his writing and reading skills. It would be some time before he became proficient.

The good work performed by Seamus Grace and Alfie became so well known that they were invited by the bishop of Ecuador to introduce the Legion into his diocese. The two worked together until Seamus was hospitalized. Alfie had to work alone among people who were ignorant of their faith and had slipped into superstition and pagan customs. Alfie persevered, trusting in the Blessed Mother for help. He wrote in a report to Ireland: "It seems such an ordinary thing for me to spread the Legion to every part of this country that it seems to me I do not have to make any act of faith. In this there does not seem to be anything of the impossible."

Alfie's charm, persistence, persuasive talents, and hard work attracted many to the Legion. The members of one presidium he started included a senator, a school teacher, working men, and a judge of the supreme court. His work among the Indians was also successful. When he discovered that most of them spoke a language called Quechua, he learned their language, just as he had learned Spanish.

At the invitation of Bishop Echeverria of Ambato, Alfie attended the bishops' conference in Quito. For a layman to attend such a conference was unheard of, but the bishop held Alfie in high regard, believing that other dioceses would benefit from this youth and his mission. At the conference, the cardinal of Quito introduced Bishop Echeverria, who told the assembly of all the good accomplished through the Legion of Mary. The bishop then invited the twenty-year-old Alfie to speak. Without a trace of shyness, the young layman spoke to a room full of ecclesiastic dignitaries. By the time he finished, all but one bishop from Venezuela had decided that the Legion of Mary should be introduced in their regions.

In many cases, the bishops of the various dioceses introduced Alfie to parish priests who were won over by Alfie's quiet nature and his devotion to his cause. Alfie saw to it that praesidia were not only established in parishes, but also in leper communities and in prisons. Both men and women prisoners attended Mass, confessed, and received Holy Communion. The conversions and attendance at the monthly Masses soon became overwhelming.

Alfie's letters to Ireland contained reports of intense activity. Now some of his legionaries were helping him in his work and soon praesidia were being set up without his help. The seed he had sown was sprouting and spreading throughout the country.

Bishops were pleased with the success of the Legion. Eventually newspapers were interested. Regular time slots on the radio were given to the Legion for news of its activities and for the recitation of prayers and the Rosary. Pamphlets were published and the Irish publication, *Maria Legionis,* was translated into Spanish.

Alfie's health began to suffer when he contracted amoebaean dysentery. Unfortunately, once contracted, this tropical disease always reoccurs. Yet, in spite of his weakness, Alfie worked long hours and usually had his supper at midnight. His health did not dampen his enthusiasm; he wrote home: "You cannot imagine all the consolation there is in this work."

With the invitation and approval of countless church ecclesiastics, Alfie eventually continued his work not only in Venezuela but also in Ecuador, Brazil, Columbia, Bolivia, Chile, Paraguay, Uruguay, and Argentina. In Buenos Aires, there was a large Russian colony of White Russians emigrants, and Alfie informed the concilium in Ireland that he had set his sights on Russia. He was already studying the language when he became ill.

Alfie grew weaker, due in part to the dysentery. He often fainted, but even when he did, he would resume his work once he had gathered a little strength. As his health deteriorated, Alfie's blood pressure fell alarmingly, and he showed signs of nervous exhaustion. Even so, he kept up his pace, and in one instance during this time he gave four talks in two days.

Alfie looked pale and had severe pains in his stomach during a visit with the archbishop of Cordoba in December 1958. After the visit, Alfie was persuaded to eat, but he became violently ill and vomited blood. X-rays showed a bleeding ulcer, and plans were made for Alfie to have surgery in the clinic of the Blue Sisters, where he received hospitality and loving care. During his stay with the sisters, friends visited frequently and the Irish ambassador called every day.

The operation revealed not just a stomach ulcer but also lymphosarkoma, an aggressive malignant tumor. All of Alfie's organs were affected: his condition was hopeless. He suffered through most of January, finally being administered the last sacraments by Cardinal Copello. Alfie died on January 21, 1959, at the age of twenty-six.

When the Legion offered to transport Alfie's body back to his native land, his grief-stricken mother replied that he should rest in the country of his spiritual conquests. A large crowd, including bishops, accompanied the body to his grave, located in the cemetery belonging to the Passionist Fathers and the Christian Brothers.

Father Counihan, S.J., who had been Alfie's confessor in Dublin, said that Alfie was "quite unique in his devotion to Our Lady and very saintly." One of the Christian Brothers of Buenos Aires wrote: "The underlying quality of his personality was surely his ardent thirst for souls. It ruled every action of his life. Fed and nourished and encouraged at the banquet table of the Lamb, urged on to ever greater efforts under the over-shadowing mantle of his Blessed Mother, he considered no obstacle too great, no hardship too severe if by overcoming those handicaps he could win just one soul for Christ."

Cardinal D'Alton of Armagh wrote: "I am certain that Our Blessed Lady has already taken to herself Alfie Lambe as recompense for his long and faithful services."

Alfie's Cause for beatification was introduced on June 17, 1987.

Venerable Anacleto Gonzalez Flores
1888 – 1927
Attorney, Politician
Mexico

The trouble really began for Catholics in Mexico in 1917, when a new constitution was accepted. The document contained five articles that were aimed at squashing the Catholic Church. Article 3 barred elementary schools from being established by clergy or religious orders. Article 5 prohibited monastic vows and abolished monastic orders. Article 24 forbade public worship outside church buildings. Article 27 decreed that all religious property including convents, monasteries, abbeys, seminaries, and all buildings connected to them were national property. Article 130 permitted the federal government to "exercise in matters of religious worship and external discipleship such intervention as by law authorized."

These laws were haphazardly enforced until 1929 when the anticlerical and fanatical Plutarco Elias Calles became president. Calles was determined to strictly enforce the unpopular constitution and the five articles aimed at suppressing the Catholic Church. Under Article 130, in July 1926, he imposed fines and jail sentences for wearing clerical garb. He forbade the clergy to vote, and required priests in charge of churches to register with the government. Article 130 was most displeasing to the bishops, who felt that the hostile regime would have so much power over the clergy that the government would be appointing and dismissing priests at will.

Catholics galvanized resistance groups to oppose the Calles regime. The National League for the Defense of Religious Liberty (LNDLR) was formed, as was the Catholic Association of Mexican Youth (ACJM). The former was composed of university students and others who furnished demonstrators and street fighters. There were many prominent Catholic leaders involved, including Anacleto Gonzalez Flores, an attorney from Guadalajara. On August 1, 1926, the Mexican bishops declared that all church bells were to be silenced in protest, and the LNDLR declared a national economic boycott, which was accompanied by sporadic fighting in various parts of Mexico. What would become known as the Cristero Rebellion would be officially launched on January 1, 1927, and that same year Anacleto Gonzalez Flores would be martyred for his faith and for his participation in the organization and enforcement of the rebellion.

Anacleto was born in Tepatilan, Jalisco, on July 13, 1888. He was baptized the next day as the second of the twelve children of Valentin Gonzales Sanitize and Marie Flores Navaho. His family was poor, and they taught him discipline, the value of work, and patriotism. As a youngster, he helped his father in his profession of making shawls. Anacleto had a brilliant mind, and from his youth he displayed the aptitude of a leader who inspired respect. He attended spiritual exercises when he was seventeen and became interested in helping his country by teaching catechism to the local youth.

A priest who was a friend of the family recognized Anacleto's intelligence and gifts and suggested that Anacleto enter the seminary. With the priest helping with his tuition, Anacleto began his studies in earnest, and within a few months was able to converse in Latin with his professor. For this ability, he was given the nickname "Maestro." In time, Anacleto realized he was not meant to be a priest, and in 1912, he left for Mexico City where he joined the Catholic National Party. The following year he began studying law at Escuela Libre de Derecho in Guadalajara. After five years, he completed his courses and received the designation "attorney superando" in 1922.

In Guadalajara, Anacleto became an enthusiastic leader of the Catholic Association of Mexican Youth and attended conferences, wrote articles, taught catechism, and founded the periodical *La Palabra*, which refuted the anti-religious articles of the 1917 Constitution. He was involved in many other social and religious activities, including the Society of St. Vincent de Paul, through which he began to visit the sick, the poor, and prisoners.

In addition to his numerous involvements, Anacleto cultivated a deep spiritual life. He started his day with Mass and the reception of Holy Communion. He dedicated time each morning to meditation and prayer, and as a Third Order Franciscan, he was faithful to the prayers and conscientiously observed the rule. He also obtained as a spiritual director, the saintly Archbishop Francisco Orozco y Jimenez of Guadalajara.

Anacleto continued to defend the rights of the people and used a philosophy of resistance based on the non-violent principals of Mahatma Gandi. In 1919, he was briefly jailed for his beliefs, but he was released and continued his work. He was a coordinator of the first Congress of the National Catholic Workers from which the National Confederation of Catholic Workers was organized.

On November 17, 1922, Anacleto married Maria Concepcion Guerrero Flores in a ceremony conducted by his spiritual director. Anacleto once said, "The family is the true unifier, energetic and vigorous in which rests all the good of society." In time, Anacleto and Maria Concepcion welcomed two sons.

Anacleto organized and served as the president of the Union Popular, an organization dedicated to uniting Catholics to protest the arbitrary actions of a government determined to erase all hint of the Catholic Church. At that time he wrote: "We are in the midst of an infamous problem . . . the country is a jail for the Catholic Church. In order to be logical, a revolution must gain the entire soul of a nation. . . . We are not worried about defending our material interests, because these come and go; but our spiritual interests, these we will defend because they are necessary to obtain our salvation. . . ."

With the organization of the Union Popular, Anacleto began to think of, and almost expected, martyrdom. The flag that was designed for the Union Popular hinted at this. Its colors were red and white with the words *Viva Christo Rey,* "Long Live Christ the King." On the back were the words "Queen of Martyrs" and at the foot of the image of Our Lady of Guadalupe was the prayer all the members were to repeat: "Humbly we ask that you confound the enemies of the Church and hear our prayer. Queen of martyrs, pray for us and for the Union Popular."

The National League for the Defense of Religious Liberty was formed in Mexico in 1925. This organization favored armed resistance, a doctrine opposed to the pacifist Union Popular. Anacleto did not agree with the new movement, but when a sacrilege in the sanctuary of Our Lady of Guadalupe in Guadalajara took place on August 3, 1926, he began to consider if perhaps an armed confrontation was in order.

In December 1926, the leaders of the Union Popular met, and Anacleto spoke saying:

> The League [the Union Popular] has begun a revolutionary adventure with a determination that may be one of the true heart. For my part, my personal position is that I may not be other than that demanded of my post. I will be with the League and I will throw on the scale all that I am and all that I have. This remains clear: the Union Popular was not made to be an instrument of civil war. Today, however, without doubt we are driven to the mountain.

Although earlier Anacleto had resisted taking up arms in the conflict, he was now ready to begin an active insurgence.

In January 1927, the guerilla war began in the Jalisco region of Mexico. Anacleto exhorted Catholics to help the guerillas, who called themselves the Cristeros, with money, shelter, food, and clothing. Catholic women, inspired by the Cristero ideal, formed the St. Joan of Arc Brigade whose aim was to assist the troops in various ways and to carry information from the leaders.

As the civil chief of the resistance, Anacleto studied the major strategies, wrote bulletins, and gave speeches. He even said that if he were martyred for the Catholic cause it would fulfill his greatest desire.

The government decided that the rebellion must be stopped. General Jesus Maria Ferreira felt that the best way would be to capture the leaders of the Union Popular and the ACJM. On April 1, 1927, the government began their hunt. Anacleto was staying in the home of Vargas Gonzalez, a home suspected by General Ferreira as a haven for the Union Popular. Troops invaded the home, but not before Anacleto managed to destroy compromising documents. The troops arrested Anacleto and everyone in the house, including members of the family, although some were set free later that day.

The prisoners were taken to the Colorado jail in Jalisco. Since Anacleto would not provide information to the government, General Ferreira ordered that he be tortured. Anacleto was hanged by his thumbs until his fingers were dislocated. His feet were slashed; still, he refused to speak. Anacleto was taken down and the torture continued, with one of the policemen hitting him on the back with the butt of his rifle with such force that it fractured one of Anacleto's shoulders.

General Ferreira quickly improvised a summary court that claimed Anacleto had caused the assassination of an American, Edgar Wilkens. Though a complete untruth, Anacleto and three other prisoners were sentenced to death. The general ordered that they be executed simultaneously, but Anacleto asked to be the last to die, so that he might comfort the others until the end.

On a day dedicated to the Heart of Jesus, the first Friday of April 1927, at three in the afternoon, the prisoners were taken out and shot. Before a loud volley of bullets sounded, the martyrs shouted the cry of the revolution: *Viva Cristo Rey*. Anacleto's desire for martyrdom had been realized. A short time later, attorney Francisco Gonzalez Nunez arrived at the jail with a stay of execution. He arrived just as the bodies of the martyrs were thrown on the patio of the jail.

The bodies were taken to their own homes. Anacleto's home became a veritable shrine, with hundred of admirers touching his body with veneration. His widow brought her sons into the room and said, "Look. This is your father. He has died defending the faith. Promise me on his body that you will do the same when you are older if God asks it of you."

The procession to the cemetery was composed of thousands who defied the presence of the police by reciting prayers and singing hymns. Although they were endangering their lives, someone called out the pledge of the Union Popular: "Humbly we pray that you confound the enemies of the Church." To this a chorus of voices answered, "This we pray, hear us!"

The next day General Ferreira announced that after a thorough investigation it was determined that Anacleto was the leader behind the shooting of Edgar Wilkins, an American citizen, and that Anacleto and his group of "fanatics" were trying to cause trouble with the United States and had acted against Mexico's interests. The widow of Edgar Wilkins, who was unsatisfied with the lie, wrote a protest to Washington, which revealed that it was well known that her husband's murderer was one Guadalupe Zuno who had killed her husband in order to rob him. Her letter helped vindicate Anacleto, who had obtained his goal of martyrdom for the faith. Anacleto was only thirty-nine at the time of his martyrdom.

The Holy See awarded Anacleto the *Cross Pro Ecclesia et Pontifice*, and another honor: a decree recognizing his valor on May 21, 1999.

Servant of God Antonio Petyx
1874 – 1935
Writer, Father of Nine
Sicily

Antonio Petyx was born into a noble family at Casteltermini. He studied with the Salesian Fathers of Randazzo in Catania, and attended the college of jurisprudence, with an eye toward a career in law. Unfortunately, the untimely death of his father prevented his graduation, as Antonio was needed at home to care for his family and manage his family's estate.

At the age of twenty-two, Antonio married M.F. Mortillare, who was also of noble birth. Their union produced nine children, and since both parents were deeply religious, they were excellent role models for their children. They instilled in their children a devotion to the daily practices of piety and the need to glorify God by visits to the Blessed Sacrament.

Three years after his marriage, Antonio entered the Franciscan Third Order. Six years after that, he joined the Pious Union of the Miseremini of St. Matthew in Palermo. Antonio's deep prayer life soon found expression in helping others when he became active in Catholic Action. He distinguished himself with his many acts of charity, as he helped the poor, assisted the young in obtaining jobs, worked in a soup kitchen, and visited the sick. In addition, he was among the founders of the Conferences of St. Vincent de Paul and was active in the social movements and the politics of the Sicilian Catholics.

Even with all his activities, Antonio was attracted to yet one more: writing for the regional daily paper, the *Messenger of Sicily*, a division of the Roman Publishing Society. Eventually he became the manager of the paper, but the failure of the newspaper in 1913 affected his entire family, which had been financially supporting the paper. Many, who spread unfair accusations about Antonio's management of the paper, misunderstood the whole situation.

Though embarrassed, Antonio accepted the trial in the spirit of humility and the love of God. The false accusations did not seriously mar his reputation, as his piety, charity, and the patience with which he bore his adversities were remembered with deep appreciation.

Antonio Petyx died October 18, 1935, much to the distress of many who looked to him as a model of lay holiness in contemporary society. The hierarchy of Sicily held Antonio in such high regard that they began the process for his beatification, which was presented to the Sacred Congregation for the Causes of Saints. In 1982, a decree was issued by the Congregation regarding Antonio's writings.

Servant of God Antonio Solari
1861 – 1945
Catechist, Founder
Argentina

Antonio Solari was born in Chiavari near Genoa, Italy but his family emigrated to Argentina when Antonio was five years old. Upon his father's death and the grave illness of his older brother, Antonio was placed in charge of the family and had to abandon his aspirations of someday entering the seminary to become a priest.

The exact nature and extent of Antonio's formal education is not known, but given his many responsibilities and the positions of honor he held, his education must have been extensive. For a time he entered the tribunals, acting as Official Mayor of Justice, and soon Archbishop Federico Aneyros of Buenos Aires appointed Antonio to a position in the curia as the Colecturia de Rentas, a position Antonio held for almost sixty years. Antonio also worked in organizing the thirty-second International Eucharistic Congress held in 1934.

In 1883, Redemptorist priests associated with the Chapel of Our Lady of Victories arrived in Buenos Aires. Antonio began a friendship with these priests and spiritually imbibed the spirit of their patron, St. Alfonsus de Liguori.

Antonio's life now encompassed his position with the curia, his work with the shrine of Our Lady of Victories, and his ministry among men and the young whom he guided toward the faith, toward reconciliation, and the Christian life.

Antonio collaborated in the foundation of the Catholic Circle of Workers with Father Federico Grotte, and began the Patronage of Apprentices of the same group. He began teaching catechism to prisoners in the jail and taught reading and writing to workers and children in Callao. He helped Father Kraemer in the Work of Christian Marriages, and gave asylum to invalid workers' families in the Home Vicentino.

Antonio's greatest work was the Conference Vicentino, a group for men who were inspired by the example of charity of St. Vincent de Paul. Antonio guided and spiritually enriched this group and took its members to visit the homes of the needy to lend them various assistances and spiritual comfort.

Antonio was an enormously active man whose heart was firmly affixed to that of Our Lord for all of his eighty-four years. He died on July 14, 1945 in Buenos Aires.

The last action taken on his Cause for beatification was made in 1998.

Servant of God Aristide Leonori

1856 – 1928
Architectural Engineer
Rome

As the son of Rafael and Anna Leonori, Aristide received an excellent education that culminated in his graduation in architectural engineering from the University of Rome. Thereafter, he engaged in an intense professional activity that brought him international fame. This gifted architect designed a great number of magnificent churches in Italy and foreign countries.

When Blessed Louis Guanella decided to build a church in Rome dedicated to St. Joseph, he chose Aristide Leonori to design it. The feast of St. Joseph was selected for a special Mass celebrating the fiftieth anniversary of Pope Pius X's priestly ordination and the twenty-fifth anniversary of his episcopal ordination. At this Mass, the church's architect, Aristide Leonori, assisted Blessed Guanella as altar server.

Besides the several churches and convents that he designed and built in Rome, Aristide received important architectural work in England, Ireland, Australia, New Zealand, and the United States. In Buffalo, New York, in 1913, Aristide constructed the gothic cathedral, and he traveled to Missouri where he designed and built the two west chapels in the Cathedral Basilica of Saint Louis. There was also work for him in Chicago and in Washington D.C., where he built the Mount of the Holy Sepulcher Church with its replica of the catacombs. Later this shrine was reproduced in Como by Blessed Guanella and Aristide. His restoration of the Cathedral of Alexandria in Egitto was remarkable, as was the Church of St. Joseph in Cairo. This church is said to be the most beautiful modern temple in the east.

In spite of his almost constant work in erecting churches, Aristide nevertheless lived a very holy life, being especially devoted to the Immaculate Conception. He was a devout member of the Third Order of St. Francis and was especially concerned for the poor. He erected a Hostel of St. Filippo for poor and abandoned children, which opened in 1885 and was so designed that each child had his own modest room. In 1893, the hostel moved to new and more spacious buildings with classrooms in which the boys learned such trades as shoe repair and blacksmithing.

In 1907, anticlerics, busy stirring up mischief, accused Aristide of mismanagement, and the hostel closed. Aristide was taken to court, where he convincingly settled the matter by proving his innocence. Pope St. Pius X came to Aristide's defense by conveying his approval of Aristide's financial dealings for the hostel, which the pope said, were above reproach. The pope confirmed in strong terms his satisfaction that Aristide's character was impeccable, that his personal piety was exemplary, and that his generosity and zeal for souls was commendable. Having placed his utmost confidence in the holy architect, the pope even suggested additional ways in which Aristide could continue his apostolate toward the poor.

In his later years, this famed architect, who had built soaring monuments to the glory of God, taught catechism to youngsters, including those preparing for first Holy Communion. No work was too humble for this son of St. Francis.

Aristide began to show the first symptoms of a serious illness in 1910. From then on until his death in Rome on July 30, 1928, Aristide suffered almost constantly. At his death he was acclaimed a saint, and the fame of his virtues quickly spread throughout the territory. So great were his many devotees that three years after his death his tomb was transferred to the Church of St. Maria of Aracoeli where it is found in the chapel dedicated to St. Peter of Alcantara.

This renowned architect, whose love of God and church is evident in many beautiful buildings, is awaiting beatification, his Cause having been introduced in 1960.

In the United States, a mosaic portrait of this holy architect is on display in Washington, D.C., in the church dedicated to the Mount of the Holy Sepulcher.

Servant of God Artemides Zatti
1880 – 1951
Pharmacist
Argentina

When Artemides was seventeen, he and his family emigrated from Italy, the land of his birth, to Bahia Blanca, Argentina. In Argentina he began at once to work with the Salesian priests in parish activities, especially in helping destitute men. Three years later, on the recommendation of his confessor, Artemides began to study for the priesthood, but as often happens when God has other plans, the course of events was interrupted. In this case, Artemides developed a lung infection (probably pneumonia), which forced him to abandon his studies. While recuperating at Viedma, Artemides realized his true vocation was to devote his life to the care of the sick. He recovered completely, crediting his quick recovery to Our Lady, Maria Auxiliatrice.

Since the priesthood was not God's plan for Artemides, he was professed as a secular member of the Salesian congregation in 1911. He took a position with St. Joseph's Hospital at Patagonia, where his talents for organization gained him the position of administrator when the founder of the hospital died For the next forty years, Artemides worked with heroic zeal at St. Joseph's. He served as a registered pharmacist, a nurse, an assistant in the operating room, the trustee of finances, and as organizer of personnel. He worked tirelessly day and night, and was a true Samaritan to the poor, especially the destitute men of the city. He performed every manner of assistance for them with remarkable care and serenity of spirit.

A lesser person might have been dispirited by the hard work. Instead, Artemides' fervor for his apostolate was apparent in his every act of charity. With the sick he not only lavished patient and loving care, but also encouraged their spiritual life to such an extent that he was considered "priestly." Others saw in Artemides' life a spirituality that they were encouraged to imitate. His active and contemplative life, his love of others, and the donation of himself to the service of the sick and the local church, as well as his Salesian congregation, gave many people an admirable model of sanctity.

His good works and holiness were already well known when Artemides died on March 15, 1951, at the age of seventy-one. In his memory, and in gratitude for all his work on behalf of the sick, a hospital in Viedma, Argentina, was named in his honor.

His cause for canonization was introduced in 1979.

Servant of God Attilio Giordani
1913 – 1972
Soldier, Railroad Worker, Missionary
Italy/Brazil

Attilio learned early from his devout and affectionate parents the virtues he would practice in life. His mother, Amalia, was a prayerful, but a sickly person. His father, Arthur, was a railroad worker who was devoted to his job, the love and care of his family, and the care of people who needed all manner of help. There were three children in the family, Attilio, Angela, and Camillo, who all thrived in the happy home provided by their parents.

Attilio was distinguished from his earliest years by his love of the Oratory of the Salesian Fathers, which he frequented as a child. When he was eighteen he was remarkable for his devotion to Jesus and the Church and his love of youth, working as a Catholic Action delegate on the diocesan level. He was an ever-joyful and enthusiastic youth leader who took great care in instructing the young on the liturgy as well as planning games, free time activities, and even theatrical plays, all done with the greatest simplicity and originality. He worked for many years in the Salesian parish of St. Augustine in Milan.

In 1934, when he was twenty-one, Attilio went into the military. During his military career, he demonstrated an evangelical zeal in helping his comrades to avoid the temptations around them. Also during his time in the military, he met Noemi, who would become his wife. She worked with Catholic children in much the same way as Attilio did in Milan. The war kept them from seeing much of each other, but their letters were frequent. Attilio expressed the most intimate feelings, never neglecting the subject of God and his religious convictions. There was also mention of his hope that God would bless their future marriage with children so he could enjoy "their innocent smiles."

Upon his discharge, he returned to civilian life. Attilio and Noemi married on May 6, 1944, and the celebration turned into a festival for the whole parish. The couple was blessed with three children: Pier Giorgio, Maria Grazia, and Paola. In describing their home, the children said: "When dad entered the house he was all ours. He did not bring to the house the tensions of his job or the problems of the world. He was pleasant, available, and open to us. He listened to us and we listened to him . . . . We were often late in leaving the dinner table because he liked to sing and talk. . . . The prayer before meals went like this: ' Thank you, Lord, for the food that you give us; please give also to those who are without. I love You. May your kingdom come.' "

The children also reveal that their father never saved money, but was generous to those in need. "His charity was translated into mutual respect, attention to neighbors, hospitality to strangers and care of the elderly." He often told the children: "If we care for others, the Lord will take care of us."

Attilio set an admirable example of kindness and loving concern for his family. Theirs was a serene life rich in faith and religious activities, which was influenced by Attilio's prayer life. Every day included meditation, Mass, and the Rosary. For himself, Attilio practiced austere penances and evangelical poverty.

Just as he never neglected his own children, Attilio was especially fond of working with young people. He was concerned about paupers, and he helped them in every way possible. It is said that in the evangelical spirit of St. Don Bosco, Attilio wanted to make of his home an oratory and of the oratory his home.

Attilio decided to become a missionary, and with Noemi and their three children, set sail for Brazil, where they settled in Campo Grande. Husband and wife promoted the Catholic faith with Attilio as a Salesian working hard as a catechist. Once again, his love of the young had Attilio producing small plays, planning sporting events, and arranging for country excursions during which he taught the young people about God and the Church. The children loved him because he "possessed a humor that never ended." He was a splendid example of one who could combine healthy fun with the deepest piety.

Attilio was the ideal husband, father, and model of Christian charity. It was once said of him, "He wants to spend all his strength on his children and those in need."

On December 8, 1972, while speaking with enthusiasm on the advantages of giving one's life for others, he suddenly began to feel ill. Calling his son Pier Giorgio to him, he told the boy, "You must pray continuously." Attilio then suffered a heart attack, and after receiving the sacraments of the Church, died with a prayer on his lips. Attilio was fifty-nine years old. Arrangements were made for his body to be returned to Milan where he was laid to rest in the cemetery in Vendrogno.

The people of Milan voiced their approval for the opening of the beatification process. The first step in the process was presided over by Cardinal Carlo Maria Martini at the Don Bosco Auditorium in Milan. Cardinal Martini, as well as Cardinal Giovanni Colombo and Monsignor Ettore Pozzoni, gave glowing accounts of the life of Attilio Giordani and the good that he accomplished for souls. His Cause was introduced in 1994 and was given final approval in 1997.

Attilio is known as "A layman keen on the education of youth," and as the "Crusader of Goodness."

Blessed Bartolo Longo
1841 – 1926
Attorney
Italy

The church of Satan shook with thunder while cries of "Blasphemy!" from disembodied spirits were heard throughout the building. The occasion was the "ordination" of Bartolo Longo as a satanic priest. The horrible noises so frightened Bartolo that he fainted from sheer fright. His mind was severely affected for some days, and because of the experience, he suffered for the rest of his life from poor eyesight and digestive problems.

How is it that a Catholic turned to Satanism and then returned to his Catholic faith is later honored in St. Peter's Basilica by Pope John Paul II?

Bartolo was born in 1841 in Latiano, Italy, to a good Catholic family and received his early training in the Piarist school of Francavill Fontana. Bartolo continued the practice of his Catholic faith until he entered college. While studying for a law degree at the University of Naples, he was introduced to members of a satanic sect.

Italy at the time was in the throes of a national revolution for the unification of the country. Anticlericalism and opposition to the teachings and authority of the pope characterized the times. Bartolo, beguiled by his evil friends and influenced by the antireligious atmosphere, joined the satanic sect and soon aspired to the satanic priesthood. While fasting and mortifying himself during his long preparation of studies, he was "ordained" a priest by a bishop of the sect. In spite of his horrible experiences during his ordination and the physical ailments he suffered as a result, it is reported that ". . . he continued for some time to exercise the office of satanic priesthood by preaching, by officiating at the rites, and by publicly ridiculing the Catholic church, its priests and all matters relating to it."

The fervent prayers of the Longo family are credited with Bartolo's conversion. Bad companions had brought him to Satan; a good friend brought him back to God. Teaching near Naples was Vicente Pepe, a citizen of his hometown, who became Bartolo's good friend. Vicente eventually lead Bartolo back to the Mother of God and the faith of his family. Vicente succeeded in placing Bartolo in the care of a Dominican friar, Alberto Radente, who helped him in the final stages of withdrawal from the sect. Bartolo was later professed a tertiary in the Dominican Third Order.

After confession and having received Holy Communion, Bartolo was convinced by Friar Alberto to make reparation for the scandal he had caused. The friar introduced Bartolo to a group of pious people who cared for the poor, the sick, and the needy. Working in this group was a rich widow, Countess Mariana di Fusco, who owned a large tract of land near the ancient city of Pompeii, that had been destroyed by the eruption of Vesuvius in A.D. 79 and remained buried in ash for almost 2,000 years.

Surrounding this ancient, excavated city were fields where 300 people lived. As an attorney, Bartolo was commissioned by Countess di Fusco to collect the rent from these poor farmers. The sad situation of the people moved Bartolo to devise means of helping them. This work lead Bartolo to become an apostle of Our Lady of the Holy Rosary. He wrote:

> One day in the fields around Pompeii called Arpaia . . . I recalled my former condition as a priest of Satan. Friar Alberto had told me repeatedly never again to think of, or reflect on, my former consecration as a priest of Satan, but I thought that perhaps as the priesthood of Christ is for eternity, so also the priesthood of Satan is for eternity. So, despite my repentance, I thought: I am still consecrated to Satan, and I am still his slave and property as he awaits me in hell. As I pondered over my condition, I experienced a deep sense of despair and almost committed suicide. Then I heard an echo in my ear of the voice of Friar Alberto repeating the words of the Blessed Virgin: "One who propagates my Rosary shall be saved." These words certainly brought an illumination to my soul. Falling to my knees, I exclaimed: ". . . If your words are true that he who propagates your Rosary will be saved, I shall reach salvation because I shall not leave this earth without propagating your Rosary." Like an answer to my promise, the little bell of the parish church of Pompeii rang out inviting the people to pray the Angelus. This incident was like a signature to my firm decision.

Bartolo organized a parish mission and invited a group of priests to speak about devotion to the holy Rosary. At the end of the mission, Bartolo wanted to exhibit a painting of Our Lady, but the one he found in a Naples shop proved to be too expensive. When he returned home he shared his disappointment with Friar Alberto, who told him of a painting that a nun named Mother Concetta had in her convent. Since he knew Mother Concetta was willing to part with it, Friar Alberto encouraged Bartolo to ask for the painting. Bartolo was extremely displeased on seeing its pitiful condition. When he hesitated to take it, the nun insisted. Her prophetic words: "Take it with you; you will see that the Blessed Mother will use this painting to work many miracles."

The painting had a less-than-auspicious journey to its new home in Pompeii — it was wrapped in a sheet and placed atop a load of manure that was being taken to the fields near Pompeii. The painting arrived on November 13, 1875, and each year the anniversary of its arrival is marked by the faithful with special prayers and observances.

Bartolo saw to the restoration of the painting and to the building of a magnificent church for its enshrinement. Substantial gifts from the wealthy and the humble pennies of the poor paid for the construction of the church. The painting, which sits high atop the main altar of the artistically enriched sanctuary, has been the instrument through which many miracles of healing have taken place. Countless visitors to the sanctuary admire the colorful painting that depicts the Blessed Mother seated upon a throne with twelve stars forming a halo around her head. On her knee is the Child Jesus who is handing a rosary to a Dominican friar, while the Blessed Mother is handing a rosary to a Dominican nun. Pope Leo XIII once stated, "God had made use of this image to grant those favors which have moved the whole world."

While still engaged in the construction of the sanctuary, Bartolo wrote books about the history of and devotion to the Rosary and composed novenas and prayer manuals for use in the sanctuary. Even with all these matters claiming his attention, he still found time to court and marry the widow Countess Mariana di Fusco on April 1, 1885.

The couple had common interests and spent their time and money in helping the many orphans who were entrusted to their care. Candidates to the priesthood and religious life were also assisted. Bartolo is credited with paying for the education of at least forty-five seminarians who often received letters in which Bartolo inquired about the progress they were making in their studies, and in which he never failed to urge them to cultivate and propagate devotion to the Rosary.

The former Satanist turned devout champion of Our Lady, the respected lawyer and protector of the orphaned, lived to the age of eighty-five, dying on October 5, 1926. His tomb and his wife's are found in the crypt of the Sanctuary of Pompeii.

The magnificent Sanctuary of Pompeii stands as a monument to the memory of Bartolo Longo. There is no doubt to whom this shrine is dedicated: a statue of the Virgin Mary holding the child Jesus is situated high atop the church. A long rosary falls from Our Lady's hand and the word "Pax" is inscribed beneath the statue. Latin words across the facade of the church proclaim boldly that the church is dedicated to the Virgin of the Holy Rosary. Twice each year, on May 8 and the first Sunday of October, great crowds of pilgrims gather here to join in the solemn prayers that Bartolo Longo composed.

Buildings for orphan children are located near the church, and in addition to their usual studies, the children are taught skills and trades that will help them later in life.

A tall, narrow obelisk-type memorial stands in the square at Pompeii. Near the top is an image of the Blessed Mother surrounded by angels. At the bottom is a statue of Bartolo Longo surrounded by his beloved orphans while on the base is inscribed the words, "Bartolo Longo, Apostle of the Rosary."

The promise of the Blessed Mother, "One who propagates my Rosary shall be saved," was realized when Pope John Paul II affirmed the salvation of Bartolo Longo's soul at the ceremony of beatification which took place on October 26, 1980.

Servant of God Camillo Edward Feron
1831 – 1908
Medical Doctor, Professor
France

We have two brothers-in-law who are on the same journey toward canonization — Camillo Feron and his brother-in-law, the Servant of God Filiberto (Philip) Vrau whose biography also is included in this book. These two men worked together in charitable organizations they founded and are now entombed together in the crypt of the cathedral in Lille, France.

Camillo belonged to a family engaged in commerce. His wife, Camille Maria Vrau, was the sister of Filiberto Vrau, and she was also prominent in Camillo and Filiberto's charitable endeavors. When she married Camillo, she obtained permission from the court to carry the last name of Feron-Vrau. Camillo and his wife had five children and lived in Lille, which is located in northern France near the border of Belgium.

Camillo was a doctor and a teacher in the Hospital of the Holy Savior in Lille, but he retired from his practice so he could devote more time to assisting Filiberto in charity work. Both Filiberto and Camillo worked tirelessly to elevate the material, moral, spiritual, and social status of the workers in northern France. For the workers, Camillo, his wife, and Filiberto established in Lille the Catholic Institute of Arts and Crafts, and in 1878, they founded the Association of the Christian Masters of the North, for which Camillo served as president until his death in 1908. They also founded the Guild of St. Nicholas for spinners and weavers. After the death of Filiberto in 1906, Camillo constructed a building for the lodging of forty workers.

In addition to helping the poor, Camillo was concerned for the Church, and he promoted the construction and the endowment of new parish churches. He and his wife also saw to the construction of the Cathedral of Notre Dame in Treille for which he served as treasurer. He also supported the Catholic University of Lille of which he was the founder of the faculty of medicine and all its complex of institutes for the relief of the sick.

Camillo died in 1908, at the age of seventy-seven, two years after his brother-in-law. Four years later, the diocesan process for his beatification began. In 1930, Pope Pius XI confirmed the decree giving Camillo the title of Servant of God.

Blessed Carlos Manuel Rodriguez
1918 – 1963
Office Clerk
Puerto Rico

Will Carlos "Charlie" Rodriguez be the first Puerto Rican saint? He might very well be since he is only one step away, having been beatified by Pope John Paul II on April 29, 2001.

Carlos was born in Caguas, Puerto Rico, on November 22, 1918. He was baptized the next year in the Holy Name of Jesus church on May 4, 1919. Life with his brother and three sisters was serene and normal. Two of his sisters married and the third became a Carmelite nun. His only brother became a Benedictine priest and was the first Puerto Rican to become the abbot of a monastery.

When Carlos was six, a fire destroyed both his father's small store and the family home. Without a place to live, his parents, Manuel Baudilio Rodriguez and Herminia Santiago, both deeply religious, were forced to move into the home of Carlos' grandmother, Alejandrina Esteras, a very devout and holy woman. Carlos's father accepted the loss good-naturedly with a constant hope that conditions would get better, but his wife, Doña Herminia, did not. She was not living in her own home, which lead her to impose upon herself and her children a strong sense of respect, almost to inhibition. Apparently, this is what caused the reserved and timid personalities of her children.

At the age of six Carlos began attending the Catholic school in Caguas. At school, he cultivated special friendships with his teachers, the Sisters of Notre Dame, as well as the Redemptorist father from whom he received his religious and humanistic education. His first reception of the Holy Eucharist marked the beginning of a love that would last a lifetime. He became an altar boy and developed a special fondness for the sacred liturgy. He completed the eighth grade at the top of his class, and not only received the first prize for scholastic achievement, but also a special prize for religion.

While attending his first year of high school at the public Gautier Benitez High School in Caguas, Carlos experienced the first symptoms of a condition that would gradually increase in severity until it would eventually claim his life: ulcerative colitis. Carlos was unable to finish his second year in high school because his sickly condition prevented his attendance. He did manage to finish the year through a self-study program sponsored by the Caguas Department of Education. He spent his third year of high school at the Colegio del Perpetuo Socorro in San Jose. He later re-enrolled in Gautier Benitez School from which he graduated in 1939 after completing both commercial and general programs. To support himself, Carlos worked at clerical jobs, but his main interest was the apostolate of making Christ known and loved as he knew and loved him.

Carlos attempted formal studies at the University of Puerto Rico. Despite missing many days for health reasons, his grades were so extraordinary that one professor, Mrs. Adrian Ramos Mimoso, wondered how he could do so well on his examinations. One of Carlos's former classmates, now an opthalmologist, once revealed that he explained to Carlos material covered during Carlos's long absences. When tested over the material, Carlos received an A. The opthamologist did not. Unfortunately, illness caused Carlos to abandon formal studies after just one year.

Though Carlos never completed college, he continued his education on his own by reading voraciously. His interests included the arts, science, philosophy, and religion. He continued learning and reportedly could remember in great detail everything that left a mark on his spirit. His brother Pepe, who became a Benedictine priest, said of Carlos: "I have known few people with such a vast and clear knowledge of religion as Carlos; a knowledge that comes not only from reading, but out of the love that penetrates far more than the intelligence."

Carlos formally studied the piano and organ and continued working on his own until he became proficient. He especially loved classical music, the works of Mozart and Beethoven, and the Gregorian Chant held a special place in his heart.

Although very virtuous, he never expressed a desire to become a priest, but it is assumed that he realized the inflammatory disease of the bowels with its persistent upset stomach would have prevented his ordination. It is known, however, that as a child he often played at "saying Mass," with his sisters as the congregation and his brother Pepe as an altar boy. Without becoming a priest, he was an apostle for many.

Carlos worked as an office clerk at the Agriculture Experiment Station in Caguas, which was part of the University of Puerto Rico. He spent his free time dispensing Catholic materials, editing Catholic journals, arranging student instructional meetings, writing Catholic articles, and giving lectures that enabled many to stand firm in the faith. His busy, virtuous life and his many accomplishments were attained despite his pain and ill health.

For several years, Carlos organized and directed a Liturgical Circle at the university. He gave lectures that were attended by not only students, but also by many of the professors and department heads. One of Carlos' "disciples" was the renowned Dr. Margot Arce de Vasquez who said, "This young man is what my good friend Gabriela Mistral used to call a 'child of the Holy Spirit.'"

Carlos also had a Liturgical Circle in Caguas, which met every week. Anyone with a question concerning morals or religion went there, and many regarded Carlos as a walking encyclopedia. Although he was very humble about all he knew, he spoke with profound conviction "as one who spoke with authority." His biographer states: "That authority came from the harmony between his word and his life: what he said was what he lived and what he lived was what he preached."

Carlos was not only knowledgeable about religious matters; he also could speak with conviction about European countries that respected the rights of Catholics to protect their most precious moral and social principles. He read papal encyclicals and the writings of St. Thomas Aquinas. He was fond of the saints, and he spoke of St. Teresa of Ávila and St. John of the Cross as though they were his personal acquaintances. He read the works of Cardinal Newman, Chesterton, and especially the works of St. Edith Stein.

When Mass was still being offered in Latin, Carlos introduced the use of the Missal to those who could not understand the beauty and significance of the Mass in Latin. Later, Carlos introduced the Liturgy of the Hours (the Divine Office). He taught many how to observe the Hours so that they benefited greatly from this liturgical prayer. His brother, Pepe, was later to comment: "The taste for the liturgical prayer of the Church that he inculcated in us was the beginning of my monastic Benedictine vocation."

Carlos realized early that the breach between our Christian culture and lay knowledge needed attention, and for this reason he began the publication *Liturgy and Christian Culture*, which he edited from the university's Catholic Center. He selected and translated appropriate articles, and he paid most of the expenses of the publication. Carlos managed to accomplish all this while maintaining a steady clerical job and feeling ill most of the time.

Carlos translated into English the Spanish books of Father Clifford Howell, S.J., *Of Sacraments and Sacrifice* and *Preparing for Easter*. Carlos made copies of the chapters and mailed them to his friends, supporters, and other interested parties, and even to the religious and clergy all over the country. Again, the expenses of copying and postage were mainly his responsibility. He organized a Liturgy Circle and the *Te Deum Laudamus* choir. As the number of his supporters increased, Carlos moved with them into the Catholic University Center and organized another Liturgy Circle, later called the Circulo de Cultura Cristiana. Additionally, Carlos was a member of the Brotherhood of Christian Doctrine, the Holy Name Society, and the Knights of Columbus. He also taught catechism to high school students and provided their teaching aids from his personal funds.

Carlos' zeal for the faith was evident in his correspondence with ministers, priests, seminarians, and laity in towns all over the island and even many in the United States. He also sent copies of articles and books to "our separated brethren." His love of Christ, the Church, and his neighbor flourished every day of his life, but especially on those days he organized that came to be known as "Christian Living Days." Those who attended recall:

> We would get together in some place outside the city and we would each bring our own snacks to share with everyone else. Charlie would give two or three talks during the day relating to the liturgical season or some religious topic or current event. The praying of the Divine Office for the laity was an important part of the agenda. We would also sing hymns in harmony with the religious feast. . . . On occasions we would pray the Rosary with emphasis on its biblical connotations . . . sometimes we had Mass and even enjoyed some wholesome recreational games.

One of those who regularly participated wrote: "Those days gave us a profound sense of unity, of great enjoyment, spiritual satisfaction and tremendous love, which transcended the moment and carried on into our daily life. As we bring back those days, we still feel that joy, that love, once again."

For these "Christian Living Days" Carlos provided everything: materials, lectures, hymns, instructions, and liturgical and biblical holy pictures. "His intention was to get us to know, love and serve Christ better," wrote one of his supporters.

While Carlos worked with Father Antonio Quevedo, S.J., of the University Catholic Center, Carlos showed an increased interest in the religious and priestly life. With Father Alvaro de Boer, O.P., Carlos collaborated in the plan of creating a religious congregation, the "Hermanas de Jesus Mediator," whose principal purpose was a socio-religious apostolate. After Carlos' death, this congregation was established in the suburb of Volcano, in Hato Tejas, Puerto Rico.

Carlos' work drew to a close during the early part of 1963. His face showed unmistakable signs of ill health, and he was extremely tired. He underwent tests, which showed serious anemia, and an exam revealed a rectal mass. Several painful biopsies later, a pathologist in the medical school ruled the biopsies nonmalignant. One doctor disagreed: "I knew only too well how often ulcerative colitis of thirty years duration degenerated into cancer." Without the microscopic evidence to support a cancer diagnosis, treatment was delayed for four months.

Although weak and very ill, Carlos' spirit was not diminished. He lived each moment quietly, with a profound joy as one who trusts in the risen Christ. He would tell his visitors, *Vivimos para esa noche*, "We live for the night of the Resurrection."

Four months after the nonmalignant biopsies, Carlos underwent surgery. In the Puerto Rico of 1963, many physicians did not consult with the patient about the surgical procedures they decided to perform. Without notifying Carlos of their plans, his doctors prepared him for a radical, seven-hour operation. The doctors confirmed Carlos' cancer, and it was necessary for them to remove numerous lymph nodes and perform a colostomy. The results of his surgery were a great shock to Carlos, especially the colostomy that not only caused painful skin irritation but also a loss of dignity and privacy. Carlos was entering his Gethsemane: he was suffering from end-stage rectal cancer.

Some months earlier Carlos had experienced joint pain, which reappeared after the surgery. He took analgesics, which caused nausea. He was already experiencing a loss of appetite, and his loss of weight aggravated his terrible pain. Carlos was moved to La Providencia, a small private dispensary, where he confided to his doctor: "I suffer not so much for myself as for so many other sick people who have no one to take care of them when they ask for something so basic as a glass of water." He never complained, instead he begged pardon for causing so much inconvenience. A visitor once commented, "I can't understand why he doesn't complain. . . . He is a very special person."

When the doctors examined him later and found tumors in his liver and throughout the rest of his body, any hope for his recovery ended. Without being told, Carlos understood, and for the most part remained silent in recollection.

Toward the end of his time, Carlos was transferred to his home in Caguas. He was so ill that he could not attend the ordination of his brother Pepe, but days later, in a heroic act to suppress his pain, he was able to sit in a wheelchair in the sacristy to attend Pepe's first Mass. This was but a momentary bit of joy. The complications of his cancer increased: dehydration, electrolytic imbalance, anemia, and an abscess that perforated the abdominal wall. One of his few comforts was gazing at his cherished crucifix.

Added to his physical pain was his spiritual distress, that which St. John of the Cross calls the "Dark Night of the Soul." Carlos felt abandoned by God, but continued to pray and plea for God's help, much the same as did St. Thérèse of Lisieux who also experienced this Dark Night on her deathbed. He continued to receive Holy Communion every day and was often visited by Pepe, who brought him a measure of spiritual comfort.

Carlos' frequent prayers were the word "*Dios*" and "Be my salvation." Eventually he was delivered from his Dark Night, and he prophesied that he would die on July 13. He lapsed into a coma and died just after midnight on the day he had indicated. He was forty-four years old.

Carlos was beatified on April 29, 2001. His process of beatification was one of the shortest in recent history. Initiated in 1992, the Decree of Heroic Virtues lead to his title of Venerable on July 7, 1997. The miracle for his beatification, the cure of non-Hodgkins malignant lymphoma in 1981, was approved on December 20, 1999.

Pope John Paul said of him during the beatification ceremony that Carlos, "Highlighted the universal call to sanctity for all Christians, and the importance for each baptized person to respond conscientiously and responsibly to it. May his example help the whole church in Puerto Rico to be faithful, living with firm consistency the Christian values and principles received during the island's evangelization."

Blessed Ceferino Jimenez Malla

1861 – 1936
Horse Trader, Gypsy, Martyr
Spain

Lively Gypsy music filled the Vatican audience hall after the ceremony in which Pope John Paul II beatified Ceferino Jimenez Malla, a martyr of the Spanish Civil disturbance of 1936-1939 who was killed for no other reason than that of being Catholic. With more than 40,000 people attending the beatification service of Sunday, May 4, 1997, the pope told the countless Gypsies present: "Ceferino sowed harmony and solidarity among the Gypsies, mediating in conflicts that plagued relations between non-Gypsies and Gypsies. . . . He must be for you an example and an incentive for the full integration of your culture in the social environment around you." The pope then added, "El Pele showed that the charity of Christ knows no limits of race or culture."

"El Pele," a name by which Ceferino was also known, lived a life of honesty, goodness, and prayer. During the three years of the Spanish Civil War, the instigators were not only interested in political pursuits, but also in the suppression of religion. During this three-year war (1936-1939), more than 7,000 religious were martyred together with many laymen. Prominent among the laymen was Ceferino, who was one of the first to die. He was arrested and martyred for defending a priest and for carrying a rosary.

Ceferino's family was nomadic, moving from village to village in Catalonia and upper Aragon. Born in 1861 at Fraga, Ceferino was the son of Juan Jimenez and Josefa Malla. He had a brother, Felipe, and a sister, Encarnacion. The family was very poor, and Ceferino frequently suffered from hunger. At a very early age he worked selling baskets with one of his uncles, and is known to have occasionally received help from the famous bandit Cucaracha, whom Ceferino met along the road while traveling with his uncle. Father Angel M. Fandos, C.M.F., who researched the life of this Blessed and wrote the first biography of him, interviewed those who knew Ceferino during those early years. Father Fandos was told, "He [Ceferino] learned to earn his bread from when he was very small, weaving creels and baskets and taking them to sell through the villages."

As to his early religious training, Father Fandos notes that Ceferino probably learned his prayers when he was small, since he prayed in the Catalan language of the district of Catalonia, the area through which Ceferino's family traveled. Father Fandos believes that Ceferino made his First Communion as a child and was confirmed, since he was subsequently admitted to the celebration of canonical marriage.

Information on Ceferino's education is non-existent. Ceferino "Never went to school. . . . Totally illiterate, he could not read, write, or do sums." Since he did not know how to write, he could not even sign his name on his marriage papers. Another person signed his name for him.

When Ceferino was about eighteen or nineteen years old, he was married in Gypsy fashion to Teresa Jimenez, a baptized Catholic. It was not until thirty-two years later that they sought permission to be married in the Church. We know that the marriage was celebrated in Lerida, the bride's native home on January 19, 1912, in the parish church of St. Lawrence the Martyr.

Ceferino and Teresa were childless, but they adopted one of Teresa's nieces, Pepita Jimenez. Ceferino always considered the child as his daughter, and he provided her with a good Christian education by sending her to boarding school at St. Vincent de Paul College, operated by the Daughters of Charity.

Ceferino's success in the business of horse trading seemed to have grown out of an act of charity. One day, the former mayor of Barbastro, Don Simon, was walking along the street when he suddenly began coughing up blood. Ceferino immediately went to him, and took the man home to care for him.

At the time, people lived in fear of tuberculosis, and Ceferino's act was considered a heroic one. In gratitude, Don Simon, a very rich man, gave Ceferino a large sum of money, advising him to go to France to buy mule wagons that the French Government was selling at the end of the World War. Apparently, Ceferino bought the wagons, sold them, and then bought a large number of mules, which he quickly sold in the village of Somontano. He repeated this operation several times, earning enough profit to be considered a wealthy man.

Once a nomad, Ceferino was now able to buy a home in the San Hipolito district where he had been living as a tenant. He also was able to establish a stable of horses, which he always kept well stocked. Several witnesses mention that both Gypsies and non-Gypsies flocked to his stable to buy horses because of Ceferino's reputation for honesty. One witness noted that "as a horse trader he didn't try to cheat and this fact brought him prestige. . . . If a horse had a defect, he would point it out. You would hear people say: 'Trust El Pele to advise you well.'" El Pele even went so far as to correct the Gypsy dealers who tried to cheat the non-Gypsies, saying it was something they should not do. For this he was very much loved and appreciated.

One very noteworthy event in Ceferino's life drew the citizens of the district to the defense of their trustworthy and generous friend. Ceferino was selling some mules at a fair in Vedrell when he was accused of selling mules that had been stolen. Called into court to defend himself, Ceferino was able to produce receipts that proved he had bought the mules in ignorance of their origins. The mules had indeed been stolen from their rightful owner, but after the judge studied the receipts, he pronounced a verdict of acquittal and gave this tribute in court: "Pele is neither a thief nor a swindler. He is *Saint* Ceferino Jimenez Malla, Patron of the Gypsies."

Many have testified that in gratitude for his acquittal, "Ceferino was seen advancing along Calle San Hipolito street to the cathedral on his knees holding two huge candles in his hands to give thanks to God for having been exonerated." His biographer writes: "If anyone else had done this he would have been considered a figure of ridicule. In the case of the Gypsy, naturally it wasn' t like that because everyone knew how serious and religious he was. Considering that this happened around 1922, we must say that already he was considered very religious."

Soon after this misfortune with the mules, the Lord gave his servant another trial when Ceferino's beloved wife, Teresa, died unexpectedly on December 4, 1922. With his wife gone, Ceferino was left alone with his adopted niece, Pepita, who was barely sixteen. To avoid scandal, he gave her in marriage to Juan Alfredo Jimenez, his nephew, son of his brother Felipe. The wedding ceremony was so sumptuous that the celebrants recalled it for many years. The newlyweds continued to live in the house with Ceferino and soon it was filled with children, all of whom Ceferino loved dearly.

Ceferino is known to have attended Mass every day with great solemnity at the Claretian church. Several witnesses who knew him said he usually sat in the last pews and recited the Rosary. Reportedly, he said the Rosary every day to keep a vow for a miracle he had obtained from Our Lady of the Rosary. At the age of sixty-five, Ceferino became a member of the Franciscan Third Order and was a member of the Nocturnal Adoration Society of his parish.

After Mass, he began his usual chores at the stable, feeding the horses, cleaning stalls, carrying water for the stock, and attending to customers. He was also a ferrier, someone who shod horses. For this he used a special tool called a "puhamante," which is now kept as a relic in the museum of the Claretian Martyrs of Barbastro.

Ceferino was no solemn saint. He attended fairs in the nearby villages and never missed the feasts organized by his fellow Gypsies. He participated in processions, and the events of the various religious organizations to which he belonged. Among these were the Nocturnal Adoration and Eucharistic Societies, the St. Vincent de Paul Society, and the Confraternity of Franciscan Tertiaries in which he was an officer. He always attended daily Mass and received the Eucharist.

In middle age, Ceferino was "tall, slim, in good health, with a strong constitution and a smart appearance." Maria de los Dolores, who knew the Blessed, recalled him as a tall, lean man and the little boys of the district saw him "as a great gentleman with an overwhelming personality, tall, thin and distinguished." Andres Jimenez, a Gypsy, adds more to the description of Ceferino: "He was a handsome man. He dressed in an elegant fashion in a suit and waistcoat. He had a watch chain that hung down from his waistcoat and disappeared into a little pocket. He went along with a walking stick."

When he was tending horses, Ceferino "went around in a smock, with a beret on his head, down-at-heel shoes on his feet, with a whip round his neck and rolled up in his hand." Father Fandos, his biographer states: "His way of dressing when he joined the caravans to go to a festival was different. Sitting on horseback or on the driving seat of a covered cart, he kept up a lively conversation with his companions while keeping a careful watch over the team of mules or donkeys he was driving. Then he wore a jacket, tie, cloth hat and boots. . . ."

Ceferino was distinguished above all for his personal qualities. According to Father Fandos: "Although illiterate and unable to keep accounts, he was gifted with natural intelligence, a great good sense, proven honesty, and a special gift for settling disputes which arose among the Gypsies and between them and the non-Gypsies. To all this must be added his great generosity, at times coming close to prodigality."

Ceferino was often called upon to exercise his gift for peacemaking. Father Fandos notes: "Never had the villages of the region known a man more honest, gentlemanly, sincere, and Christian. In public and private, he showed himself respectful, humble, cheerful, peaceable, helpful and generous. For everyone he had a greeting, a smile, time for a pleasant conversation, a courteous invitation, a promise. . . . I heard of nothing blameworthy. Where the other Gypsies were concerned, he always treated them with great cordiality . . . calling them 'Tato,' a term of affection which the Gypsies use for each other."

Alejandro Moca Sese, a friend of Ceferino's, once declared before Father Gabriel Camp, "Ceferino was such a good man it was difficult to think of any sins, lies, or faults. He always seemed to be preserved by grace. . . ."

While working as a horse dealer, Ceferino cultivated a friendship with Don Nicolas Santos de Otto, a professor who taught at the University at Oviedo, and who had an estate at San Esteban de Liters. The professor had a great influence on Ceferino, who endeared himself to the professor's family. Toward the end of his life, Ceferino devoted himself completely to the Otto family and became the trusted caretaker of their house.

Professor Otto knew Ceferino fifteen years. The professor declares: "Ceferino was a man who was very firm in his religious convictions. . . . He always carried his rosary with him, and you would often come across him saying it. When he was walking along the street, on his own or together with others, he always recited it. He was present every time he could at the Viaticum for the sick, at Mass, at the Forty Hours Prayer, as well as other religious ceremonies in which he was a devoted participant and was thought of as such."

Ceferino was not ashamed to show his faith. He was first in processions and always carried a lighted candle. When the Franciscan Third Order was canonically erected, Ceferino was seen holding in his hands the Franciscan banner. The seminarians present noted this and commented very favorably on his humble devotion.

Ceferino detested blasphemy and would courteously confront those who were engaged in such behavior. He would give them a little talk about God or about priests, asking the guilty to refrain from such practices especially, "When I'm around, don't talk badly about God or about priests." With such a polite and Christian attitude, the guilty seemed never to be offended.

His love of the poor was outstanding. During the last years of his life, when Ceferino was living in near poverty, he continued to give alms to the poor in whatever way he could. Many witnesses speak of his generosity. Jose Cortes Gabarre declared: "I have seen on various occasions how he welcomed beggars into his house, gave them clothes in good condition and money, and he did all this in a very friendly way, treating them with affection."

Another witness reports that "poor Gypsies would go to him and he would take them into the house, feed them and treat them with great affection. . . . When it snowed, he would go round the villages to see if there was anything the poor Gypsies might need. He ruined himself sharing his goods with poor Gypsies."

Jose Castellon reported that "his charity was such that there was no Gypsy in Barbastro or outside the city who did not have recourse to him or that he did not assist morally and materially." Because of his honesty, his generosity, and his love and care of the poor, Ceferino was regarded as a saint even during his lifetime. But his financial situation was ruined by his generosity so that he had to sell his house.

Ceferino sought to inspire the local children, and he often gathered them together for religious instruction. Donna Gloria Castellon testified for the process of beatification that "Ceferino often got the children of the neighborhood together and took them out into the country, ostensibly to gather 'cenojo' an edible herb, but really to give them catechesis by telling them stories from the Bible and from Spanish history, and to get them singing church songs. He would exhort the children to respect nature and he would finish by giving each one a piece of chocolate."

The peace in Barbastro ended when rumors of unrest spread through the area. Don Nicolas Santos de Otto, at whose estate Ceferino stayed, asked Ceferino to go into town and bring back the news. Ceferino never returned. The Spanish Civil War had begun, and Ceferino was swept up in it. After the celebrations on Saturday, July 18, the feast of St. Christopher, the People's Front seized power, and armed men with rifles began walking the streets. Gypsies went into hiding, priests were arrested, and people were seized for no reason.

The exact date of Ceferino's arrest is debated, but experts place the date between July 19 and July 25. As he was headed to Mass that morning, he saw a young priest trying to free himself from the hands of militiamen. El Pele approached with the words, "Help me, Holy Virgin! So many men against one, and him innocent too!" Another witness claims that Ceferino's words to the soldiers were "Help me, Holy Virgin! Aren't you ashamed to take an innocent man like that? He hasn't done anything, and so many of you to do it."

The militiamen threw themselves on Ceferino and, while searching him, found in his pocket the little instrument he used in the care of the horses and a rosary. The rosary alone was sufficient reason for the men to take him to the Capuchin convent where at least 350 detainees were kept, among them many of the Claretian Fathers. Ceferino was to stay there until the day of his martyrdom. Two of the prisoners who were spared almost at the last moment report that Ceferino "lived in a continual atmosphere of prayer," and that "in prison he used to pray and recite the Rosary."

Ceferino's adopted daughter, Pepita, brought him food each day and cautioned him that by continuing to pray the Rosary he was putting his life in danger by demonstrating his faith. She begged him many times in tears not to recite the Rosary because they would kill him for it. All her appeals were unsuccessful. One of the witnesses said that Ceferino would not hand over his rosary "because the rosary signified his faith in Christ, and reciting it was prayer."

The exact date of Ceferino's martyrdom is also uncertain, although it is reported to have been August 9, 1936. One night the revolutionaries took twenty-five prisoners to the Barbastro cemetery to be shot. Among them were priests, religious, and especially selected Christians, including Ceferino. About three in the morning, the innocents were lined up against the wall of the cemetery. While shouting, "Long live Christ the King" and holding his rosary high in the air, Ceferino, and the others, were shot. Some did not die from the first volley. According to Jose Castellano, a certain revolutionary named Bellostas, who seems to have been the leader of the group said: "The Gypsy's still alive, he's the best," and shot Ceferino again, killing him. Ceferino died with his rosary in his hand.

The bodies were stripped of everything and were dropped into a common pit. According to Mariano Carruesco Arnal, one of the gravediggers, the bodies were covered with quicklime and with water to speed decomposition and then covered further with mud. Ceferino's remains were not to be recovered.

Blessed Ceferino was killed exclusively for religious reasons. He was never involved in politics, nor had the revolutionaries any charge against him except that he prayed the Rosary in prison and had defended a priest. Ceferino, seventy-five years old at the time of his death, and all those who died with him were always regarded as martyrs of the faith.

When Ceferino was beatified, Archbishop Giovanni Cheli, who was then the president of the Pontifical Council for the Pastoral Care of Migrants and Itinerant Peoples, said that "Ceferino was poor during much of his life, but rich in charity which he used to help countless others. Poor, but rich in virtue. Humble but great in the faith."

Servant of God Claudio Lopez Bru
1853 – 1925
Attorney
Spain

Claudio Lopez Bru, the second marquis of Comillas, was born in Barcellona, Spain, to a very religious family. His father rose from almost poverty to the peak of riches and honors, not through favoritism or what might be considered luck, but through hard work and business acumen. After a series of trips to Cuba and the Philippines, Claudio's father settled in Barcelona, where he married and raised his family.

Claudio received a Christian education from his parents and excelled in his school studies. He completed all his subjects with high marks, and went on to obtain a degree in law. At twenty-eight, Claudio married Maria Gayon, a woman of exceptional qualities. Much to their regret they remained childless, but they saw in the poor and unfortunate children of their country the children they never had.

At the death of his older brother, and then that of his father, Claudio inherited his father's title and a huge fortune. His family now consisted of his mother and his wife. Claudio took his new responsibilities seriously, and he sought ways to help others. He created new jobs for the unemployed, built houses for the many unfortunates of the city, organized labor unions, opened schools and sanatoriums, and even distributed his own possessions. He did everything according to the spirit and social doctrines of the Church.

Claudio conducted a pilgrimage in 1894 to visit Pope Leo XIII and gave a great part of his inheritance to the seminary opened by Pope St.

Pius X, which was later raised to the rank of pontifical university. Reportedly, Claudio's many activities were made possible by his deep spiritual life, which included daily Mass and Holy Communion, the recitation of the daily Rosary in the midst of his family, and a life of austerity and penance.

Claudio died in his home in Madrid at the age of seventy-two. His last words were: "I confide myself to the mercy of God."

Blessed Contardo Ferrini

1859 – 1902
Professor
Italy

The city of Milan claims as its native son Contardo Ferrini, who was born in that city on April 4, 1859. His father was a teacher of mathematics and physics. Little is known of his mother, although both Contardo and his father seem to have lived under her domination. This might account for Contardo's abnormally sensitive nature and his perception of the world as hard and hostile. He was highly intelligent, and at the time of his first Holy Communion, he was already greatly influenced by Scripture and by St. Augustine's *Confessions*.

At school and at the university, Contardo impressed most of his classmates as being irritatingly self-sufficient and withdrawn. Inwardly, however, he was suffering for his refusal to approve or imitate the lifestyles of those around him who took his high standards, especially concerning purity, as criticism of themselves. Consequently, Contardo had few friends, but one who shared his high ideals and who understood him was Achille Ratti, who later became Pope Pius XI. Like the future pope, Contardo was an ardent mountaineer, and may have enjoyed the sport in the company of this good friend.

When Contardo's mother and her friends attempted to interest him in various marriageable young ladies, he made it clear that he was not called to the married state, nor did he feel that he had a religious vocation. He was to remain single all his life.

He studied law at Borromeo College in Pavia, and received his doctorate in 1880. He went to Berlin, Germany, for post-graduate study. Contardo knew a dozen languages, some of which helped him tremendously in his studies of the Scriptures. He specialized in Greek and Roman law and was recognized as one of the outstanding authorities in the field. For this reason, the University of Pavia created a special chair for him in 1883. In 1887, Contardo was made professor of Roman law at Messina, and in 1894, he returned to the University of Pavia. The following year he was elected to and served on the Milan City Council.

Contardo was a profound scholar, an inspired and talented teacher who demanded much from his students. In turn, his students greatly admired him as a sterling example of a life of holiness lived in the midst of intellectual pursuits.

Contardo not only engaged in scholarly and legal pursuits, but he also was active in social and charitable endeavors. He worked for the Society of St. Vincent de Paul in both Berlin and Milan, and was associated with the Ambrosian Library. In addition, he helped found the St. Severinus Boethius Society for university students.

As a Franciscan tertiary, his interior life was distinguished by a great devotion to the Mass and the study of the Scriptures. Although his life was difficult, restricted, and lonely, Contardo accepted his lot with patience, virtuously observing the precepts of the Church.

Contardo died of typhoid fever in 1902. Soon after his death, Contardo was put forward as a candidate for canonization. Among the witnesses who testified to his virtues were his friends and colleagues and Achille Ratti, the future Pope Pius XI.

In 1927, twenty-five years after his death, Contardo Ferrini was given a glowing tribute by Cardinal Carlo Salotti during the funeral services the cardinal conducted for Joseph Moscati, a physician and professor of medicine (Moscati's biography is given in this book). During the funeral oration, the cardinal drew a parallel between Contardo, the professor of law, and Joseph Moscati, the professor of medicine. The cardinal ended the oration by saying:

I agree in thinking that we are in the presence of a new Contardo Ferrini. Two men of similar sentiments: two truly worthy scientists; two sterling characters: two devotees of fervent and sincere piety: two pure souls, who remained untouched by the filth of our times and by the lusts of the sense: two professors of lay universities, who have sanctified their chairs by the purity of their teaching: two apostles who have left their mark on this generation. Perhaps God wishes to glorify them together, so that they should be an example to our century, and so that there should be some recognition of what science and a good Catholic laity is worth when placed at the service of a noble cause and the realization of the evangelical ideal.

Contardo Ferrini was beatified in 1947, forty-five years after his death. Joseph Moscati, who died in 1927, was canonized in 1987.

Saint David Roldan
1907 – 1926
Martyr
Mexico

Saint Salvador Lara
1905 – 1926
Martyr
Mexico

Three laymen martyred during the Mexican revolution were canonized on May 21, 2000 together with a group of twenty-two other martyrs who were members of religious orders. These laymen of Zacatecas were killed for belonging to the National League for the Defense of Religious Liberty (LNDLR) whose goal was to defend the rights of the Catholic Church by peaceful and legal means. From 1926 through 1929, the Church in Mexico was severely persecuted. Church buildings were seized by the government, priests went into hiding, religious ceremonies were forbidden, and Catholic people lived in fear. Mass was secretly offered in the people's homes.

Manuel Morales, president of the National League, called a meeting on July 29, 1926. In addressing the gathering he said, "The League will be peaceful, without mixing in political affairs. Our project is to plead with the government to order the repeal of the constitutional articles that oppress religious liberty." (Manuel's biography is included in this book.)

Attending the meeting was **David Roldan**, vice-president of the National League and a member of the Youth of Catholic Action. David was born in Chalchihuites, Mexico. Idealistic and virtuous, David entered the seminary to study for the priesthood, but had to leave because of the poor financial situation of the family. He worked as a miner, but in his free time, he often helped Father Batiz with his pastoral duties (Father Batiz also was canonized). At work, David was highly regarded by his co-workers and supervisors. He was very active in the Church, and is known for having gathered signatures on a petition that requested the repeal of the anti-religious laws by peaceful and legitimate means.

Salvador Lara was also a person of high ideals and was a fervent member of his church. He, too, entered the seminary in Durango, but had to leave for similar reasons — the poor financial situation of the family. After leaving the seminary, Salvador worked to support those who depended upon him. Father Batiz welcomed Salvador's help in the affairs of the parish, and he admired Salvador's work as president of Catholic Action and as secretary of the National League. When Father Batiz was arrested, Salvador called a meeting to find a way to free the priest by legal means. Soldiers learned of the meeting, and they broke into Salvador's home and arrested the officers of the National League. Before leaving the house, the soldiers gave Salvador's mother unfounded hope for his return by telling her the prisoners would be taken to Zacatecas to present their declarations. At headquarters David Roldan, Salvador Lara, and Manuel Morales were placed in a cell with Father Batiz.

On August 15, 1926, the four prisoners were put in two cars for the journey to Zacatecas. In the mountains near Puerto Santa Teresa, the cars stopped and the prisoners were taken out. A proposal was made by the guards: the prisoners would be set free if they declared their acceptance of President Calles' anti-religious laws. All four refused. Father Batiz and Manuel Morales, the twenty-eight-year-old president of the League, were taken forward. Father Batiz pleaded with the guards to free Manuel since he had children to support, but Manuel refused saying, "I am dying for God and God will care for my children." The two were then shot.

David Roldan, nineteen, and Salvador Lara, twenty-one, were led forward. While bravely facing their executioners they cried out, "Long live Christ the King and the Virgin of Guadalupe!" Reportedly, Salvador's cry was so intense and so loud that the executioners were unnerved, but fired their weapons, nonetheless. One of the soldiers, who admired Salvador's heroism, looked at the body and lamented, "What a pity we had to kill this man, so grand and strong."

David Roldan, Salvador Lara, Manuel Morales, and Father Batiz were all beatified on November 22, 1992. With twenty-five other Mexican martyrs who were members of the clergy and religious orders, they were canonized on May 21, 2000. Pope John Paul II advised during the canonization ceremony: "May the example of these new saints, a gift of the Church in Mexico and to the Universal Church, spur all the faithful, using all the means within their reach and especially with the help of God's grace, to seek holiness with courage and determination."

Servant of God Diban Ki-Zerbo
1880 – 1980
Shepherd, Slave, Catechist
Africa

This candidate for canonization spent his whole life in an area north of the present state of Ghana in eastern Africa. His village is referred to as Zizin-Da, and it was here that he was born into a large family. Little is known of his early years except that he served the family as shepherd during the rainy season and was accustomed to a great deal of freedom.

In 1896, when Diban was almost twenty, the French colonized the country and subjected the villagers to various harassments, including the burning of their millet fields. To keep Diban from starvation, his parents sent him to live with an uncle in Bouare, a village to the north. Unfortunately, while in Bouare, Diban was captured by native slave traders who sold him for a few bars of salt. After a time he was sold again, this time for a number of goats.

For several months Diban was kept in chains, his left wrist chained to his right foot. When his owners finally thought they could trust him, Diban was unchained and assigned such menial tasks as pasturing sheep or working in the fields. He worked so diligently and carefully that his master's wife wanted to reward him by letting Diban marry and have children. There were many women slaves who greatly admired him since he was handsome, strong, and athletic. The young girls even composed songs in his honor that they frequently sang for him. Diban was not interested. He had vowed never to take a wife while in captivity, or to be any part of the trade in human beings.

One day when his master was away, Diban decided to escape. He ran two days and a night when, thoroughly exhausted, he decided to rest. He then climbed a tree for a better view of his surroundings, and was greatly disappointed to see his master coming directly toward him. Diban's master ordered him to come down from the tree, and when he did, Diban's master struck him so hard on the back of his neck that Diban fainted. Diban was beaten and returned to the village where he was forced to work, despite the pain he endured.

Diban made a second attempt at escape, this time at night. He was pursued by torchlight, and when he was captured, he was dragged back to the village. This time he was tortured: his arms and legs were tied behind his back with water-soaked ropes that shrank as they dried and cut into his flesh. Diban afterward declared that he had never suffered so much.

Diban had a simple love of the "God of my Fathers," that sustained him, and helped him believe that one day he would indeed escape his captors. One night in a dream he saw a beautiful young woman, surrounded by a bright light. She held out her hands to him and seemed to call him to her. Just as he was getting ready to move toward her, he awoke. Diban believed the woman was telling him to try again to escape.

One day, as he was pasturing his master's flock, Diban was thinking of escaping when suddenly, out of nowhere, a man appeared before him. The man wore a wide belt and carried a rod. The two men looked at one another for a time before the man asked if Diban had come alone. Then, just as suddenly as he had appeared, the man vanished.

Diban left immediately in the direction he thought the visitor had come from. Diban went south to Kabara, to the Niger River where a fisherman offered Diban hospitality and hid him when the master's brother came looking for him. The next day, another fisherman took Diban to an encampment of white men who were members of a missionary order known as the White Fathers. The first priest Diban met was Father Garlantezec, who took Diban to the mission at Segou on March 11, 1899. When Diban went into the chapel of the mission, he saw the image of the young woman he had seen in his dream. He then learned that she was the Mother of Jesus, who loved him deeply.

Diban joined the group of young men who had helped build the mission. He soon distinguished himself by working as a mason and as a cook. Diban studied the Catechism, and 1901 was baptized. Soon after, he began training to be a catechist. Diban was given the name Alfred when he was baptized, but Father Ficheux of the mission decided to add the name Simon, after the apostle, because of Diban's warm heart, his faith, and his hard work.

In 1903, Father Dubernet, Superior General of the mission, asked Diban if he had ever thought of getting married. There many young girls who had been rescued during a siege who were now living with the White Sisters, so Diban had many young ladies to choose from. In 1904, he married one of these girls, Louise Coulibaly.

When a mission was started at Ouagadougou, Diban and his wife moved there to help with the work. For this work, Diban became known as one of the founders of the Church in his own country. Soon there was a church, a missionaries' residence, a school, and a dispensary. And in 1905, Diban and his wife welcomed their first son.

After a time Diban entertained the thought of visiting his birthplace. He had heard that, although his mother had died, his father was still living. The village happily welcomed his return, and encouraged him to stay. The name of the man who had captured him and kept him in slavery for so many years was revealed to him, and Diban was advised to seek him out and take revenge. Diban resisted saying, "Never. I forbid you to touch him . . . I have forgiven him." With these words, he demonstrated a love for God and man that was to remain with him throughout his life.

Diban returned to his missionary work and moved from Ouagadougou to Navrongo, and after his work was completed there, he moved to Reo and then to Toma. Unfortunately, while he was in Toma, his beloved wife died. Her death left him alone to raise three small children, Maurice, Marie, and Georges. After a long period of mourning, Diban thought it best, for his children's sake, that he remarry. He took his time in choosing another wife, finally settling upon Folo Ki, who would take the name Theresa at her baptism. They married in 1917.

The First World War caused difficulties in Diban's village, and he returned amid rumors of villagers being forced to fight in the "White Man's War." Diban was placed in charge of the defense of his village, but as soon as peace was restored, he returned to his charitable endeavors at the mission of Toma. Courageous and very active, he worked hard in various endeavors as a farmer, gardener, mason, cook, tailor, nurse, carpenter, catechist, choirmaster, spiritual advisor, and, in his free time, as a hunter.

When the White Fathers temporarily left the mission, Diban organized classes and prayer services on Sundays. On Thursdays, he supervised catechism lessons for women. On Tuesdays and Wednesdays, there were catechism classes for boys and girls. He continued this activity for ten years, until the younger catechumens were sufficiently prepared to help, and then to replace him in the spiritual formation of the village.

According to Theresa, Diban had little time to himself as he was often summoned to help those in distress. He was most often called upon to tend the sick, and he was so successful that many considered him a doctor. He was gentle, patient, and radiated peace, which helped the worried and the sick enormously. He spoke of the love of God, and if the patients were receptive, he prepared them for baptism. His life was permeated by faith and nourished by the Holy Spirit.

Diban found great consolation in prayer, saying that prayer was like air and food for the Christian, the very substances of life. He worked among the sick for many years, knowing that God was always there looking down upon him and his efforts. He often climbed the hill to the church where he spent time in adoration before the Blessed Sacrament. At home in the evenings, he gathered his family for prayers, hymn singing, and meditations on the Bible. The Rosary was often recited, and there was conversation about the important events of the day.

In Diban's village there were many non-Christians who tried to protect themselves from evil by wearing rings, bracelets, or pendants that had been consecrated to unknown deities. Diban vigorously denounced such activities saying, "I have never been afraid of anything, not threats nor evil actions. I have never worn an amulet nor worshiped false gods. Those I know who protected themselves by believing in fetishes are now dead, but the Lord has kept me alive. . . ."

Diban's biographer and friend, Father Gabriel Pichard, states: "Alfred lived in the presence of God through his faith. He viewed the realities of his family life, that of the village and the whole world openly, illuminated by a hidden light that enabled him to always adjust his life to the will of God. . . . At first sight there was nothing extraordinary about him, except for the fact that he experienced the simplest things in life in the true spirit of the Gospel. I think that sometimes this must have taken heroic courage."

It seemed the good Lord wanted Diban to be officially recognized for his work in establishing so many missions and for his successful catechetical work. This acknowledgment came about when Diban's son, Professor Joseph Ki-Zerbo, took his father to Rome in 1975 where they met with Pope Paul VI. Diban was more than one hundred years old at the time. A photograph taken in the pope's reception room shows Diban sitting on the throne while the pope raised his hand in blessing.

Another pope would recognize Diban's achievements. On May 10, 1980, Pope John Paul II, who was paying his first visit to Burkina Faso, celebrated Mass in the huge square at Ouagadougou. At the time, Diban lay dying in the town's hospital. Since the pope could not visit the dying man personally, he sent Cardinal Gantin to give him a rosary and his blessing.

Diban Ki-Zerbo is known as the founder of the Church in his region of eastern Africa. The last action taken on his Cause for beatification was made in 1998.

Servant of God Dino Zambra

1922 – 1944
Student, Soldier
Italy

Dino was undoubtedly proud that his paternal grandmother, Marguerita De Lellis, was a direct descendant of the great saint of charity, St. Camillus de Lellis. His parents, Gerardo Zambra and Elena De Giorgio, both deeply religious were, in turn, proud of Dino's intelligence and his early interest in religious matters. His mother educated him in the faith, in human values, and in the value of generosity in money and services to the poor.

Soon after his reception of first Holy Communion and Confirmation at the age of seven, Dino showed signs of a deep interior spirit. This was demonstrated when he fractured his right arm and was taken to the hospital. His mother marveled that Dino did not utter a single complaint when the accident occurred, or when the arm was being set. When she asked if his injury hurt, Dino replied: "Yes, mother, it hurts a great deal, but I am thinking of Jesus and all that he suffered."

From the first elementary class to the third year of high school, Dino was always first in his class. He is remembered as being brilliant and always available to help his slower companions with their lessons.

As a member of a noble and rich family, Dino could have availed himself of an easy life, one of safety and convenience. Instead, when he was eighteen, he left home for Milan to enroll in the Catholic University of the Sacred Heart. His quick mind, his modesty, and his quiet behavior earned the deep respect of his teachers and fellow students.

During his years at the university, Dino worked tirelessly for the Association of St. Vincent, winning the confidence and esteem of the poor. He also participated in the "Group of the Gospel" with great enthusiasm. He began to keep a diary, which was published after his death, which shows the progress of his spiritual life. For a time he considered becoming a religious, but his tender letters to his fiancée indicated he was called to the married life.

Dino was called to military service on February 10, 1943, and departed for Ascoli Piceno, Italy. After a few months, he was transferred to Grottaglie and then to Oria where he became gravely ill. He was sent to the Ospedale Sanatoriale in Lecce where he won the respect of doctors, nuns, and his nurses with his patience, good humor, and graciousness. Unfortunately, Dino succumbed to his ailment at the age of twenty-two.

His family, worried that they had not heard from him in sometime, went to all the military places he had served and learned of his death. They arranged for the exhumation of his body and its removal to the Church of St. Maria Arabona in Lecce. During the days when it was lying in state, the citizens kept vigil day and night.

The Cause for Dino Zambra's beatification was opened on the diocesan level in 1961. The last action taken on his Cause was in 1998.

Servant of God Dominic Cesari
1912 – 1949
Postal Employee
Italy

Dominic was born into a religious family. He spent almost all of his childhood in the care of his maternal grandparents, who raised him in a spirit of prayer and faithfulness to the teachings of the Church. When he was eleven years old, he began studies at Montalto Marche Seminary. During the next seven years, Dominic distinguished himself as a person of great piety with perhaps a vocation to the religious life. At eighteen, he was admitted to the Missionary Institute of the Consolata in Turin, but had to leave after four months for reasons of health. When his health improved, Dominic entered the order of the White Fathers at their seminary in Rome, and from there he was sent to the general curia in Algiers. Five years later he left the order, agreeing with the superior that he did not have a true vocation.

After returning to his family, he attended a school in Spoleto. When the war began he enlisted, and was wounded in battle and taken prisoner. His imprisonment began in Porto Bardia, but he was soon sent to a prison camp in Egypt, and then to another in Bombay, India. He was transferred from the Bombay camp to another located in the fields of Yol, near Punjab, on the slopes of the Himalayas.

During his long and severe imprisonment, Dominic was a model of true charity and Christian goodness. He encouraged others to pray and begged them to be firm in the faith. He strengthened his fellow prisoners by his example and with words of encouragement. He was often ridiculed by the guards and by some of the prisoners, but he continued, nonetheless, in exhorting all to depend on the mercy and love of God.

After six years of imprisonment, Dominic was released. He returned to Italy, but seemed to have difficulty adjusting to his freedom. At first, he occupied himself in small and humble jobs, making himself useful to whomever asked him for help. Finally, in the autumn of 1947, he accepted a position in Rome in the orphanage of St. Giuseppe, founded by Blessed Louis Guanella. After a year, Dominic resigned to accept a position with the local post office. Soon after, his health began to deteriorate, though for a long time he lived in great pain without complaint. In 1949, he was hospitalized in Rome and died March 9, at the age of thirty-seven.

The Cause for his beatification was opened in 1967. The Sacred Congregation for the Causes of Saints carefully studied Dominic's spiritual writings and declared him a Servant of God in 1974.

Servant of God Edward Ortiz de Landazuri
1910- 1985
Medical Doctor, Father of Seven
Spain

Edward Ortiz de Landazuri said the most painful experience of his life took place when his father, a military man, was arrested at the beginning of the Spanish Civil War. His father was arrested not because he was a member of the military but because he was a Catholic. Edward and his mother were permitted to spend the night before the execution with his father, which Edward said were the most excruciating hours of his life. The experience marked the beginning of a religious crisis that brought Edward back to God.

Edward was born in Segovia, Spain, in October 31, 1910, and received his medical license 1933. He began to practice medicine at the Hospital of the King at Madrid, and then went to Germany to complete his medical studies, obtaining his final degree in 1940. He then practiced in the Hospital Clinic of Madrid for the next six years, until accepting the chair of General Pathology of the Faculty of Medicine of Cadix. Soon after, he left this position to work in the Pathology Clinic of Medicine of the University of Grenada. He taught until 1958 when he moved to Pamplona to organize a department of medical pathology at the University of Navarre. Edward was named head of the Internal Medicine Services of the Hospital of Navarre and was in charge of a sixty-bed pavilion. It was here that he stayed until his retirement.

On June 17, 1941, at the age of thirty-one, Edward married Laura Busca Otaegui, a pharmacist he met in 1935 when he worked at the hospital in Madrid. The couple had seven children who were the joy of their father's life.

Edward was always anxious about his spiritual progress. In June 1952, he asked to be admitted to Opus Dei. His admission was the beginning a serious effort to continually improve his spiritual life while following the path opened by its holy founder, St. Josemaria Escriva de Balaguer, whom Edward deeply admired. Little by little, conscious of divine grace, Edward acquired a simple and strong piety.

Edward had a peaceful and joyous attitude and worked with a surprising intensity. His work day began early with Mass and often ended well past midnight. He was friendly with everyone, and was for his students both a master and a guide. He was pleasant and worked hard to please God by using the talents God had given him. To his patients, Edward was a true friend, someone who was interested in their personal lives as well as their physical and spiritual conditions.

As a member of Opus Dei, Edward advanced quickly in the spiritual life, which had a pleasant and benevolent effect upon his family, friends, colleagues, students, and patients. Edward's every effort seemed to turn his soul increasingly toward God. Hundreds of students and medical graduates and an estimated 500,000 patients came under Edward's care.

In 1983, at the age of seventy-three, Edward stopped teaching. Shortly after, he was diagnosed with a cancerous tumor, which proved extensive and incurable. The doctor recognized the gravity of his situation and accepted it, uniting his sufferings to the sufferings of Our Lord. In spite of his illness, Edward's last two years were ones of intense professional activity and earnest preparation for his soul's encounter with God.

In May 1985, Edward entered the Academic Clinic of Pamplona, where he had worked with devotion on countless patients. There he died, repeating the phrase: "Senor, increase faith in me, increase hope in me, increase charity in me so that my heart looks like yours."

One of Edward's colleagues, Dr. Landazuri, a profoundly Christian doctor said of Edward: "He was a person with a great capacity for friendship, friends that he cared for and to whom he wrote frequently. . . . Many people who knew him said that he was a saint."

Edward's holiness became well known, and many who sought his intercession received favors. Reportedly, these favors have become more numerous every day, which prompted the appointment of a vice-postulator. The Cathedral of Pamplona was the site of the opening of the Cause of beatification. The archbishop appointed the tribunal that conducted the first session of the process into the life and virtues of this holy doctor.

Venerable Egidio Bullesi
1905 – 1928
Sailor, Ship Designer
Italy

Egidio lived only twenty-three years, but in that short time, he accomplished a great deal in the world and attained great sanctity for the next.

Born in Pola, Italy, to Francis and Maria Bullesi, Egidio was the third of nine children. He was exuberant, impulsive, cheerful, and intelligent which he proved while attending school. In 1914, during World War I, Egidio's mother, worried for the safety of her children, took nine-year-old Egidio and his siblings to Hungary and then on to Austria. Egidio's father Francis stayed behind and worked in Pola.

As for so many, the war proved a great hardship for the Bullesi family. Mother and children did not return to Pola until 1919. Egidio and his family enjoyed a time of relative peace, though the family's financial situation impelled the thirteen-year-old Egidio to look for work. He found work as an apprentice on the docks of Pola, where he heard language that he never heard in his devout home. Nevertheless, with courage, he maintained his high ideals and in time gained the admiration of his fellow workers.

Following the example of his sister, Maria, Egidio began to spend his free time engaged in the activities of Catholic Action, working with young people. He also joined the Third Order of St. Francis in 1920 when he was fifteen.

At nineteen, Egidio enlisted in his country's navy, and served with 1300 other seamen on the ship named the *Dante Alighieri*. During his two years of military service, Egidio set a fine Christian example. He avoided bad speech, and corrected the language of his friends with charity and courtesy. He was punctual at his work, and gladly discussed religious problems with those who approached him. He continued his apostolate of helping others with great success while completing his studies to become technical designer.

After the navy, Egidio went home to his family and to a position as a designer at the shipyard of Monfalcone (Gorizia). He resumed his apostolate among the workers, and spent his free time in helping the poor through the activities of the Society of St. Vincent de Paul.

Egidio was diagnosed with tuberculosis at the hospital in his hometown of Pola. He spent a year in the hospital, while his family alternated between hope of a recovery and disappointment. He accepted his illness with admirable courage and Franciscan serenity, offering his life for the benefit of missionaries. He became gravely ill in 1929, and he died on April 25, four months short of his twenty-fourth birthday.

Egidio was buried in the habit of a Franciscan tertiary. His body was laid to rest in the communal cemetery of Pola. Many, including members of the Catholic Action and sailors around the world, soon knew his reputation of sanctity.

His Cause for beatification was introduced by the Curia of Trieste in 1974. As part of the process, Egidio's remains were exhumed and taken to Barbana, in northeastern Italy. The Cause was completed in 1977. Venerable Egidio now awaits beatification.

Venerable Ezequiel Huerta Gutierrez
1876 – 1927
Singer, Choir Director, Father of Ten
Mexico

Ezequiel Huerta Gutierrez was born on January 7, 1876 to Isaac Huerta and Florencia Guiterrez Oliva. A pleasant, idealistic, and very sociable child, Ezequiel helped in his father's store. Sometime very early in his youth, Ezequiel was riding with his father and several others in a wagon filled with barrels of tequila. Isaac, a deeply religious man, suggested to his son that they recite the Rosary. One of the other men grumbled aloud about the praying. A few miles down the road, a wheel came loose and the wagon overturned, throwing everyone and everything to the ground. The only one who was hurt in the accident was the man who grumbled. From then on, the Gutierrez family custom before leaving on any trip included reciting the Rosary.

The family home was in Magdalena, but when Ezequiel and his brother, Salvador, were sent to school in Guadalajara, the mother suggested they sell their house and move, which they did.

Ezequiel had a beautiful tenor voice. He studied music and singing with an Italian master and learned the main parts of several operas. He also formed a large choir, which sang in the churches of Guadalajara, and they went from church to church to sing the praises of God at various services and festivals. When an Italian opera company came to town and their star became ill, Ezequiel was selected to replace him. Ezequiel was such a success that he was offered a contract to sing with the company. He refused, saying that his voice was dedicated to the service of God.

104

When Ezequiel was twenty-eight, he married Maria Eugenia Garcia. They were a happy and religious couple who welcomed ten children into their home. Ezequiel dearly loved his wife and children and was a dedicated family man who was generous and affectionate. Ezequiel's daughter recalls that her father rose early each day and sang as he bathed and then tended the flowers in the garden. He then left for Mass with some of the children. She also reports that he said the Rosary every day, and that he received Holy Communion with the utmost concentration and devotion. He joined the Franciscan Third Order in 1925, and he faithfully observed all the devotions and the rule of this venerable order.

Ezequiel was so idealistic that he did not like to charge for singing at church services. Two of his brothers, Jose and Eduardo, had become priests, and Ezequiel left his brothers to make financial arrangements with the various churches for his singing. His dear wife meticulously managed what he earned. When the religious persecutions in Mexico from 1923-1926 closed churches, Ezequiel found work as the custodian of the church of San Felipe Neri.

General Ferreira, who organized the persecution, suspected the two Huerta family priests of being instigators of the rebellion. He also thought that Ezequiel's wife was a member of the Cristeros, a movement which opposed the persecution. Active members in the resistance were two of Ezequiel sons, Manuel and Jose de Jesus (whose biographies are given elsewhere) who were members of the Union Popular and who participated in a number of battles in the Jalisco region. When Ezequiel's wife, Maria, and two daughters attended a secret Mass, they were arrested, but, thankfully, were soon released.

The police came to search Ezequiel's home, looking for members of the resistance. Though they found nothing suspicious, Ezequiel was arrested, nonetheless. Tearful and emotional, the children kissed their father farewell for the last time.

A young seminarian friend of the family, Juan Bernal, was present during the inspection of the house, and he provided testimony about Ezequiel's last hours. At the prison, Ezequiel was questioned by Sergeant Felipe Velazquez. Velazquez wanted information about Ezequiel's two brothers who were priests, about his two sons who were fighting in the resistance, and about the Cristero movement. Ezequiel said nothing, and was beaten until blood began to appear all over his body. When the sergeant threatened to torture the two priests and even to hang Ezequiel by the legs, Ezequiel said nothing but began to sing "My Christ lives, my King lives." He was beaten so badly for singing that afterward he could barely make a sound. Finally, Ezequiel was carried to a cell where he joined Juan Bernal, the young seminarian. Without a complaint about his condition and the cruel treatment he had endured, Ezequiel told Juan Bernal where Marie could find some money he had saved for her.

Ezequiel was martyred on April 3, 1928, in the cemetery of Mezquitan. With eight companions who were also martyred for the faith, Ezequiel now awaits his eventual beatification. Two of his fellow martyrs were his sons Manuel and Jose.

The Decree of Valor for Ezequiel was declared by the Congregation on May 21, 1999.

Servant of God Filiberto Vrau

1829 – 1905
Founder
France

This Servant of God, together with his brother-in-law, the Servant of God Camillo Edward Feron, founded so many organizations and saw to the building of so many religious structures that one is amazed so much was completed during a lifetime.

Filiberto (Philip) Vrau was born into a wealthy family. His father was an industrial financier in the city of Lille. The Vrau family firm manufactured the famous "fil au chinois" sewing thread which helped underwrite the Vrau family's generosity and that of brother-in-law Camillo Feron, who married Filberto's sister.

Even though Filiberto had received a Christian education, he abandoned the practice of religion and went searching for something to ease his uneasy soul. He even explored spiritualism, but at the age of twenty-five he experienced a complete conversion. From that moment on, he developed a great devotion to the Eucharist that influenced his entire life, including his efforts to establish Nocturnal Adoration. He experienced a great deal of satisfaction when he organized in Lille the first International Eucharistic Congress.

The city of Lille at the time had annexed four suburban communities that needed places of worship. Filiberto and Camillo financed the building of six new churches and the Cathedral of Notre Dame de la Treille. The brothers-in-law also financed the building and maintenance of Catholic schools — twenty-eight schools for boys and forty-four for girls. The crown of their school building efforts was the creation of the Catholic University, a huge endeavor in which they enlisted the help of prominent citizens. A school of law was started, then schools of literature, science, theology, and medicine, which included hospices, clinics, and hospitals. In all of their efforts, Filiberto and Camillo did everything according to the spirit and social doctrines of the Church; chaplains assumed the responsibility of overseeing the moral and religious integrity of their projects.

Additionally, Filiberto Vrau was active in the field of Catholic publications and in the Conference of St. Vincent de Paul. He also organized the Circle of Catholic Workers and a guild that was conceived as a religious association between the owners of various firms and the workers. Filiberto established the only professedly Catholic commercial school in France, a Catholic school of arts and crafts for higher industrial studies, and a Corportion of St. Nicholas for spinners and weavers with a co-operative fund supported by monthly assessments on both employers and employees. Both Filiberto and his brother-in-law were always concerned for the religious and social needs of workers.

Filiberto died in 1905; his brother-in-law Camillo surviving him by three years. These Servants of God, whose days were full of works for the Church, have not been separated in death. Their remains are entombed in the chapel of the Catholic University of Lille.

Filiberto Vrau's Cause of beatification was introduced in 1930, the same year as that of Camillo Feron.

Blessed Francis de Paula Castello y Aleu
1914 – 1936
Chemist
Spain

Francis' father, who worked for a hydroelectric company, died two months after the birth of this Servant of God. Francis's mother Theresa was a teacher, and to her fell the responsibility of caring and educating her three children, Theresa, Marie, and Francis. Francis proved to be an intelligent child and showed a fondness for religion at an early age. While his mother prepared him for his first Holy Communion, he answered the questions in the Catechism without hesitation and without mistakes.

Francis was born in Alicante, in the southeastern part of Spain, but the family moved to Lerida to be closer to his mother's teaching position. Francis began his secondary studies at the age of eleven at the school of the Marist Brothers. During this time, Francis made his first steps in the apostolate. Four years later he received an urgent call to go to his mother. She died before he reached her. The fifteen-year-old Francis keenly felt the loss of his mother, but he assumed the responsibilities of the house and the care of his sisters.

Francis began his studies in chemistry at the Institute of Sarria operated by the Jesuits. One of his teachers, Father Roman Galan, invited Francis to undertake spiritual exercises, which proved to be enlightening and a decisive experience. Afterward, Francis knew how to balance his studies with an intense apostolic activity. He joined the Federation of Young Christians, a perfect apostolate for this young man who knew how to speak to the young and who set an example of strong piety and ardent generosity. Francis engaged in other apostolates, and taught the faith wherever he went. He avoided making enemies by avoiding passionate political discussions, especially those before the beginning of religious persecutions and the Spanish Civil War.

After obtaining his degree in chemistry, Francis began working as a chemist in the Cros Factory of Lerida, and with his earnings he provided for the expenses of his sisters. Francis became engaged to Maria Pelegri, but their plans for marriage were thwarted in 1936 when twenty-two-year-old Francis was called to military service in the Red Revolution. He was incorporated in an infantry unit that occupied a small fort in Lerida. He was able, however, to eat his meals and spend the night at home. On July 18, 1936, Francis was ordered to another barracks, but soon found himself in prison as part of the religious persecution. The churches of the city were burned and priests were murdered; the city was described as something of hell having fallen to the wild instincts of men without control. Francis' prison cell was dark, with only two small windows for light. One of his companions later testified that Francis kept his good humor throughout the ordeal, putting his faith before all else.

Francis was transferred to the city jail in Lerida on September 12. Here he was mockingly called "fascist," with the Popular Court claiming he had "fascist ideas." Standing before the judge he was asked, "Are you fascist?" The young Catholic militant answered, "I am not, and I was never a member of the political left."

The court based these false accusations on the fact that Francis possessed grammar books in German and Italian; therefore, he must be a fascist if he had books in these languages. Francis answered the charge: "These grammars permitted me to perfect myself in these languages which are necessary for my profession, that is all."

Then came the question: "Are you Catholic?" To this Francis answered without hesitation: "I am. And I am proud of it." He was promptly condemned to death. Francis faced the condemnation with a courageous smile and without becoming disturbed.

The judge, to give some semblance of legality to the case, invited Francis to defend himself. Francis replied, "Of what good would it be? It is useless because I am being condemned for being Catholic. I gladly accept the verdict. The biggest happiness in this world is to die for Christ. I would give my life a thousand times for this cause and without hesitation."

Francis and his companions were returned to prison to await the execution of their sentences. Joy permeated the soul of this Servant of God who, with his companions, began to sing hymns. During the next few hours, Francis wrote letters of farewell to his family. Three of his letters are preserved: one to his sisters, another to his spiritual director, Father Galan, and the third to his fiancée. To his sisters he wrote: "Divine Providence wanted to choose me as a victim for poor sinners. I absolutely do not want you to cry for me because I am so happy. . . ." To his spiritual director he wrote that he was prepared to die and that he was calm and happy. "In a short time I will see the Father's glory. Thanks be to God." He asks that the priest give his farewell to the members of the Federation and to various people whom he mentioned.

His letter to his fiancée was very poignant. Since her two brothers had been murdered for being Catholic, Francis wrote that she should be proud to have had two brothers and now her fiancé condemned for the sake of God, and he spoke of his intense joy at dying for the cause of the faith. He then told her, "If you can, get married soon. From the height of heaven I will bless your union and your children. I don' t want you to cry. No. I don't want it. So be proud of me. . . ."

The time soon came when Francis and his prison companions were driven to the place of execution, the cemetery of the city of Lerida. Several armed militiamen came with them. During the ride the group sang the Credo, "I believe in God," from the sacred liturgy.

We know from a witness, Henry Foles, what then took place: The prisoners lined themselves in a row with Francis in the middle. They joined hands and then Francis exclaimed in a strong voice, "I forgive you all." While Francis' eyes were raised to the heavens and his lips were moving in prayer, the weapons fired. The eight innocent Catholics fell to the ground. The witness approached Francis to see if he was still alive. Francis was found with his head turned to the right, his eyes half open and on his face a sweet, angelic smile. It was 11:30 p.m., September 29, 1936. Francis was only twenty-two years old.

The Cause for the beatification of this heroic martyr was introduced in 1986. The document *Positio super Martyrio* was given in 1992.

Frank Duff
1889 – 1980
Legion of Mary Founder
Ireland

Frank Duff's family was considered wealthy. His father, John Duff, had reached the higher echelons of civil service, and his mother was an accomplished pianist and singer who, like her husband, had inherited a sizable fortune. Frank, the eldest of the family's seven children, learned from his father to appreciate the beauty of the Irish countryside. Frank developed a life-long enjoyment of bicycling from the time he spent cycling about the picturesque highways and byways with his father. From his mother he learned Irish songs, and since she read to the children in the evenings, he learned to appreciate literature. Although not considered exceptionally holy people, both parents are said to have been "honest-to-goodness Catholics," who taught the children their prayers, trained them in the virtues, and made certain they attended Sunday Mass.

When Frank was about nine years old, the family moved to a large house in County Dublin. Frank began to attend private schools, including one run by the Holy Ghost Fathers. Frank did not like school: he had a strong dislike for mathematics, preferring history and languages. He was sent to Blackrock College, and by the time he was thirteen, Frank was studying five languages: Irish, English, Greek, Latin, and French. He was an enthusiastic participant in athletic and sporting activities, especially cricket. He received a permanent injury from a cricket ball: during one match a ball struck him behind the left ear, knocking him unconscious and permanently impairing his hearing. His hearing loss would prove a significant handicap.

At the age of eighteen, Frank finished his schooling and like his father, secured a position in civil service. His father suffered ill health, and had to retire, and his mother's inheritance was greatly reduced. Frank was suddenly the breadwinner of the family. He made a name for himself, and received a salary increase, when the state's Department of Finance adopted a new mathematical system invented by Frank.

At the age of twenty-four Frank joined the St. Vincent de Paul Society, which drastically changed his life. The poverty in Dublin at the time was appalling. Great numbers were unemployed and families lived in one-room tenements in the slums experiencing hunger, squalor, religious neglect, and often drunkenness and depression. Frank and his fellow St. Vincent members were determined to help with not only the physical needs of the poor, but also with their spiritual needs. When the society distributed money and food to the destitute, they included medals, scapulars, and holy water. Many are said to have returned to the sacraments by Frank's gentle appeals.

Frank was told that a proselytizing center had been set up where almost 150 poor people were offered a free breakfast on the condition they took part in a Protestant service. Because many Catholics were attending these services, Frank, with a fellow Catholic Joseph Gabbett, decided to counteract the problem. They rented a large, unused stable and invited the same people to have breakfast and hear a sermon, which was almost always about the danger of betraying their religion by attending Protestant services. Frank would sometimes speak to the group, but mostly he washed dishes and swept up. When World War I began,

Frank and Joseph visited the barracks, talked with the men about the Catholic faith, and distributed the brown Scapular of Our Lady of Mount Carmel and the Miraculous Medal. They also arranged for priests to hear confessions.

When Frank was about twenty-seven he joined the Third Order Carmelites and began to recite the Divine Office. He once remarked, "I have looked on the Divine Office as pure communication with God." Toward the end of his life he once confided, "Since I first started saying the Office in 1917, I have never missed a line of it." Between 1914 and 1922 it is reported that he spent nearly three hours a day praying in church, this in addition to his fulltime civil service job. Some years later, in a letter to Pope Paul VI, Frank wrote, "I have said five decades of the Rosary daily, without ever omitting it, since the year 1914."

The course of Frank's life was greatly influenced when he read St. Louis Marie de Montfort's *True Devotion to the Blessed Virgin*. From this book came the idea for the Legion of Mary. On September 7, 1921, in the presence of Father Toher and Frank Duff, and with a statue of the Immaculate Conception in their midst, thirteen ladies attended the first meeting of the Legion of Mary. From the beginning, the apostolate had a pastoral nature in helping the poor and sick. The women would incorporate into their lives what they had learned from the *True Devotion* and they would look to Our Lady for guidance.

While the Legion would undertake all kinds of apostolic work, the group looked to a pressing problem first — prostitution. Because of cruel poverty, many young girls had resorted to selling themselves. Thirty-one street girls lived in one house of evil reputation, and Frank and five sister legionaries worked to persuade the girls to attend a retreat in a nearby convent. Within a few days of the start of the retreat, all of the girls, with the exception of two Protestants, had confessed and received Holy Communion. Frank and the Legion saw to the complete rehabilitation and physical care of all of the girls.

At the time, St. Vincent de Paul Society was open to men only, but the Legion of Mary was open to both men and women. The Legion spread quickly across Ireland and into Scotland and then England. When the St. Vincent de Paul Society was unable for various reasons to open a hostel for homeless men in Dublin, local government officials sent for Frank. They liked his work in rehabilitating street girls, and they offered him the large North Dublin Union Building and the funds to repair and alter the building if he would open the hostel. On March 25, 1927, the feast of the Annunciation, the Morning Star Hostel opened to two hundred homeless men. The Legion presidium that was formed to take charge of the hostel was the first men's presidium of the Legion to be organized in Dublin. Because of their efforts, and those of Frank Duff, it is said that only God knows the number of men reclaimed from degradation and the mire of sin and vice.

When the government saw the successful outcome of the hostel for men, another building of the Old North Dublin Union complex was given to the Legion for the care of destitute women and unmarried mothers. After Frank and others performed the necessary alterations, two hundred women and children were admitted as permanent residents at the Regina Coeli Hostel. Legion sisters were placed in charge, and they established a routine of daily Mass and Holy Communion and the recitation of the Divine Office as well as the Rosary and the Legion prayers. The residents were asked to perform necessary chores and were given spiritual instruction. Not only did the residents attend Sunday Mass, but many also attended *daily* Mass. The boys were trained as altar servers and all the children attended school. Frank established his headquarters at the hostel, and from there, for the next forty-five years, he directed the widely expanding organization.

Even though the Legion operated in parishes with the approval and guidance of the priests and the archbishop, some priests objected to the Legion, claiming the Legion took over the functions of the priest and were "busy-bodies." Finally, in 1931, certain influential people persuaded forty-two-year-old Frank to journey to Rome to seek the approval of the pope. During a meeting with Pope Pius XI, the "Pope of Catholic Action," Frank Duff outlined the history and objectives of the Legion and answered questions. When the pope asked what he could do for him, Frank answered: "If we could say that it was the personal desire of Your

Holiness that the Legion of Mary would spread over the whole world, this would be a great mode of propaganda for spreading the Legion." To this the pope answered simply, "With all my heart I express that desire."

That same year the Legion was invited to open a presidium in New Mexico. Soon the Legion was established in St. Louis, Los Angeles, and San Francisco. Before long, the Legion spread throughout the United States and then Canada. The *Queen* magazine, and Father Roger Mary Charest of the de Montfort Fathers, promoted the Legion of Mary's goals of the sanctification of its members and true dedication to the apostolate with special emphasis on true devotion to Mary. The growth of the Legion in the United States was phenomenal. Also, presidia were started in Australia, New Guinea, many islands in the Pacific, and in Africa.

All the while that Frank was founding hostels and overseeing the world-wide work of the Legion of Mary, he was still employed fulltime in the civil service. With all the duties that demanded his attention, Frank thought of retiring. His income after retirement would be greatly reduced and because he still supported his widowed mother and a sister, he sought their advice. With their approval, Frank finalized his retirement plans and was then able to devote more of his time to the Legion of Mary.

The center of Frank's life was the Mass, but there were other devotions that he dearly appreciated, especially the holy Rosary and the Rosary of the Seven Dolours of Our Lady. Frank also participated in a yearly pilgrimage to Lough Derg, an abandoned, ancient monastic settlement. The grueling pilgrimage consisted of fasting, walking barefoot, an all-night vigil, and certain penitential exercises. Frank began the yearly pilgrimage in 1915 and continued his yearly trek for forty-nine years. In addition to the pilgrimage, he made yearly retreats.

When Cardinal Pacelli (Pope Pius XII) was elected the successor to Pope Pius XI, Frank received an invitation to visit Rome. After learning of this, the papal nuncio in Dublin entrusted Frank with the responsibility of delivering to the pope all the official documents relating to the apparition of Our Lady at Knock, Ireland. Frank Duff considered this a rare privilege. Remarkably, the appointment with Pope

Pius XII was set for April 28, the feast day of St. Louis Marie de Montfort. At this meeting, the pope gave his ardent support and encouragement to the Legion of Mary.

Frank suffered a mild stroke during his later years, which kept him bedridden for five months. His confinement gave him time for reflection. After his recovery, Frank received an invitation from the Vatican to attend Vatican II as an official lay observer. Cardinals, bishops, and religious superiors recognized him and approached him with open arms and warm greetings. Later he was to exclaim: "It was thrilling to have all those bishops from the ends of the earth greeting me eagerly because I represented the Legion." At one point during one of the Council sessions, Cardinal Heenan of England drew the attention of the 2,500 bishops to the presence of Frank Duff in their midst. A sustained applause was offered as a sincere gesture of gratitude for all that Frank Duff had done for the church. Frank gave no less than thirty-two formal addresses to various groups during Vatican II and was privileged to have a private audience with Pope Paul VI, who expressed his appreciation for what the Legion of Mary had already accomplished.

The golden jubilee celebration of the Legion of Mary was held in Dublin on Sunday, September 7, 1971, with a solemn high Mass concelebrated by many spiritual directors of the Legion together with archbishops and the papal nuncio. Frank was then eighty-two years old and the Legion had spread throughout the world.

In 1979, when Frank was ninety, he consented to make a series of videocassette recordings. In these recordings, he demonstrated his keenness of mind and his indomitably cheerful spirit. These recordings have been distributed throughout many countries where thousands who never met Frank Duff can hear his words of wisdom and witness the gentle spirit that guided the Legion.

In 1979, Frank Duff and three Dublin legionaries went to Rome to assist at Pope John Paul II's Mass in his private chapel. Afterward they had a specially prepared Irish breakfast with the Holy Father who gave every possible encouragement to all Legion undertakings. At the end of their meeting, the Holy Father bade Frank farewell with the words,

"Remember, victory comes through Mary." The pope knew very well the good that resulted from the activities of the Legion, since years earlier, when the pope was the archbishop of Cracow, he had encouraged the establishment of the Legion in his archdiocese.

Frank's cheerful disposition endeared him to many and helped him to overcome many difficult situations. His love of the outdoors went with him his entire life, as did his love of bicycling. He bicycled until the day he died.

Frank Duff received his eternal reward on Friday, November 7, 1980, at the age of 91. His body lay in state in the Regina Cocli Hostel Chapel where people from all states of life visited, including government officials, bishops, priests, religious, countless legionaries, the rich and poor, schoolboys and girls, and the residents from the three hostels. A cardinal, three archbishops, other bishops, and the Legion's spiritual directors concelebrated the funeral Mass. During the Mass, four extra deacons were required to distribute Holy Communion to the crowds who gathered outside the chapel. A telegram of sympathy was received from Pope John Paul II in which he joined in praying for the eternal repose of Frank's soul.

Those who knew Frank Duff claim that he was a very ordinary man who was very close to simple, ordinary people. But Frank was an ordinary man who accomplished extraordinary things. According to the postulator of Frank's Cause for canonization, Dominican Father Bede McGregor, "Frank empowered a tremendous number of ordinary young men and women to become apostles, not just in their own place of origin, but throughout the world."

Frank Duff wrote his own account of the founding of the Legion in his book, *Miracles on Tap*. He also wrote many articles, booklets, and the Legion Handbook that embodies the philosophy, spirituality, and rules of the Legion of Mary. Frank received many awards during his lifetime, but perhaps the greatest was when Monsignor Rothlauf called him the "Magnifier of Mary." He has since been called "Ireland's Greatest Export."

Servant of God Franz Jägerstätter
1907 – 1943
Mine Worker, Farm Worker
Austria

In the same district of upper Austria where Adolf Hitler was born (Braunau) and where Adolf Eichmann, the administrator of the infamous "final solution of the Jewish question" spent his childhood (Linz), is the village of St. Radegund, where the rebel-peasant Franz Jägerstätter lived in sharp contrast to the principles of these two promoters of evil.

Franz was the son of Franz Bachmeier, a farmer who died in World War I. The father's death left Franz's mother in an awkward situation — unmarried and pregnant. Franz's mother eventually married Herr Jägerstätter who adopted the illegitimate boy and, as was the custom, gave his farm to his adopted son when Franz came of age.

While in school, Franz was a very good student who excelled in many subjects, but especially in reading and religion. His conduct, however, was less than acceptable. Some say he was a little wilder than most young men his age. He seemed to always want to be the first to try something new, and the villagers remembered him as always ready for a fight and "a little wild in his ways and in his style of living." One villager remembered that Franz had the reputation of being one of the most accomplished fighters in town in his frequent battles with young fellows of neighboring villages over the attention of the local girls. For one such fight, Franz and his opponent were arrested and spent several days in jail. The fight divided his village, and for a time Franz was banished. He returned when tempers settled.

Franz's interest in the ladies got him in deeper trouble when he was thought to have fathered an illegitimate child. Many of the villagers believed he was not the father, while his friends believed he was. Whether he was or he was not, Franz voluntarily supported the child, a fact confirmed years later by his widow and in letters he wrote from prison.

In addition to his "weakness" for the ladies, as the villagers and his friends called it, Franz was known as a proficient sportsman, a young man who loved dancing, bowling, and card-playing. Perhaps the most vivid memory of his neighbors is that Franz was the first in the village to own a motorcycle. After its acquisition, Franz would leave home for a few days without telling anyone where he was going. His journeys often took him to visit a friend in Salzburg, who reports that Franz was a happy young man who took part in dances, harvest festivals, and similar social events.

Franz had a reputation as a young man of many faults. Later in life, he admitted regret for his past, and he wrote on many occasions against immorality. Franz's change of heart and conduct is given in a long letter he wrote in 1936 to his godchild whose father had died. In attempting to take the place of the father, Franz counseled the boy in matters appropriate to a boy of fifteen or sixteen:

> Should it be that temptation is ever so strong that you feel you must give in to sin, give some thought then to eternity. For it often happens that a man risks his temporal and eternal happiness for a few seconds of pleasure. No one can know whether he will ever again have an opportunity to confess or if God will give him the grace to repent of his sin. Death can surprise us at any minute, and in an accident one very seldom has time enough to awaken repentance and sorrow. This much I can tell you from my own experience.

When Franz was about twenty he left the village for almost three years to work in the iron mines in the Steiermark region of Austria. In the socialist environment that was quite hostile to Catholicism, Franz apparently realized how precious his faith was, and he began to grow more in love of God and in the practice of virtue. When he returned home, the change in Franz from a wild young man to one of virtue was so sudden that many villagers were surprised. As one put it, "It was almost as if he had been possessed by a higher power." He even reported to the parish priest that he was thinking of joining religious life. Father Karobath discouraged him, pointing out to Franz that he had an obligation to continue the operation of the farm for his parents. Some believe that Franz then chose a bride whose characteristics were in keeping with his own spiritual beliefs when he married the deeply religious Franziska in 1936.

Although generally liked, some villagers believed that Franz went to extremes with his newfound practices of virtue and was a fanatic. He was known to have sung hymns while he worked and tended cattle, or while walking to and from the parish church. Some villagers remember Franz saying the Rosary while plowing and even interrupting his farm work to say prayers or read a little of the Bible. Franz said gambling was a vice and refused to play cards, though he willing joined the game if assured they would not play for money. He also resisted visiting the local taverns to avoid becoming involved in political arguments that always seemed to develop when Franz was present.

Franz adopted another form of self-denial: According to a neighbor, when Franz began to receive the Holy Eucharist on a daily basis he would fast until noon as a special mark of respect for the sacrament. He was known to pack a knapsack with food and meat, and to distribute these to the poor. His wife quietly condoned the practice, even though they lived simply and almost in poverty themselves. Franz is known to have had a deep devotion to the Blessed Mother and to have often visited her shrine at Altötting. His wife sometimes accompanied him, riding on the back of the famous motorcycle.

When the sexton of the village church died in 1940, Franz assumed his responsibilities, holding that position until he departed the community for military service. He discharged his duties conscientiously, objecting strongly to people talking and gossiping in the sacristy. He attended to the cleaning of the church buildings, assisted in the services, kept altar boys under control, and maintained a number of organizational duties. Franz refused to accept donations for assisting at such private functions as funerals and weddings. His dedication and the exceptional manner in which he performed his duties are recognized on a marble marker on his grave that identifies him as *Leherbauer*, meaning "sexton."

By all accounts, Franz was a good farmer. After his conversion, some thought that Franz must have neglected his farming duties in order to carry out his religious activities, though his family says that after his conversion Franz reorganized his work schedule and became more efficient. Franz was an exemplary neighbor who was always on hand whenever help of any kind was needed. He was also known as an excellent husband and father as well as a good friend.

Shortly before the Nazi invasion of Austria, Franz spoke out forcefully against the regime. After the forces of Adolf Hitler crossed the Austrian border in 1938, the people of Austria voted almost unanimously to incorporate Austria into Germany. What distressed Franz even more were the number of Catholic clergymen who actually praised the Nazi Party for its many good works, an action that influenced the people to give the Nazis the almost unanimous victory at the polls.

Although he was strongly encouraged by many, including Father Karobath, to vote for the Nazi Party, it is common knowledge in St. Radegund that Franz did not cast one of the "yes" votes, but is believed to have cast a "void" ballot, an action that could be traced to dissenters. To Franz, a yes vote represented a betrayal of Church and nation.

Franz refused to cooperate with the Nazis, including refusing to contribute to the "little red collection boxes," which supported many of the Nazi-sponsored welfare or patriotic organizations. The only time he did contribute was for the benefit of the police. He may have felt a need to help these defenders of law and order since he had given them trouble in the past.

In 1940, Franz was ordered to report for military training in the German army. He immediately set about seeking the advice of priests and even the bishop as to whether it was morally acceptable to fight in the

Nazi organization. After prayerful consideration, he reported for training, knowing full well the act of defiance he would eventually take. Before long, and at the request of the mayor of St. Radegund, Franz was returned home to care for his family and his farm.

On March 1, 1943, Franz received a letter requiring him to report to the German army. Before he left, he wrote a letter to his wife encouraging her to accept whatever would come in the spirit of penance, relying upon the good Lord for help. In this farewell-sounding letter, Franz asked his wife to tell his daughters often about the Child Jesus and heaven. "Learn to become a family loving one another and forgiving whatever may come. Forgive all those who might cause you hardship and me, too." Apparently, he knew the criticism she would encounter because of the action he would take: the absolute refusal to fight in what he considered an unjust war that opposed his Catholic faith and introduced National Socialism.

Franz's refusal to fight was well known in his village, and his family was subjected to severe criticism, as he had expected. Because he faced imprisonment and death for refusing to fight, some said he was neglecting his responsibility to his family. Franz countered the criticism in one of his letters: "Again and again people stress the obligations of conscience as they concern my wife and children. Yet, I cannot believe that, just because one has a wife and children, he is free to offend God especially in all the things he would be called upon to do. Did not Christ Himself say, 'He who loves father, mother or children more than Me is not deserving of My love?' "

His critics charged that Franz was mentally deranged and was, in effect, committing suicide. Regardless of the harsh comments, and even though he was encouraged by some priests and even his mother to cooperate, Franz stood firm.

In a letter to a priest friend, Franz begs for prayers, saying that no one can dispense him from what he viewed as: "A great danger to the health of my soul that this 'gang' presents. As it is, it is so hard to come even one step closer to perfection. Is it even conceivable to try in such an outfit? Everyone tells me that I should not do what I am doing because of the danger of death (in prison); but it seems to me that the others who do fight are not completely free of the same danger of death. . . . I believe it is better to sacrifice one's life right away than to place oneself in the grave danger of committing sin and then dying." Franz then begs for a remembrance at Mass, "as long as you are permitted to offer Mass."

At the Ennis Induction Center Franz was immediately placed under military arrest when he refused to cooperate. The following day he was taken to the military prison at Linz. He was left with the impression that his execution could take place at any time.

In his first letter home he sent greetings, "From my new home. Just don't forget me in your prayers and everything will turn out for the best according to God's will. . . . May God give you everything that you desire for yourself — as long as it is not likely to be a hindrance to your eternal welfare. For the sorrows of this world will quickly pass." He then asks his wife for a few necessities — soap, a work shirt, etc. — and concludes by asking that she enclose in her letter, "one of those little pamphlets about the visitation of the Blessed Mother in Portugal."

During the early days of his imprisonment, he was encouraged in his position by other prisoners, and is believed to have converted two condemned men. He expressed the opinion that he could accomplish more among the bitter and disillusioned prisoners than he could ever hope to do in the army.

In another letter to his wife he wrote: "I am always troubled by the fear that you have much to suffer on my account: forgive me everything if I bring injustice down upon you." He then tells her that he declared himself ready to serve in the medical corps because he would then be performing a charitable service, but changed his decision when he realized that he would only be replacing someone else who would be doing the killing for him. His change of decision mattered little: his request for medical corps duty was denied.

Throughout his imprisonment, Franz was well aware of the liturgical observances and the feasts of saints, as he mentioned them in his letters. He was also keenly aware of the farming activities that should be taking place. Two weeks after his arrest he wrote: "Now it is almost time to be sowing the oats. The weather must really be glorious. Whenever you have questions about the farm, write me so that I can help with my advice. Needless to say, I am always ready to do so — though I would much rather be helping you in person." His letters speak of yearning and sadness at being unable to help at home: "If it were possible for me to get a leave to clear away some trees, you would also have the straw in the cow barn changed. If the weather stays like this, you will begin mowing the hay by Easter and will be able to have fresh feed. Yesterday we already saw apricot blossoms in our prison garden."

Probably the saddest of his letters is one in which he instructs his wife, "I think it is better for you to tell the children where their father is. . . ." He then addresses some words to his three little daughters, Rosalie (born in 1937), Marie (born in 1938), and Aloisia (born in 1940): "I thank you from the bottom of my heart for the greetings you sent me. It makes me very happy that you pray for me so often and that, as I hope, you have become better children. . . . It would make me so happy if I could see you again — I would gather you all together so that you would soon learn not to fight among yourselves any more. Also, you must not lie, and at mealtime you should always be satisfied with what you get. Then, I believe, the Heavenly Father will grant that I can come home to you someday, even though it may not be right away. . . . I greet you, my dear little girls. May the Child Jesus and the dear Mother of Heaven protect you until we see one another again." One can read through his letter the heartache his sacrifice produced.

Franz's letters were filled with prayerful comments about his trust in God, of upholding the faith, of praising God, and offering all pains and sorrows as sacrifices. He writes: "One week passes after another; the important thing is that we do not let a single day go by in vain without putting it to good use for eternity." And again: "It is good that man cannot see into the future. This way we can take each day just as God sends it to us." To his wife who had assumed his sexton duties, he does not forget to instruct her, as she would soon be decorating for the May devotions: "Do this in honor of our beloved Mother of God. She will surely not abandon us." Franz also notes in his letters that from time to time he was permitted to receive Holy Communion from a visiting priest.

After a few months, Franz was transferred to the Military Investigation Prison (Berlin-Tegel) in Berlin. Here Franz was counseled by the prison chaplain to cooperate, but Franz, the chaplain reports, would not be swayed. Franz said the regime was evil as expressed by the Church and was engaging in fighting an unjust war. Under the circumstances, he found it impossible to accept service.

Franz's trial was set for July 6, 1943. When his attorney saw that the courtroom was already in use, he persuaded the court to assign court officials to persuade Franz to change his position. Since the prisoner was sincere and humble, the court agreed. So it was that Franz, a peasant farmer, was confronted by two high-ranking officers who were in a position to impose a death sentence. Arguments were presented until the officers' appeals reached a point where they were pleading with the prisoner not to force them to condemn him to death. The trial was brief, and the sentence was swift: death.

Several days later Mrs. Jägerstätter received the dreaded news and she, together with the parish vicar, journeyed to Berlin for a final, twenty-minute visit with her husband. She later wrote: "With heavy hearts we had to take leave of each other."

Franz's final letters home were heartrending, but filled with confidence in God, of his willingness to give his life for a just cause, and a plea to his wife for forgiveness. As a final word to his children, Franz wrote: "Now, my dear children, when Mother reads this letter to you, your father will already be dead. He would have loved to come to you again, but the Heavenly Father willed it otherwise. Be good and obedient children and pray for me so that we may soon be reunited in heaven. . . ." His final letter was written on a special form provided for this sad purpose by the authorities, who would send it to the prison authorities and then to the military court. The letter would then be mailed to the family as notification that the execution had taken place.

On the night before the execution, Prison Chaplain Jochmann again visited Franz. The chaplain found Franz completely calm and prepared and without a word of complaint. On a table was a form, which, if he would sign it, would save Franz's life. Franz again refused. The next morning Franz declined to read some pamphlets the chaplain offered him and instead read for a time from the New Testament. Later, he walked calmly to the scaffold. He was thirty-six years old.

The chaplain, who witnessed the execution, commented later to a religious sister: "I can only congratulate you on this your countryman who lived as a saint and has now died a hero. I say with certainty that this simple man is the only saint that I have ever met in my lifetime."

Franz's body was cremated. A Sister George located the urn containing the ashes and took them to St. Radegund for burial. Since there was a transportation delay, she writes that she had the urn in her room for several days, and adds, "I can testify that I found extraordinary help in a spiritual matter through Jägerstätter's intercession. . . . In our eyes, Jägerstätter, whom we knew only from the chaplain's account, was one of God's special friends."

Although the villagers at the time did not regard Jägerstätter's actions as heroic, they eventually grew to appreciation his courage and convictions. So it was that in December 1984, responding to a nationwide petition, the president of Austria issued a special posthumous Award of Honor to Franz Jägerstätter. Franz is now regarded as a national hero and a Catholic martyr, and his story has become widely known through radio and television dramatizations, which have inspired millions.

Franz's grave is located against the west wall of the St. Radegund village church where visitors from around Austria and the world frequently pause for a prayer of intercession. In 1999, a stained glass window was installed in the Newman Centre of the University of Toronto recognizing this farmer who died for his faith.

The postulator for his Cause for beatification writes that Franz Jägerstätter: "Can be considered as a martyr of faith and justice in the sense of the ecclesiastical tradition. He was faced with the alternatives: God or idol; Jesus Christ or Fuhrer."

Blessed Frederic Ozanam

1813 – 1853
Attorney, Founder of St. Vincent de Paul Society
Italy/France

A relic of St. Francis Regis is credited with the miraculous cure of the child, Frederic Ozanam. The frail five-year-old was suffering from typhus and was near death when his father, a physician, entered the parish church where Mass was being offered. Realizing the uselessness of the medicines he had given his son, Dr. Ozanam and his wife took their son to the chuch to offer prayers to St. Francis Regis for the child's recovery. Madame Ozanam reported that as soon as the saint's relic was placed on the child, the fever left him. A witness to the event enthusiastically confirmed the miracle.

Frederic was born in Milan in 1813. His family consisted of his devout parents, an older sister Elisa, brother Alphonse who was to become a priest, and brother Charles who was to follow his father in the medical profession. Frederic's father was known to have treated countless poor patients without charge, and Frederic's mother, also known for her charity, frequently visited the sick. Sometimes, without their knowing, husband and wife would meet in the same house of the needy.

Frederic's early education took place in the scholarly atmosphere of the Ozanam home with his sister handling the major tutoring, his father teaching him Latin, and his mother teaching him religion. When Frederic was six, Elisa contracted meningitis and died. Her death caused him great grief. By the age of nine, he was prepared to enter the Royal College at Lyons, which offered an elementary grades program. Radicals at the school who challenged the faith sowed doubt in the mind of a then fifteen-year-old Frederic, a doubt that would last but a few months but which struck him deeply. He once wrote: "The horror of those doubts that eat into the heart, pursuing us even at night to the pillow we have drenched with tears." One day during a walk, he visited the Church of St. Bartholomew. He drew near the tabernacle and pleaded for the gift of impregnable faith. Spiritual direction from Abbé Noirot settled his doubts.

At the age of eighteen, Frederic finished his studies. His father envisioned Frederic as a magistrate or judge of the royal court, even though Frederic seemed to have preferred a literary career. His father finally persuaded him to clerk in a law office in preparation for a legal career. Frederic also began training for a literary career by writing a defense of the faith that was published in the newspaper, *Le Précurseur*. Although the paper had an opposite view, the article, which was against a group known as the Saint-Simonians, was very well received. In Frederic's words, the Saint-Simonians, "Regarded Christianity as having been quite all right for past ages, but entirely inadequate to solve the world's present problems."

Frederic entered the university at the Sorbonne in Paris as a law student, and he soon became aware that most of the students were aggressively anti-Christian. Frederic actively sought out Catholic friends, finding three. He and his friends began a counter-offensive to the anti-Christian students and the many anti-religious professors. Frederic and his friends addressed formal protests to each professor who, in the face of opposition, modified their position so that many of the students, noting the change, returned to the faith.

While at the university Frederic stayed in the home of a devout Catholic, Monsieur André Marie Ampère, France's foremost mathematician and physical scientist. Through Ampère, Frederic was introduced to many distinguished men of science and letters.

As he walked to and from the university, Frederic sometimes walked through an area of the city that was crowded with the poor who lived in squalid conditions. One day as Frederic and his friend Jules Devaux walked through the area, Jules suggested they visit Sister Rosalie, a Daughter of Charity. Sister Rosalie worked among the poor and provided nursing care and a pharmacy that distributed free medical supplies. In addition, she provided a clothing dispensary, a nursery for children of employed mothers, and had established a trade school to help the children find employment when they were older. Jules Devaux helped Sister Rosalie, and after Frederic accompanied Jules on one of his visits to the sick, Frederic felt called to serve, too. When his studies permitted, Frederic went to Sister Rosalie for assignments, even helping her and others nurse the sick during the pestilence of 1832 that spread quickly through the slums.

In 1833, seven young men gathered to consider Frederic's idea of forming a union of charity. Though the writing of a constitution and bylaws would be delayed until the association had been functioning for some time, the group chose the name Conference of Charity. Under Sister Rosalie's influence, these young men pledged to offer material, moral, and spiritual assistance to the poor. At this time, Frederic was only twenty years old. In addition to his full-time studies, he went enthusiastically to his assignments, visiting the sick, seeing to the needs of many a poor family, and busying himself with finding homes for orphans.

At first the Conference of Charity was to consist of only the original seven members, but when appeals for help started coming from other parishes, the Conference of Charity decided to open its membership to every Catholic student who was unquestionably zealous in the practice of his faith. Father Faudet was the first of thousands of parish priests who welcomed the future St. Vincent de Paul Society.

At the age of twenty-three, Frederic received his doctorate in law, which qualified him to lecture as a member of a university faculty. He was determined to practice law as his parents had always hoped he would, but before doing so, he continued his studies for a doctorate in literature. Doctorate in hand, he returned to Lyons where he supervised the founding of a Conference of Charity. Later in the year, he began practicing law. Although he was not completely happy with law as a profession, he felt it a privilege to represent the poor to whom he afforded the greatest consideration. During one court session in 1837, he pleaded twelve cases and won them all.

While in Lyons, twenty-four-year-old Frederic served as the director of the Society for the Propagation of the Faith, founded by Pauline Jaricot in Lyons in 1921. Also, to supplement his meager earnings from his law practice, Frederic began writing again. One of his earlier works, a critical political essay entitled "The Two English Chancellors" which contrasted the characters and careers of Thomas Becket and Francis Bacon, had been published as a book, and was a huge success. Now he wrote a more scholarly brochure entitled "Church Property" and a larger work, *Origins of French Law*. The latter work was in defense of the faith. He also used his pen to promote the Society for the Propagation of the Faith.

Frederic began teaching law rather than practicing it when he became a member of the faculty of the University of Lyons. A short time later, on Easter morning while in Paris, Frederic received Holy Communion with 150 members of the Conference of Charity. The organization was growing: there were Conferences in fifteen French cities with fifteen new Conferences forming and more than two thousand young men as members.

Frederic, uncertain as to whether or not he should join the religious life or marry, went to his confessor, Abbé Noirot. Noirot strongly advised him to marry. Not long after, Frederic met his future wife Amelie Soulacroix when he visited her father on university business. Amelie was educated, charming, and devout, and after several visits to the Soulacroix home, Frederic abandoned all thoughts of a religious vocation. When an offer of a professorship at the Sorbonne in Paris was extended to him, Frederic extended a marriage proposal to Amelie. Amelie accepted Frederic, and Frederic accepted the Sorbonne. At twenty-seven he was the youngest man ever admitted to the Sorbonne faculty.

The couple was married by Frederic's brother Alphonse, now a priest, and spent their honeymoon in Rome. One summer, years before, Frederic had traveled to Italy with his father and had met with Pope Gregory XVI. He met with the pope again during his honeymoon trip. When the couple returned to Paris, they rented a small apartment five blocks from the Sorbonne and close to the Church of St. Sulpice. Their life was quiet and pleasant, with Frederic continuing to publish his writings to considerable scholarly and critical acclaim.

In addition to teaching, studying, and writing, Frederic also made weekly conference visits to the poor and contributed generously to their needs. After several years, just when the happy couple thought they would be childless, Amelie gave birth in 1844 to a daughter, Marie. Marie was to be their only child.

Frederic began to notice that he was tiring more quickly than usual. He developed a fever, but kept working, even taking on a literary mission to Italy for the Sorbonne. While in Rome, Frederic, his wife, and daughter met with Pope Pius IX. Frederic presented the pope with a report on the Conference of Charity — the Society of St. Vincent de Paul — and how it had grown. The Society had spread to England, Ireland, Germany, and Scotland, and in 1845 reached the United States. In 1846, the Society spread to Canada and Mexico.

Weakness and fever continued to haunt him, though he persisted in writing and promoting the Society. Frederic was calling upon Christians in France to vote for the new National Assembly, and when it was firmly established, Frederic joined the reorganized National Guard, which was organized to prevent a loosely organized army from inciting riots in an effort to overtake the national government by force. Before he left for duty, Amelie presented him with a scapular of Our Lady of Mount Carmel that she had made herself as a sign that she was placing him under the protection of Our Lady. When the turmoil was over, Frederic returned to his teaching, writing, and charitable assignments.

Frederic's health continued to decline, and by 1849 he was refusing all writing and speaking invitations. He managed to continue attending a weekly meeting of the Society, and his charitable visits, until he was stricken with pleurisy. He rallied, and again was able to attend Mass at his favorite church, that of the Carmelites, and to continue supervising the opening of other chapters of the Society. When sickness again visited him, Frederic began writing *LeLivre des Malades,* a book of Scripture passages that had always strengthened and consoled him. This, as well as many of his writings, was meant to save souls for Christ.

At the age of forty, Frederic's condition was diagnosed as tuberculosis, which later attacked his kidneys. Hope for a cure was unrealistic. After twelve happy years of married life, he thanked his dear wife for all the happiness she had provided and died after pronouncing this final declaration: "I love Him so . . . My God, my God, have pity on me."

The tomb of Frederic Ozanam is located in the crypt of the Church of Carmel at the Catholic Institute in Paris surrounded by a mural depicting the Good Samaritan. He was beatified by Pope John Paul II during his visit to Paris on August 22, 1997.

Frederic Ozanam is regarded as the principal founder of the St. Vincent de Paul Society. What began with a twenty-year-old college student and six others is now 875,000 members strong. The St. Vincent de Paul Society has 47,000 confraternities in 131 countries on all five continents.

Servant of God George (Jerzy) Ciesielski

1929 – 1970
Professor of Engineering
Poland

George Ciesielski was born in Cracow on February 12, 1929, and as a child, he soon displayed a quick and intelligent mind. He advanced rapidly in his studies and attended Cracow Polytechnic Academy where he excelled. During his summer vacations, he liked to organize educational sightseeing tours for his fellow students with an aim at inspiring them, in quiet terms, to practice virtue and to prepare themselves for the future.

George was known to have said: "The future is uncertain . . . speculation on the past is of dubious value. What is left is the present. It seems to me that it offers wide opportunities of action. It can start anywhere, so long as it does start and continues. . . . Would it not be right to ask oneself each morning: how can I serve God today?"

George carefully considered his vocation: "Each of us was granted his own path, his vocation. Keeping faith with that vocation is the

135

meaning of my existence. Your glory and our earned right to eternal happiness. Give me, Lord, the understanding of my calling for each day and give me Your grace to fulfill my vocation faithfully." The vocation, which he chose, was that of matrimony. He married in 1957 and the couple had three children.

In 1960, George received his doctorate in engineering from Cracow Polytechnic Institute and in 1968, he became a professor. While at the institute, George invented a method of binding structural cracks in cement with a special binding substance. In addition, George was renown for his construction of the foundation of the largest sports complex in Katowice, which was erected over a site of abandoned mines. Other buildings in the area had collapsed, but George's method of laying the foundation proved to be successful. In 1969, when George discovered that Sudan, Africa, was in need of qualified engineers, he moved to Khartoum where he became a lecturer at the University of Khartoum.

Throughout his life, George was a good Christian and an admirable example for others to follow. He never argued with others and always presented his ideas rationally in the form of dialogue, realizing that someone else might have a better idea than his own. He was always eager to help others and never sought an expression of gratitude. He said, "The work performed must be perfect; it should be performed well as a condition of meeting the transcendental goal. Salvation does not depend on the kind of work one does or the help one gives to another, but on how it is done."

This Servant of God was known as a gifted and patient instructor who respected all his students, Christian or Muslim. In reference to the Muslims he said: "They too are my brothers because we have the same Father in heaven." Some of his Muslim students are known to have called him "Rajul Allah," which means "Man of God."

Both in his professional and family life George consciously realized a Christian calling. He was a man of prayer, devoted to the Eucharist and to the word of God. Each day he attested to his faith, believing that it was a Catholic's duty to seek sainthood through patient, devoted, and systematic work, as well as through self improvement, helping others, and a deep prayer life.

George was teaching at the University of Sudan in Africa at the end of his life. On October 9, 1970, George took his three children boating on the Nile River. There was an unfortunate accident, and George and two of his three children were killed. He was forty-one. Almost immediately, George was regarded as a saint, and his Cause for beatification was introduced.

"Life ends inevitably in death. . . . After death is the judgment. . . . That judgment is the final evaluation of one's entire life," George said. "Would it then not be logical to apply the criteria of the Last Judgment in our daily life, so as to remember always what is awaiting us in the decisive moment?"

The last action taken on his Cause for beatification was made in 1995.

Servant of God George La Pira
1904 – 1977
Mayor, Professor, Ambassador of Peace
Italy

Those who knew George La Pira in his youth would probably never have expected him to one day be on a first-name basis with heads of state. Born into a family of humble means, George worked his way through college, studying accounting first and then jurisprudence. He graduated with honors, and began a long, active career teaching law at a Roman university. During his time as a professor, he became interested in St. Thomas Aquinas' *Summa Theologica*, which gave him a monumental theological vision of Christianity. Reportedly, George is said to have experienced "a particular clarity made of logical thought and the persuasiveness of conclusions," as he read this great work of Christian theology.

Encouraged by his friends, Joseph Lazzati and Contardo Ferrini (whose biographies are included in this book), George was drawn to the Secular Institute of the Kingship of Christ, an institute inspired by Franciscan ideals that operated within the Catholic University. George's involvement with the institute inspired him to join not only the Franciscan Third Order, but the Dominican's as well. When his classes permitted, George prayed and studied from dawn almost to the afternoon, when he devoted the rest of the day to meetings with young people. He was active with them in the organization of Catholic Action, which, among other endeavors, was devoted to being charitable and helpful toward the poor. He founded various Catholic groups for artists, students, and various professions in which he faithfully participated.

Sometime around 1936 George began living in the historic monastery of St. Mark's in Florence, the center of religious art and Florentine history. At times, when George lived elsewhere, he still considered the monastery his true home. George wrote for various publications, and in 1939, he founded and wrote for a magazine named *Principi*, which set the Christian premise for an authentic democracy. When the content centered on the evils of racism and the German dictator, and denounced the invasion of Finland and Poland, the fascists suppressed *Principi*. When he discovered that the secret police were searching for him, George escaped first to Siena and then to Rome.

After Italy was liberated by the Allies at the end of World War II, George decided to work for the good of men by entering politics. In 1946, George was chosen a deputy to the "constituent" meeting of the Christian Democratic Party. Because of his cultural and moral contributions, George became one of the greatest craftsmen in the formation of the new Italian Republic. He was re-elected in 1948 and was elevated to Secretary of State.

With three others, George founded the magazine *Social Chronicles* in which, among other religious articles, he published a beautiful commentary on the dogma of the Assumption of Mary.

In 1951, George decided to devote himself entirely to establishing peace in the world. He visited Stalin in 1951 hoping he would cooperate in establishing peace in Korea. That same year George was chosen mayor of Florence, much to the approval of the poor, and during his years as mayor, 1951 to 1957 and 1961 to 1965, he did a great deal to improve the city. He restored old neighborhoods, sought employment for the unemployed, preserved the jobs of two thousand workers, and opened international markets. Under his administration, public jobs of every type were made available. New schools were built, hundreds of roads were restructured and modernized, the poor were cared for and the hungry fed. The town theater was restored, as was the Historical Center. George is credited with transforming the city from a center of tourism to one of culture, peace, and Christian civilization.

George La Pira began a dialogue among Christians, Hebrews, and Muslims within the Conferences for Peace that he promoted in Florence between 1952 and 1956. He also spoke in Geneva in 1954 in a session of the International Committee of the Red Cross. He attended many conferences that sought to ensure peace in a world threatened by atomic destruction. In 1959, he was invited to speak at a conference in Moscow that was attended by the hierarchy of the Soviet Union. To this group George proudly announced:

I am a Christian believer. I believe in the presence of God in the history, in the incarnation and resurrection of Christ, and I believe in the historical strength of prayer; therefore, according to this logic, I have decided to contribute to the peaceful coexistence among East and West as Mr. Kruschev says. I suggest making a bridge of prayer between West and East to sustain this peace. . . . We must provide peace to the people, to build houses, to nourish the fields, to open shops, schools and hospitals, to reconstruct and to open the cathedrals . . . then our bridge of peace between East and West will become unshakable. And we will work for the greater historical ideal of our age, a peaceful time of human advent and Christianity.

We are told that the Soviets were astonished, and they were undoubtedly greatly annoyed when he added: "As you have removed from the Mausoleum of the Kremlin the dead body of Stalin, in this way you must also remove the dead body of atheism. It is an ideology that belongs to the past."

George La Pira also visited the United States where he encouraged the approval of laws dealing with the civil rights of ethnic minorities. While in the United States he conferred an honorary citizenship of Florence on the Secretary of the United Nations, U. Thant. George went to Tunisia in 1969, and from there went on to Helsinki, Bruxelles, Budapest, and Vienna in preparation for the conference in Helsinki. In 1973 he visited Hanoi, seeking peace in Vietnam.

George had contact with many heads of state including Nikita Kruschev, John F. Kennedy, Anwar Sadat, Chou En-lai, Abba Eban, and General DeGaulle. George also knew, visited, and wrote to Pope Piux XII, Pope John XXIII, and Pope Paul VI.

George's Christian inspiration was sustained by the prayers of cloistered nuns who prayed for the success of all his endeavors. They also prayed for him when he became ill and after he died on November 5, 1977, at the age of seventy-three. Shortly before his death George wrote to Pope Paul VI and received from the pontiff, "a long, affectionate and immediate answer."

According to his wishes George La Pira, although born in Pozzallo di Ragusa, Sicily, was buried humbly in the cemetery of Rifredi in Florence near the grave of the Rev. Facibeni, a saintly priest who had dedicated himself to the care of orphans and the poor.

The memory of George La Pira is very much alive today. This Servant of God wrote many books on political and religious subjects that are still in print. Additionally, he inspired the creation of the Association Georgio La Pira, which is very active in caring for the poor. The association is based on the voluntary service of their associates who distribute meals to the poor without distinction of faith, race, or nationality. It also provides housing at night for the homeless among many other services.

George La Pira was a spiritual man of cheerful faith closely united to Jesus and spiritually dedicated to the Blessed Virgin. His life of dedication to others and the virtues he practiced to a heroic degree prompted Cardinal Silvano Piovanelli, the Archbishop of Florence, to begin the diocesan process for his beatification. The Cause was accepted by the Congregation for the Causes of Saints in 1986.

Venerable Giacomo Gaglione
1896 – 1962
Victim Soul
Italy

Giacomo Gaglione was born a healthy child to Valerio Gaglione, an attorney, and his wife Amelia Novelli in Marcianise near Caserta. Giacomo's early years and adolescence were uneventful; later he would distinguish himself in the sport of bicycling.

Just as he was about to graduate from high school, at the age of sixteen, Giacomo experienced the first signs of an illness that would intensify and immobilize him in bed with paralyzed legs. The young man was not pleased with his situation, and struggled to deal with being the victim of an irreversible handicap. His attitude changed after he met St. Joseph Moscati, a well-known Catholic physician at the university in Naples (Moscati's biography is included in this book).

Giacomo felt blessed after meeting the sainted physician, and Giacomo was further blessed when, at the age of twenty-three, he met Padre Pio, the stigmatist of St. Giovanni Rotondo. The influences of these two Christian men helped Giacomo understand his illness not as misfortune, but as a gift from God. Giacomo abandoned himself to the divine will and participated in pilgrimages to Lourdes, Loreto, and Pompei. When he was about fifty-two years old, after a number of these pilgrimages, he founded an organization that he named the Apostolate of the Suffering. The bishop of Caserta, Monsignor Mangino, gave his full approval for the apostolate that was established to help patients accept and even to love their physical sufferings.

Giacomo worked tirelessly in the apostolate, even writing different books of meditation on the subject. Through the apostolate, he met many people who not only benefited from his example and his writings, but also asked him for prayers. Four years after initiating the Apostolate of the Suffering, Giacomo founded another organization, Hosts Upon the World.

After suffering for fifty years, Giacomo died at Capodrise at the age of sixty-six. His mother and his sisters Rosa and Nicoletta had assisted him throughout his illness.

Cardinal Corrado Ursi signed the decree for the introduction of the Cause of beatification. The *Decree super Virtutibus* was given February 17, 1994.

Servant of God Guido Negri
1888 – 1916
Military Captain
Italy

Of the twelve children born to Evangelist and Ludovica Negri, Guido was the last. He was born at Este near Padua and proved a happy and intelligent child. After finishing all the preliminary studies, he enrolled in the University of Padua and eventually earned a degree in literature.

Guido joined the military service and soon became an officer in the infantry. The men, who frequently criticized him, did not appreciate his Christian conduct. At the beginning of the Italian-Turkish war, Guido was sent to Treviso, where he also expressed his religious and patriotic feelings. In order to make the officers and soldiers understand his views, he gave a lecture entitled "Weapons and Literature" during which he expressed the opinion that only faith inspires true love of country. Thereafter, the men were less critical, and many came to appreciate and respect his opinions.

However, the men did not know how really virtuous Guido was. He engaged in almost continuous penance and fasting, and he even submitted his body to scourging. Every Friday of the year, and especially during Passion Week, Guido wore sackcloth under his clothing. In addition, he became a Dominican tertiary and was solemnly professed by the general of the Order of Preachers, Padre Giacinto Cormier. Guido faithfully observed all that the Dominican rule recommended.

When the war against Austria began in 1915, Guido was sent to Alto Cadore where he performed his duties with the perfect conscience of a soldier and a Christian. His careful obedience to commands earned a promotion to captain with the command of the fifth company of the 228th regimental infantry. During an assault on the Colombara Mountains where the enemy was entrenched, Guido was struck in the heart by a bullet and died. The "Holy Captain" as he was known, was buried on the field with sincere reverence by his soldiers. His body was later removed to a cemetery at Este where his grave immediately became the destination of pilgrimages.

In the great plaza of Este, the "Holy Captain" was posthumously awarded the country's Silver Medal of Valor for his bravery during his last battle. He received additional recognition when he was invoked during the Third National Congress of the Third Order Dominicans at Bologna in 1935. The diocesan informative process for his Cause of beatification was begun by the bishop of Padua who saw to its introduction.

Servant of God Isidoro Zorzano
1902 – 1943
Industrial Engineer
Argentina/Spain

Isidoro was a schoolmate of Josemaria Escriva, Founder of Opus Dei and remained his close friend throughout his life.

Isidoro was the third of five children born in Buenos Aires, Argentina. His family relocated to Spain when he was just three. For high school, Isidoro attended the General and Technical Institute of Logrono and later obtained a degree in Industrial Engineering from the Central School of Industrial Engineera in Madrid. After the completion of his studies, Isidoro accepted a position with the Andalusian Railway in Malaga.

On August 24, 1930, Isidoro decided to visit his friend, the future St. Josemaria Escriva, in Madrid. During a lengthy and profound conversation, St. Josemaria confided the inspiration he received on October 2, 1928, to found the Opus Dei. This was the first time Isidoro learned about the organization that his friend had founded two years earlier.

St. Josemaria advised that no one need abandon the world as if it were an obstacle to living one's faith. Within this new path, ordinary work itself would become a means of holiness and service to the church. Realizing that this was the channel for his desire to seek higher spirituality while continuing to work at his profession, Zorzano immediately asked for admission. From that day forward, Isidoro dedicated himself completely to God.

Isidoro returned to Logrono that same night, his life flooded with new light and meaning. He later wrote to his friend St. Josemaria: "I'm completely reassured now. I have a sense of well-being and peace that I've never experienced before." Except for occasional visits to Madrid during the first five years of his vocation, Isidoro was physically separated from the founder, but in their correspondence St. Josemaria continued to lead Isidoro toward ever-greater intimacy with God.

With the approach of the Jubilee year declared by Pope Pius XI in 1933, Isidoro prepared for a pilgrimage to Rome to obtain the Jubilee indulgence. He wrote to St. Josemaria in August of that year: "I plan to saturate myself well with the spirit of the catacombs, to live the early times of Christianity." One of Isidoro's companions at that time noted, "He had a great desire of gaining the indulgences from the Holy Jubilee, keeping in mind the basilicas he had to visit . . . and the prayers he had to recite which his confessor had indicated." Reportedly, Isidoro "gained the Jubilee indulgences with great fervor, as was his most ardent desire."

Second to his desire of obtaining the indulgences was his wish to meet with the Vicar of Christ. Because of the multitude of pilgrims, it was almost impossible, but in the end Isidoro reported: "We were received in audience by His Holiness." Isidoro thus became the first member of Opus Dei, with the exception of the founder, to meet personally with a pope.

Also in 1933, Opus Dei opened the Dios and Audacia Academy in Madrid. Isidoro frequently visited from Malaga, and was greatly admired by the students for his simplicity. The founder even had plans of making Isidoro the director. One student later wrote, "I was not yet a member of Opus Dei when I met Isidoro Zorzano in March 1935. He was quite young looking. Many of us thought he was just another student. And this made the friendship and confidence a whole lot easier."

St. Josemaria once wrote: "With order your time will be multiplied, and you will be able to give more glory to God by doing more work in His service." Realizing the value of this instruction, Isidoro became very orderly through constant effort. One of those who knew Isidoro at this time wrote: "In the midst of his many occupations he dedicated a daily half hour to mental prayer in the morning and another half hour in the afternoon. He did this with great devotion and recollection. He also attended daily Mass and received Holy Communion." He became very punctual in the fulfillment of his schedule. He would awake at 5 a.m. or earlier so as not to omit any of his planned spiritual exercises before reporting to work. His schedule was described as very meritorious and full of sacrifices because at all moments he sought only to give greater efficacy to his work and more glory to God.

Isidoro knew that he could not limit himself to practicing the virtue of organization; he had to teach it to others. When Opus Dei founded the students' residence at Valencia, the founder arrived to inspect it. Upon seeing the disorder in which they were working, he expressed to his assistants his desire to send for Isidoro so that "we may learn from him how to do things well. . . . So Isidoro arrived and we learned many things from him. He tried to teach with his example without giving arguments or long explanations . . . he reminded us of the value of little things which are converted into great things when we offer them to God. He helped us make good use of time."

One of the founder's assistants wrote: "One thing about him that I admired more and helped me more . . . was his extraordinary order and care for little things. . . . In general, order requires effort and for this I frequently had recourse to Isidoro."

Another piece of advice given by St. Josemaria was that of a daily examination of conscience. The founder wrote: "Examination of conscience — a daily task. Bookkeeping is never neglected by anyone in business. And is there any business worth more than eternal life?" He also wrote: "Do not neglect the few moments of mental prayer every day. At night the examination which is a question of three minutes. With these, your Rosary and, above all, your frequent Communion, nothing and no one can overcome you."

Isidoro struggled to live this advice. He once noted, "I do not neglect the daily examination; it is indispensable; it is the only way of polishing the rough edges of our soul and making sure we are always on the right track."

Isidoro had always wanted to move to Madrid to be closer to his friend, St. Josemaria, and this became a reality in 1936 at the beginning of the Spanish Civil War. Staying in Malaga had become impossible for Isidoro as a group of revolutionaries had sentenced him to death for being Catholic. Isidoro asked for a leave of three months from the Andalusian Railway, the firm for which he was then working. He was let go from his position when soldiers began searching for him, surely to imprison and assassinate him. His reputation for holiness was such that he would undoubtedly have been one of the first victims.

The next year, 1937, St. Josemaria and other members of Opus Dei took refuge in the Legation of Honduras. Isidoro is known to have visited them often to bring them all kinds of relief. St. Josemaria eventually returned to Madrid, and in April 1939 the war ended. With peace restored, Isidoro was reinstated in his job with the railway company.

In October 1937, an Opus Dei residence was opened and Isidoro was installed as administrator. In addition to this work, Isidoro seems to have had time to indulge in one of his few pleasures — mountain hikes with his friends. During these walks, they felt inclined to open their hearts to him, to discuss their problems, and to obtain advice. When they paused to rest, Isidoro would invite his companions to pray with him. His first apostolate would seem to be among the members of Opus Dei, especially those whose spiritual care St. Josemaria entrusted to his friend. These included a professor, a doctor, a teacher, and many others.

When Isidoro was about forty-one, his health began to decline. Eventually persuaded to enter the hospital, his condition was diagnosed as Hodgkin's disease, a malignant, progressive, sometimes fatal disease that causes enlargement of lymph nodes and other organs. For six months, Isidoro endured great suffering, and when his condition became critical, St. Josemaria administered the Anointing of the Sick. The two long-time friends had their last conversation on July 14, 1943, with St. Josemaria asking Isidoro to pray for certain intentions when he reached heaven.

Isidoro passed to his eternal reward on the eve of the feast of Our Lady of Mount Carmel, July 15, 1943. The next day, the feast of Our Lady, St. Josemaria celebrated Mass for Isidoro's soul. That same afternoon Isidoro was buried in the Almudena Cemetery in Madrid.

Immediately after his death, his reputation for holiness spread with requests for prayer leaflets and biographies. Five years later, so many answers to prayer were reported that the information process for beatification was started with Monsignor Leopoldo Eijo y Garay, Bishop of Madrid, presiding. The end of the diocesan investigation took place on June 17, 1994. Isidoro is now known as the Servant of God.

During his last illness, Isidoro gave us this thoughtful consideration: "God will always be faithful to us, even if we are not always faithful to him. What a friend! When we undergo suffering that seems impossible to bear, how reassuring it is to know that God always gives us the strength we need. All we have to do is fulfill his will at every moment."

Blessed Ivan Merz

1896 – 1928
Professor, Writer
Croatia

His many activities for the good of the church were such a profound influence upon the young people of his day that his memory is still inspiring present-day youth and inclining many to a closer relationship with God.

We cannot lay the spark of Ivan's love of the church on his early upbringing. He was raised in a liberal home where religion was considered a mere tradition, a formality, while the values of this world were highly rated. Ivan's father was a military officer in the then Austro-Hungarian Monarchy and was the chief of the railroad station. His was a secure financial position, which provided Ivan, who was born on December 16, 1896, with a happy, carefree childhood. Ivan's mother maintained her home in an upper middle class fashion and provided Ivan, an only child, with great love and attention.

In Banja Luka, the city of his birth, Ivan attended elementary school and graduated in 1914. He would later say that it was not the official religious instructions in school that eased him to the Catholic faith, but a secondary school teacher, Dr. Ljubomir Marakovic. Ivan said: "A Catholic layman has saved me for eternity." Professor Marakovic, Ivan's Croatian language teacher, directed Ivan through an interest in art and literature to moral and religious values. And it was because of Professor Marakovic's recommendation that Ivan kept a spiritual diary from which we can trace his spiritual development. Ivan's biographer, Reverend Bozidar Nagy, S.J., writes: "There are few people even among the saints and those chosen by God whose spiritual development and ascent to God can be as closely followed as that of Ivan Merz." Ivan's diary was maintained for eight years and filled twenty notebooks.

At the age of sixteen Ivan was attracted to a young lady, Greta Teschner, whom he met through friends of the family. Greta was also sixteen and Ivan, a chaste and sensitive young man, fell deeply in love with her. Unfortunately, their friendship was short lived. During the summer, while Greta was on summer vacation, she permitted a man to seduce her. When this man refused to marry her, she ended her life in despair. Afterward, Greta was occasionally mentioned in Ivan's diary. When he was eighteen he wrote on July 8, 1914: "Everything is passing. I hardly loved anything as deeply as I did Greta, and all the same, it has passed; I remember, it has refined me, but again, one can live without it too." The tragic loss of Greta served to bring Ivan to a higher and more exalted love, which he discovered in Jesus Christ and in the Catholic Church.

Ivan wanted to study art and literature, but his parents disagreed with this decision, believing him more suited to a military career. To please them, Ivan enrolled in the Military Academy at Wiener Neustat. He endured for only three months, having neither the liking nor the talent necessary for such a career. The experience, however, proved beneficial as Ivan was exposed to another side of life. He wrote in his diary on October 15, 1914: "The new officers were taking their vows to sacrifice all they had for God, the Kaiser, and their country, and all the colleagues got drunk like animals. God is cursed here in Croatia; the speech is vulgar. . . . Some of them sit on the floor drinking champagne out of bottles. Yes, these are the very same people who made fun of me yesterday for studying Latin, for striving for the spiritual."

Despite a temporary weakening of the faith, all was to be restored in greater measure and his prayer life increased in doubled portions as indicated by another entry in the diary dated October 24, 1914. In speaking of prayer he writes: "This conversation with the Almighty, this connection, the recognition of the Almighty, this is religion. Religion without prayer is dead. However, prayer is not measured by its length and it does not need to be read out of a book. Conversation from one's own feelings, meditation about the Scriptures and of the intentions of the Almighty, this is prayer."

When Ivan returned to Banja Luka for Christmas in 1914, his parents realized he had no interest in a military career and did not press him to return to the academy. Instead, he was permitted to study in Vienna, where he began studies in law and literature.

In Vienna, his cultural horizons expanded. He attended the theatre, concerts, and operas and read a great deal. All the while his spiritual maturity developed. Occasionally, the memory of Greta was resurrected. Yet he found joy in the Eucharist and made many notations about it in his diary as he did on January 27, 1915:

> I cannot comprehend that Christ, the Lord-Creator, He towards whom everything is aimed, whom man feels walking and sleeping, He who is strong and almighty, who puts the universe into motion, He who watches over every blade of grass and each little worm, that Christ whose hands and feet were pierced by nails, who was spat at, He who restored to life the dead and who loved children, and who at his own death darkened the sun and shook the earth, that He will be mine, He will talk to me, a man for whom I alone know rightly. For all this, just for this I know that it is Him, because He has shown in this His great love.

He was to write again: "He whom we feel around us, of whom our reason says is eternal, whom the soul unintentionally desires, He will doubtlessly be just. This brings us to a personal God. He does exist, and I believe this firmly, and even during the most difficult moments of temptation and doubt, I believe that He is the only, eternal, great God. And if He exists, it follows that our life has a purpose."

During the summer of 1915 and World War I, Ivan was drafted. While awaiting his assignment, he spent time with his parents in Banja Luka and continued to study literary works. He continued to write in his diary, which indicated that he felt a desire to perfect his soul and his character. He felt weak, and in sincere prayer, he turned to God for help. After thoughtful consideration, the eighteen-year-old made a vow of chastity, promising to be chaste before marriage. The vow was taken on the feast of the Immaculate Conception, December 8, 1915. He wrote: "I made my vow of chastity before marriage to the Blessed Virgin. . . . Maybe it will last as long as I live." This little premonition was fulfilled when he later took a vow of perpetual chastity.

Ivan was told to present himself for training in the army in February 1916. Unable to muster any interest in military training when he was attending the military academy in his youth, he now applied himself diligently to military life during the eight weeks he spent at Lebring, near Graz. He was then taken for further military training to Graz and Slovenska Bistrica. After passing an officer's exam in January 1917, Ivan was given command of a group of soldiers and they were sent to the front. Ivan participated in all the battles on the Italian front, staying there until the end of the war.

Ivan was exposed to the sufferings, death, and other horrors war brings. The Catholic faith, from then on, was more than ever the highest priority in his life. He wrote to his father: "I am grateful to God for participating in the war, because war taught me many things that I would not have conceived otherwise. . . ."

Even under the stress of wartime conditions, Ivan made a number of entries in his diary, many of which concerned his condemnation of war. His diary and correspondence indicate that he never took up arms or shot at the enemy. His greatest distress at this time, as noted in the diary, was an inability to attend Mass and receive the Eucharist.

Following the war, Ivan resumed his studies in Vienna, concentrating on literature and Roman and German languages. His diary no longer shows traces of spiritual conflicts — the war seemed to have had a positive effect on the development of his personality. His love of liturgy increased during this time, and to share with the young his love of the Catholic faith he joined an association called "Croatia" which was an organization of Croatian Catholic students. He soon became the secretary, gave lectures, and talked with his colleagues about the best way to engage in apostolic work when they returned to their home country.

In his diary, he discusses his immense joy after making the ninth Holy Communion for the first Friday devotion of the Sacred Heart. He expounded in his diary on his love of liturgy, saying: ". . .Liturgy is the greatest work of art that exists in the world, and in addition it is a central art since it presents the life of Christ who is the center of history . . . Liturgy is the expression of the spirit of the Church. . . ."

A scholarship made it possible for Ivan to leave Vienna for Paris, where he pursued his studies for two years at the Sorbonne and at the Catholic Institute. Besides his studies, Ivan collected material for the dissertation of his Ph.D, which he would receive later in Zagreb.

In Paris Ivan led a very spiritual life, to the admiration of his friends and the many people who took notice of him. Soon after his arrival, Ivan and his friends joined the charitable organization of St. Vincent de Paul. For his part, Ivan cared for a poor family in one of the suburbs of the city.

Ivan made few entries in his diary at this time probably because he was having difficulty with his eyes, which were threatened with blindness. In spite of this difficulty, he completed his studies. For a young man who loved to read literature and study, it must have been a great trial for him to restrict his reading. However, Ivan noted that he was able, somehow, to translate Paul Claudel's *Way of the Cross*.

Ivan was deeply impressed by a visit to Lourdes, and in a letter to his parents in which he encouraged them to deepen their religious life, he wrote: "You know that university life in Vienna, the war, my studies and finally Lourdes have convinced me completely of the truthfulness of the Catholic faith and that my whole life, therefore, evolves around Christ the Lord . . . the Catholic faith is my life's vocation and it must be the same for each man, with no exceptions."

His prayers for his father's return to the sacraments were answered in January 1921 when his father received Holy Communion for the first time in twenty years. His mother, however, still declined an active participation in the life of the church.

When Ivan finished his literary studies in Paris he settled in Zagreb where his parents had moved, and found employment as a teacher of French and German languages. This was to be his profession for the rest of his life. He soon received his Ph.D from the Zagreb University; his dissertation was on the influence of liturgy on French writers.

For six years, Ivan lived with his parents in a house named "Starcevicev Dom," and all the while he had a deep influence on the lives of many. As his close associate, Marica Stankovic wrote: "A new man appeared on our horizon. A man came for whom faith was not tradition but life, and who did not consider Catholic activities as a kind of sport but as a battle for immortal souls."

Soon after his arrival in Zagreb, Ivan joined the activities of a youth organization that would develop into the Association of Croatian Eagles. He held the offices of secretary and vice president until the end of his life. It is said that Ivan's greatest merit consists in the fact that he introduced into the Eagles' organization the ideals of Catholic Action that Pope Pius XI had proposed.

In his position as secretary and vice president, he attended meetings, engaged in detailed correspondence, visited branches of the organization in various cities, and gave lectures. The postulator of Ivan's Cause writes: "Ivan's aim was to help the young people receive cultural and religious education as well as a correct orientation in life. Ivan's presented in his program the development of spiritual life, the importance of the Eucharist, enthusiastic love toward the church, cooperation with bishops and priests, carrying out the pope's directions regarding Catholic Action, and the religious duties of the members of the Eagles organization."

To many of the young Ivan was a genuine friend, giving advice when asked, helping financially when needed, and finding employment for others. Ivan worked hard for the organization as his notes indicate, but unfortunately, one year after his death, the government in Belgrade prohibited the organization. The young, however, still inspired by Ivan, quickly joined societies of prayer and apostolic work so that the influence of this holy young man continued.

One of Ivan's friends wrote: "Ivan, with a new zeal and a fully conscious experience as a layman set forth the beauties of Christian truth, the magnitude of the church for the life of every Catholic, the value of liturgy for personal spiritual life, the importance of the papacy for Catholics and for nations, he emphasized the necessity of the engagement of laymen in the apostolate of the church, but always in collaboration and subordination with Church hierarchy; He spoke in favor of un-political activity of Catholic organizations, making efforts to promote the supernatural, spiritual well-being of their members."

Much of this Ivan emphasized with his more than three thousand pages of writings. His works had a profound influence on the Croatian Catholic public, on public opinion, and on ideological movements. It is with good reason Franjo Kuharic, Archbishop of Zagreb, called Ivan a "Masterpiece of the Holy Spirit."

Ivan was such an inspiration that in 1975 Dr. Marin Skarica, a priest from the Split Archdiocese, wrote a dissertation on the basis of Ivan's writings and defended it successfully at the Papal Liturgical Institute Anselmianum in Rome. This was the first Ph.D dissertation written on Ivan Merz, and was entitled, "Ivan Merz, Promoter of Liturgic Revival in Croatia."

Ivan's personal schedule of religious activities involved daily attendance at Mass and daily reception of the Eucharist. Ivan meditated each day for at least three quarters of an hour, which included liturgical meditation on the text of the daily Mass. He prayed the breviary and was fond of the daily recitation of the holy Rosary that he had grown to love after his visit to Lourdes. In fact, he was often seen praying the Rosary while going from one place to another. Once, when he had conducted pilgrims to Rome, he was found reciting the Rosary at the foot of his bed at two o'clock in the morning. He often stated that the Rosary was his second best friend. His first friend was the Eucharist.

Ivan once gave this advice: "When life is hard for you and when you meet with trouble, take the Rosary of Our Lady and it will comfort you and give you strength to endure all in peace with a complete surrender to the Will of God."

His prayer life consisted of frequent adorations before the Eucharist. Many priests, who left us touching testimonies of the piety with which Ivan received the sacrament, noted this love. One of Ivan's close friends wrote: "Whoever found himself in church with Merz would feel, by watching him, the real presence of God. He knelt in such complete humility, honor, and with a heart that pointed to the presence of the holy, chaste, just, endless Deity in front of whom one must fall on knees offering one's whole soul just like Ivan was doing." He once wrote in his diary, "The Holy Eucharist is the essence of life!" and "In Holy Communion the soul celebrates its triumphs; it becomes similar to its Divine Groom; it becomes divine itself."

Ivan made a spiritual retreat nearly every year. He would retire from the world alone or with others, into solitude and silence, under the direction of a priest. His notes taken during those retreats were later published in three books. During the retreats or during other times of thoughtful prayer, he drafted a number of rules, including: to lie on a very hard bed; to feel hunger on Fridays; to go without any food or drink for twenty-four hours once a month; to give away any surplus goods to the poor; to accept gladly humiliation in front of other people; never to devote myself to too great an extent one-sidedly to science; to practice bodily penitence, fast, and other self-denial for the many sins committed in the world; never to complain about food; to carry out my duties as consciously as possible and to consider this as the cross of my life. Ivan also tithed, giving ten percent of his earnings to the poor.

Father Don Ante Radic remembers how Ivan was always ready to help his fellow man, and of one particular beggar Ivan met. This beggar was so deformed that people were turning away from him. Ivan, without hesitation, approached the man, gave him a generous gift, and engaged in a lengthy conversation with him. The man, already a Catholic, was given fatherly advice to attend Mass and receive Holy Communion frequently. Ivan ended by inviting the man to his apartment. All who witnessed this exchange were edified at seeing this example of love for one's neighbor.

Ivan's love of the Blessed Virgin is well documented in his diary and in the numerous articles he wrote about Our Lady of Lourdes. He is also known to have given lectures with slides about Lourdes, not only in Zagreb, but also in other cities all over the country. He even had a statue of Our Lady of Lourdes in the corner of his room with a small light burning constantly in front of it. Our Lady seems also to have influenced the vow of chastity before marriage that Ivan took when he was nineteen years old. This vow was pronounced on the feast of the Immaculate Conception, December 8. Eight years later he took a vow of perpetual chastity, also on the feast of the Immaculate Conception.

At Zagreb, while still teaching, all Ivan's free time was devoted to the education of Croatian youth in Catholic organizations, especially the Association of Croatian Eagles to whom he gave the slogan, "Sacrifice-Eucharist-Apostolate." These are the words engraved on his tombstone.

It should be noted that Ivan spoke ten languages and was prepared for four professions. It seems that he was almost always studying. After he received his Ph.D in 1923, he began the study of philosophy under the guidance of Father Alfirevic, S.J., and continued the studies for two years. He also studied important papal statements and encyclicals, beginning with Leo XIII to the pope of his time, Pius XI. He obtained material from around the world and collected more than 1,200 books for his library. His spiritual director, Father Josif Vrbanek, S.J., wrote that Ivan was a teacher, a writer, and a military officer and that he had the knowledge and virtues required for the priesthood.

Ivan was always ready to defend the Church, whether in writing or through defensive lectures. His defense could be physical, too, as was the case with a church in Stenjevec. Members of the "Old Catholic" sect intended to seize the church and occupy it. Ivan, with members of the Eagles and others of the faithful, stood in front of the church's doors. Ivan endured insults and humiliations, with some would-be invaders even spitting at him. In spite of all the abuse, Ivan and his friends successfully protected the church.

For a time Ivan considered the possibility of becoming a monk or entering the Jesuit Order. After careful reflection and a spiritual retreat in the fall of 1923, he realized clearly that God wanted him to stay in the world and to work for His kingdom as a layman.

Throughout 1925, Ivan edited the column "Eternal Rome," which appeared in a periodical *For Faith and Hope*. The column gave Ivan an opportunity to express his love of the Catholic Church and of the pope who is Christ's visible representative on earth. Because this was also a Holy Year, Ivan, together with other members of the Association of Croatian Eagles, organized a pilgrimage to Rome for one hundred young people. Every year thereafter a "Day of the Pope" celebration was held to commemorate the trip. The celebration became increasingly festive and was celebrated not only in Zagreb, but also all over Croatia where there were young people inspired by Ivan's example and ideals.

As secretary and vice president of the Association of Croatian Eagles, Ivan was in almost constant communication with priests and bishops, many of whom later spoke of him as being an inspiration. One priest wrote: "He was not only a friend to me, but I also considered him as my spiritual guide." When another priest was unjustly libeled, Ivan did all he could for him, and so grateful was the priest that he called Ivan a "consoling angel."

Because of his work with Catholic youth, and because of his good example, there were numerous vocations as a result. After his death, thirty people credited their vocation to the influence of Ivan Merz.

As noted, Ivan did a great deal of reading and studying, all with eyesight that had troubled him since childhood. In addition, he had severe sinus problems, and later in life, he developed problems with his teeth. During the last year of his life, he was seriously ill with an acute inflammation of the mandible cavity for which he had to undergo surgery. Ivan also had to undergo nose surgery. He developed an acute streptococcus inflammation of the lower jaw, which he accepted as his cross for the conversion of his mother who was now praying the Rosary, and for the young people for whom Ivan had been working.

According to his spiritual director, Father Vrbanek, Ivan knew he would soon die. Ivan arranged his affairs, wrote his will, and composed this text as an inscription for his tombstone: "Died in the peace of the Catholic faith. My life was Christ and death was my gain. I am expecting the mercy of the Lord and I am in undivided, complete eternal possession of the Most Sacred Heart of Jesus. I am happy in peace and joy. My soul is reaching the goal for which it was created. In God the Lord."

Ivan developed meningitis after his unsuccessful surgery. Father Vrbanek administered the last sacraments, and afterward, because Ivan could not speak, the priest asked him: "You are sacrificing your life for the Croatian Eagles aren't you?" Ivan nodded his head in confirmation.

A few days later Ivan received a telegram from Rome in which the Holy Father sent his blessing. Ivan was still conscious when they gave him the news and this, from the pope he loved so much, was a consolation in his last moments.

In the presence of his parents and closest friends, Ivan died on Thursday, May 10, 1928. News of his death spread quickly as the bells of the Zagreb cathedral tolled in tribute. Previously, the bells of the cathedral tolled only at the death of a bishop. Soon after his death, the *Catholic Weekly* wrote, "He was never dressed in a priest's robe, but he was a pillar of God's church!"

Three days later Ivan was buried in the Mirogoj cemetery with the ceremony conducted by Bishop Dr. D. Premus. Numerous delegates of various Catholic organizations from all over Croatia attended the service, which was witnessed by an estimated 5,000 people. Ivan's body was exhumed in 1977 and placed in the Shrine of the Sacred Heart of Jesus in Zagreb, the church he regularly visited during the last six years of his life.

Ivan's first biography appeared four years after his death, and numerous books and articles have followed throughout the years. Many people stated that Ivan's influence was more powerful after his death than during his lifetime, and this can be substantiated by the ceremonies observed on the anniversaries of his death.

Having died with the reputation of a saint, many began to pray to him for his intercession. One of the most outstanding answers to prayer took place in favor of a girl named Anica Ercegovic of Sunja who had multiple physical problems including tuberculosis of the lungs, inflammation of the joints, grave rheumatism of the whole body, and a serious heart condition. For six years, she received medical treatments without success. After she started a novena for the intercession of Ivan Merz, she visited his grave and returned home completely healed.

Ivan Merz has been the subject of many highly scholastic works. During the fiftieth anniversary of his death, the second dissertation on this holy young man was written and successfully presented by the postulator of Ivan's cause, Father Bozidar Nagy at the Papal University Salesianum in Rome. It is not only the Church and the Croatian youth and the people who hold Ivan Merz in high regard. Witness the postal service of the Republic of Hrvatska, which issued a postage stamp in 1996 depicting Ivan Merz with hands joined in prayer.

Although the Association of Eagles was disbanded in 1929, it was reorganized in the 1930s under the name "The Crusades." The organization existed in Croatia until 1945 when the communists disbanded it. It was again renewed in 1997 under the name Eucharistic Youth Movement, a name suggested by Pope John XXIII. More than 80,000 boys and girls in Croatia have benefited from the influence of this outstanding organization that now exists in more than fifty countries.

The 100th anniversary of Ivan Merz's birth was solemnly observed in 1996 in Zagreb, Paris, and Rome and his death is commemorated each year with Mass and solemn ceremonies conducted by the local bishop in Zagreb. Perhaps one of the most touching tributes to Ivan Merz was given at the time of his funeral when a wreath was placed on his tomb by the youth from Vinkovci. On the silk ribbon hanging from the wreath were words that have continued to speak for many: "Thank you, God's eagle, for showing us the way to the sun!"

Ivan Merz was beatified by Pope John Paul II in 2002.

John Bradburne

1921 – 1979
Vagabond of God
England/Africa

John Bradburne's holy life was reason enough to initiate his cause for beatification, but when miracles of an extraordinary nature took place while his body was awaiting burial, the cry for his recognition by the Holy See became widespread. Known as a vagabond, a pilgrim, and a relentless searcher for God, John was born in Cumbria, England, the son of an Anglican minister and had two brothers and two sisters.

During his youth John learned to love nature and classical music, and while he was in school he learned to play a wind instrument. Later he developed a love of poetry, a love that would lead him to become a prolific poet. During his school years, he was a member of Officers' Training Corps, where he developed some knowledge of military life. After graduation, when unrest developed in India, John volunteered to serve, and he was immediately accepted into the Indian Army. He received his commission as second lieutenant in 1940 along with his brother Philip. Philip and John sailed together as far as Bombay; John was destined for Malaya. After serving in Burma and enduring two bouts of malaria, John was discharged from the Army in 1945.

War had not dampened John's love of life. According to Father John Dove, S.J., who wrote a biography of John, John was, "The life and soul of a party with his antics and ready wit. . . . He was an affectionate person who enjoyed the company of the young belles . . . he was always generous giving more than he ever received. . . ."

As for religion, in those days everything in nature spoke to him of God. He was Anglican, but no one noticed any formal approach to religion. Although Protestant missionaries tried to interest him, John asked about the Church of Rome, and continued to seek God as the Spirit directed him.

When he returned to England, John secured a job with the Forestry Commission in Somerset. He was attracted to a special young lady and contemplated marriage, but after serious consideration, John realized he was not meant for the marital state. This sociable, joyous, fun-loving man was meant to seek God.

In 1947, John went to Buckfast Abbey where he received instructions in the Catholic faith and was baptized. Since the Benedictines would not accept him as a member until two years after his conversion, John went to work, finding employment as a prep school master teaching English.

John's devotion to Our Lady was just beginning when he decided to visit Lourdes. It is said that he went straight to the baths and drank gallons of Lourdes water. He was to write later: "Lourdes worked a miracle in my body and soul: of that I am now sure. Our Lady has done the same for countless others, but that does not lessen the miracle, it increases its wonder." He returned to England where he signed on as an assistant stoker on a coal-burner fishing boat. He finished his seafaring journeys in early 1950 and began studying the history of the strict Carthusian Order. John made his way to the English Charterhouse at Parkminster, Sussex, where he stayed seven months as a working guest.

After his stay in Sussex, John went to Rome, and then on to Naples, Athens, Cyprus, and to the Holy Land where he visited all the places sanctified by the presence of Our Lord. He then went to Louvain, Belgium, where he entered the order of Our Lady of Mount Sion. Here John considered becoming a priest, but after eighteen months in Louvain he decided he was not suited to the sedentary religious life. He wanted to imitate the example of St. Benedict Joseph Labre, that is, the life of a pilgrim in search of God and sanctification. In 1952, he left Louvain for Jerusalem by way of Rome. While visiting the Parrochia Mater Dei in Palma, John took a private vow to Our Lady never to wed in this world, but to serve her and her Son as a celibate.

After his travels, John returned to England. His father's death caused him to consider the religious life again, and this time he entered Prinknash Abbey in Gloucester as a postulant in 1955. One year later, on Good Friday, John decided he should move on. He joined the Third Order of St. Francis and never again entered a religious order. Each time John left a religious house, he did so with the admiration of the abbots who wrote glowing references and told of their disappointment and sorrow at his departure.

John moved to London where, because of lack of funds, he became a street musician, staying with friends and taking many and varied jobs. At one point, he worked as one of the sacristans at Westminster Cathedral. He lived in the bishop's residence for two years working as caretaker and serving Mass for visiting bishops and cardinals. But in 1962, he was off to Africa and the missions of Zimbabwe. He worked with the Franciscan Fathers doing odd jobs and helping in the schools. At the mission in Gandachibvuva he first lived in the priest's house, but then he built a hermitage, furnished with the poorest accessories and pictures from a calendar. At night he usually visited the chapel for prayer, and he was often seen praying there during the day. His example greatly edified those around him, and together with his winning personality and cheerfulness, he won the admiration and love of all who knew him.

At a mission in Silveira, John served as typist, secretary, sacristan, doorkeeper, guest master, bell ringer, keeper of the watchdogs, and watchman. After a time he moved on again, choosing to return to England to visit his mother. Then, once again, he journeyed to the Holy Land and back to Africa. He heard of a village known as Mutemwa, which in the Shona language means: "You are cut off." Mutemwa was a leper colony of eighty to one hundred lepers, most of whom were pitifully deformed and horribly disfigured. The government provided huts, small rations, clothing, blankets, and medicine, but the poor lepers received no attention or loving care. John was contacted by missionaries to see if he would move to Mutemwa and work as a kind of supervisor. John agreed.

In all, John would spend seventeen years in Africa. Father Desmond O' Malley, O.F.M., remembers when John arrived in Africa the first time in 1962 that John said he had three wishes: the first, to serve and live with lepers; the second, to die a martyr; and third, to be buried in the Franciscan habit. At the time of his first visit, he did not know there was a leper colony in Africa, and the country was at peace. With his return in 1969, he would fulfill his first — indeed all — his wishes.

John went right to work for Mutemwa, first asking the All Souls Mission eleven miles north to accept the colony as one of their missions. He asked to have the sisters' help in the small hospital at the colony, which they began to do regularly. John visited every hut and soon got to know the name of each leper and his needs. A priest visited the colony once a week for Mass and confessions, but John conducted all other services. He read the Bible, recited morning prayers, administered the Blessed Sacrament and played the harmonium. When a leper died, if a priest was not available, John conducted a simple service and comforted his friends.

Each day, following morning prayers, the lepers filed past "Baba" (Father) John to ask him for various medicines, ointments, or aspirin which John kept in large basket. Everyday John made his rounds, visiting each leper to make certain they were well. He bathed those who needed bathing, built fires, made beds, changed dressings, and distributed food. Those lepers who were seriously ill received extra loving attention from "Baba" John, including extra food and even sweets. In the afternoon, there was the recitation of the Rosary, and later in the day, John conducted evening services. John treated his charges with dignity, lavishing love and attention that was welcomed whole-heartedly.

Although John had joined the Franciscan Third Order, he had never been officially clothed in the habit. To John's great delight, he was finally given the habit while at Mutemwa. Father Sean Gildea, O.F.M., the Superior of the Franciscans in Zimbabwe and one of John's good friends, was deeply moved by John's truly Franciscan mode of living and his tender care of the lepers and said: "John is more Franciscan than the whole lot of us put together."

By late 1978, the War of Liberation that had raged around Mutemwa for years came to Mutemwa. Rhodesian security forces tried to prevent villagers from feeding the guerrillas by burning granaries, destroying whole villages, and by inflicting cruel beatings and torture. Eventually the leper colony, although isolated, was also in danger. John was urged to leave, but he refused. On Sunday, September 2, 1979, the guerrillas came for John. He was accused of having a transmitter radio and of being an informer. When his captors found no transmitter, he was taken to a secluded, guarded hut some miles from the colony where he said the Rosary and awaited his death.

Three days later, in front of an assembly of more than five hundred people, John was given a "trial." Many spoke favorably of John, but at one point, John knelt down, raised his arms, and in a loud voice recited the Our Father in the Shona language. Finally, the guerrilla commander decided that John was an innocent man and should be released. John was then invited to minister to refugees in Mozambique, an act that could have saved his life, but he politely refused to leave his flock of lepers. John was set free, but as he began his journey back to the leper colony, the guerrillas who had arrested him followed him.

An elder who went along with John said that as they walked John began to perspire profusely and stopped along the way three times to kneel and pray. During each pause, the guerrillas argued as to whether or not they should kill him. During the third pause for prayer, they pulled John to his feet. One of the guerrillas, who had an automatic weapon, opened fire. John fell to his knees and then to the ground, dying as the elder said, like a lamb, quietly and without complaint. John's second wish had been granted: he had died a martyr.

Immediately, strange things began to happen. The elder, who was not a Christian, reported that the group decided to hide the body so the security forces would not find it and kill them and the villagers in the area. As they were crossing the road with the body, they heard people singing. Frightened, they dropped the body and ran. Later they went back, only to find a large white bird hovering over the corpse. It moved up and down over the body as though to guard it. They again fell back in alarm. After gathering their courage, they went back a third time, finding this time three beams of light ascending from John's body, meeting at a height and descending as one beam. The colors seemed to be blue, red, and white. John had always been deeply devoted to the Holy Trinity. The elder and the others fled in total fright.

Father David Gibbs and a nursing sister found the body the next morning. Later it was revealed that John had been shot in the back — an exit wound produced a large gash in his abdomen. Twenty-four spent bullet cartridges were found at the scene.

A Mass of the Resurrection was planned at the Silveira mission with Archbishop Patrick Chakaipa as the celebrant. It was a glorious funeral Mass with two choirs singing John's favorite classical hymns and was attended by his many distraught friends and numerous priests.

During the service, a wonder was witnessed. After three lilies were laid on the coffin at the request of a dear friend who knew of John's love of the Trinity, a drop of blood fell from under the coffin. Father Michael O'Halloran placed a clean chalice purificator cloth over the drop, but then another drop fell and then another. In all, three drops fell. After the service, the coffin was opened, but no source of blood was found. However, John's wish to be buried in the Franciscan habit was remembered. So it was that the three drops of blood resulted with

John's body being re-clothed in his beloved habit. His third wish was now realized.

The mortuary report at this time should be noted. When the body was first examined, "All the wounds were covered with cotton wool as a matter of formality. The state of the cadaver was seen to be excellently preserved . . . the wounds were clean, clear, and dry (no fresh blood was seen) and there was no discoloration." Still, the blood on the chalice purificator was known to be fresh, bright, and crimson. The inside of the casket was examined, but no moisture or blood was present. It was finally declared that "Blood is never like that from a dead body."

John's body was buried in the Chishawasha Mission Cemetery in Salisbury where it rests beside the remains of Dominican sisters, Jesuit priests, and religious brothers. Since his death in 1979, John has become known worldwide with many favors being credited to his intercession.

Venerable Jorge Vargas Gonzalez
1899 – 1927
Electrical Engineer

Venerable Ramon Vargas Gonzalez
1905 - 1927
Medical Student
Mexico

These two brothers vigorously opposed the persecution of Catholics initiated by the Mexican government during the years 1926-1929 and because of their efforts, both died as martyrs in defense of the faith.

Jorge and Ramon were two of the eleven children born to Doctor Antonio Vargas and Elvira Gonzalez. Both brothers joined the Catholic Association of Mexican Youth (ACJM) and were great admirers of the resistance leader, Anacleto Gonzalez Flores, whose biography is included in this volume. During the religious persecution in Mexico, the Vargas family gave refuge to a number of priests and seminarians, including the future bishop of Culiacia, Father Lino Aguirre. Jorge once told Father Lino that it was not safe for him to go about the city by himself, and offered himself as a bodyguard. After his day's work, Jorge, dressed in overalls and riding his bicycle, accompanied the priest on his secret ministerial visits.

Jorge and Ramon's sister Maria Louisa remembers that the family once had in their house several priests and the resistance leader Anacleto Gonzalez Flores. There was great danger in hiding Flores, but the family would never have considered refusing him. While he was there, Anacleto suggested that Ramon, the idealistic medical student, might like to work among the wounded resisters. Ramon declined, saying he was a man of peace.

Taking Anacleto into the house would prove a grave decision. Early on the morning of April 1, 1927, there was a tapping on the window of the pharmacy that was attached to the family's house. The secret police had surrounded the house, and demanded to be admitted. They took as prisoners Anacleto, three Vargas brothers, and several others, transporting all to the Colorado jail. The mother and sisters were also arrested, but the valiant mother called to her sons as they were taken away, "My sons, until Heaven!" Other relatives were also arrested, but were released later that day. When the police raided the house, Ramon could have escaped. When asked why he did not, he replied, "I told myself, my mother and my brothers are prisoners, am I to run away?"

In jail, the new prisoners encountered Luis Padilla Gomez (his biography is included in this book). He had been arrested that morning and joined the others in the same interrogation room. All were horribly beaten, but following the example of Anacleto, they remained steadfast and silent. When the torments were suspended, four of the five prisoners were condemned to death. Florentino Vargas, a brother of Jorge and Ramon, was set free since the police thought, erroneously, that he was under age. After reciting an act of contrition in loud voices and with cries of *Viva Cristo Rey*, "Long Live Christ the King!" the battle cry of the resistance, Jorge, Ramon, Anacleto, and Luis were executed.

When word circulated that the prisoners had been killed, three of the Vargas sisters went in search of their brothers and were told of the execution. Their mother, who had realized the awful truth, bravely said: "I already was afraid of this, and because of it I have offered them to Our Lord. They are already in heaven. We are going to make preparations to receive them as martyrs."

The bodies of Jorge and Ramon were returned to their family, but Florentino was missing. Thinking he too had been martyred, they were overjoyed when, after some hours, he returned home. The heroic mother then said: "Ay, my son, how close you were to the crown of martyrdom. Now it is your obligation to live so as to merit it."

Hundred of people came during the night to press medals and rosaries to the bodies of the martyrs. The following day, they accompanied the bodies to the cemetery.

Jorge and Ramon, as well as Anacleto and Luis Padilla Gomez, are awaiting beatification. Their Cause was enhanced when the diocesan Decree of Valor was issued on May 21, 1999.

Servant of God Joseph (Giuseppe) Lazzati

1909 – 1986
Vatican II Attendee
Italy

Joseph Lazzati was one of eight boys born to the Catholic Lazzati family in Milan. Throughout his life, Joseph spoke little about his early years except to say that, at an early age, he belonged to the student association known as Santo Stanislaus and took part in the group's spiritual exercises when he was twelve. He took part in the exercises every year until he was twenty-one. Dan Andrea Valsecchi, an Ambrosian priest, wrote about meeting an eighteen-year-old Joseph, at a Santo Stanislaus retreat in Biandino, high in mountains. The priest wrote:

> I have known Lazzati during the month that I spent in holiday in Biandino. What struck me about Lazzati was the allurement of saintliness that he gave off. I wished to stay near him in the chapel of the House. I saw him stay a long time on his knees and every day he said the breviary in Latin, like a priest. Besides,

he daily participated in Mass and went to Holy Communion. This modest attitude, this way of controlling himself, this evangelic conduct didn' t forsake him during all the day — these qualities made me want to hold a dialogue with him. I've always seen him quiet and a good mixer, measured in his gestures and in his words. . . .

That same year Joseph began studying arts and philosophy at the Catholic University. In 1928, when he was nineteen, Joseph read for the first time the biography of Blessed Pier Georgio Frassati (whose biography is included in this book) who had died three years earlier. From then on, Blessed Pier Georgio became the model for Joseph's life.

While at the university, Joseph wondered: "God calls me, but to do what?" He finally decided: "I've selected the single state. I enjoy every moment the greatness and the beauty of the grace of God, that is, thanks to chastity I' ll be able to join more and more with him, because to him I consecrate soul and body and to exercise an apostolate more generously and effectively."

After he graduated with honors in 1931, he was called to military service, but he still had time to assist one of his professors, Don Ubaldi, a Salesian priest. Another priest urged Joseph to participate as a diocesan assistant with the Ambrosian Youth of Catholic Action. Joseph agreed, and was soon elected diocesan president of the Milanese Youth of Catholic Action, and soon he began to write booklets for the instruction of new members.

Joseph continued his studies and became a university lecturer in Ancient Christian Literature. He was also named a regular teacher of the faculty of literature. About the same time, in 1939, he founded an association of consecrated laymen and offered his vocation to Cardinal Schuster who recognized the new movement, at a time when the Code of Canon Law did not recognize consecrated laymen. The new organization became known as the Secular Institute of Christ the King.

Joseph also became involved in politics during the war years of 1941-1943 when the fascists presented a new and powerful political presence. A group of university professors, including Joseph, went to a meeting in Rome where they and others attempted to create a new Christian political party with Servant of God Alcide De Gasperi, whose biography is included in this book.

During August 1943, Joseph was recalled for military service and arrived at Bolzano. When the news of the September 8 armistice reached them, the Germans asked Joseph and his fellow soldiers to collaborate with them. Each soldier was asked to choose between being faithful to the royal army or to join the re-forming fascist army. Joseph and many others stoutly refused to join the fascist army, for which they were promptly placed in prison. Joseph was moved from prison in Poland to prison in Germany. In one prison labor camp, Joseph worked in a condition of slavery which he said made him better understand the humiliation of Christ, who took the shape of a slave to save us from sin.

From the beginning of his imprisonment, Joseph wanted to offer his fellow prisoners help and moral support. He organized meetings known as Groups of the Gospel, which helped many who experienced a lack of confidence and despair. One of the prisoners, Alessandro Natta, later wrote: "My thoughts return to the hard days in which I knew Lazzati. He was, like me, a young officer deported to concentration camps in Germany. . . . We attempted to diffuse among the prisoners a new concept — antifascism and democracy — of country and civil engagement, a trust in the national rebirth and in the social ransom of the Italians . . . the fellows of different philosophies and political convictions we confronted with enthusiasm of building about character, basics, and the idea of a new national community."

Finally, Joseph was released from the prison and went home to Milan where he was greeted by Cardinal Schuster. Lazzati was soon called to become vice-secretary of the Christian Democratic Party. In addition, he was elected town councilor and as a representative to the Constituent Assembly. Soon after, he was elected national-councilor. The list of organizations he helped develop, the national committees he belonged to, and his writings, including the review *Cronache Sociali*, are extensive.

Although seriously engaged in politics, Joseph did not neglect his spiritual life. One of his political friends wrote that he and Joseph lived in the same rooming house in Rome. They had adjoining rooms with walls "of thin boarding." He wrote that, because of the thin walls, "We heard the passing rhythms of life." He also was able to hear Joseph's movements: "Lazzati never left his prayers. Many times a day, also during the more difficult of the political and parliamentary times, he was always praying, not with scruple but with courtly reserve and loving fidelity."

During the first months of 1948, "Ambrosianeum," an organization that became a "studio of theology for the laity," was created. Joseph was chosen president the following year. With his return to Milan, Joseph resumed his intense activity with Catholic Action and with new centers of formation for laymen. Now he was engaged in conferences and debates, and he taught courses about the engagement of Christian men in the world. He also became friendly with the new Archbishop Giovanni Battista Montini, the future Pope Paul VI. Archbishop Montini entrusted the diocesan Catholic newspaper, *L'Italia* to Joseph, and although Joseph had no technical training, for three years he proved himself a competent journalist and editor.

During this time, Joseph published a small book, *Maturity of the Laity*, a collection of previously published lessons, conversations, and articles. A copy went to Pope John XXIII, and Cardinal Montini conveyed a thank you from the Holy Father to Joseph: "The Holy Father knows and esteems your zeal in the varied forms of the apostolate. . . ."

After his term at the diocesan paper was completed, Joseph was designated diocesan president of Catholic Action for the years 1964-1967 by the new archbishop of Milan. Joseph continued to write, and a collection of his articles was published by the Catholic University under the title *Church, Laity and an Historical Pledge*.

In 1965, the University of the Sacred Heart elected Joseph the headmaster of the Faculty of Letters and Philosophy. Three years later he became rector, a position he held until 1983. The spiritual director of the university once wrote that Joseph, "Had to do difficult mediations, and it seemed to me that always he did it with dignity and prudence, with patience and wisdom."

When his term as rector ended in 1983, the Holy Father, Pope John Paul II, wrote Joseph a long note of gratitude and conferred on him a special honor. His letter ended, "I have decided that you should receive the Great Cross of St. Gregorio."

In the last years of his life, in spite of a terrible sickness, Joseph wrote a trilogy, a synthesis of his thought on the laity and the Christian laity. It would be his last. Joseph was hospitalized, and at the hospital he met Father Bonato, who was in the hospital delivering a series of conferences to the nursing nuns in preparation for the feast of Pentecost. Father Bonato visited with Joseph and was deeply impressed with his calm attitude toward dying, as Joseph called it "sister corporal death." Father Bonato frequently visited Joseph and heard his confession. After one confession, Joseph pressed the priest's hand and said: "Father, let me kiss your hand, so I can kiss the Church." Father Bonato admits that he wept, and then, at Joseph's invitation, they spoke at length about Jesus. The priest wrote: "I can't easily forget what happened in that room. To me it was a taste of paradise . . . he had been 'always' to me an essential point of reference in my life . . . I thank God to have known and loved him. . . ."

Joseph Lazzati died at dawn on Pentecost Sunday, May 18, 1986. His Cause for beatification was introduced in 1994.

Joseph Lazzati, so active in the growth of the church and the transformation of the country, was also active during Vatican Council II. Pope John Paul II, in addressing the administrators, faculty, staff, and students of the Catholic University of the Sacred Heart during their Jubilee pilgrimage to Rome, on April 13, 2000, said: "I remember in particular Professor Joseph Lazzati, rector of the university in years past, who, during the Council, made an enlightening contribution to the discussion of several topics. I hope that you will be able to emulate his wisdom and integrity of life."

Saint Joseph Moscati
1880 – 1927
Medical Doctor
Italy

Two special church years are noted in the biography of Joseph Moscati, doctor, professor, and scientist. He was the only layman beatified by Pope Paul VI during the Holy Year of 1975, and he was the only layman canonized by Pope John Paul II during the Marian Year of 1987-1988.

Pope John Paul II described physician Joseph Moscati as "the concrete realization of the ideal of the lay Christian." Dr. Moscati began life in Benevento, Italy on July 25, 1880. He was the seventh of nine children born to pious Catholic parents, Rosa and Francis Moscati. His father was a magistrate who was later to become president of the Court of Assize in Naples. In the pleasant environment of their devout Catholic family, Joseph and his brothers and sisters grew to be testimonials to their parents' mutual love. Obedient and docile, they were nourished by prayer and good example.

Joseph's earliest education was received at home. In 1889, he was also enrolled in the school of Victor Emmanuel. He was prepared for his first Holy Communion by Monsignor Henry Manrano with his first reception of Our Lord taking place on December 27, 1890, when Joseph was ten years old.

Joseph was described as friendly to all during his primary and secondary education, though he was sometimes shy and seemed unwilling to associate much with others. He was, nevertheless, well liked by his companions and earned the esteem of his teachers. Said to be "a little outspoken," he was "of a gentle and kindly disposition, deeply sincere and serene." Because of his intellect and uprightness of character, as well as his practice of virtue and prayer, his professors frequently presented Joseph as an example to his companions. Joseph was blessed with a quick mind and a keen desire for advancement in his studies. In grammar school, his high marks were such that he was given a yearly scholarship. After brilliantly completing his studies in the higher grades, at the age of seventeen Joseph received a first-class, classical diploma and began considering the choice of a career. He would not study law, as had his father, but after praying for guidance, he decided upon a career in medicine and entered the University of Naples.

Joseph kept his same pattern of habits. He avoided frivolous amusements and applied himself to his studies. He started each day by attending Mass and offering prayers.

While engaged in his first year at the university, Joseph suffered the loss of his beloved father. Although he was intensely grieved, Joseph consoled his mother and family by declaring, "God takes the place of those whom he has taken to himself."

During the first year of his medical studies in 1898, Joseph won the annual prize for the best results in zoology. During the second year he studied anatomy, physiology, and pathology and frequented hospitals, laboratories, and clinics. He is said to have been so absorbed in his studies that he failed to notice the activity around him. Professor Bevacqua related that while Joseph was under his instruction in the medical clinic he was impressed not only by Joseph's serious, composed, and attentive attitude but also by the ease and spontaneity with which he answered all the questions, even the most difficult ones more experienced pupils were unable to answer. Joseph gave his answers in a quiet voice, which the professor interpreted as Joseph's way of preventing the humiliation of the older students.

When he was only twenty-three years old, Joseph was awarded a degree in medicine and surgery with the highest honors on August 14, 1903. He next entered a contest to prove his suitability for the post of Coadjutor Extraordinary in the United Hospitals. He won this "with such ease as to dumbfound both his examiners and his companions." He then began his terms of service in the infirmaries and casualty departments of the hospitals.

Joseph's commitment to the welfare of his patients was demonstrated in April 1906, when Mount Vesuvius began to erupt. Alarmed, Joseph quickly left for the nearby town of Torre del Greco, where elderly invalids were being tended at a branch of the United Hospitals. Through a thick rain of ash, Dr. Moscati helped to evacuate the inmates while encouraging and comforting them. Joseph was barely out of the hospital with the last patient when the roof of the building collapsed. Joseph proved to be a true instrument of Providence in the evacuation.

During another calamity, an outbreak of cholera in 1911, Joseph again showed himself self-sacrificing and devoted to duty. He worked tirelessly to curb the spread of the disease in the overcrowded slums of Naples.

The year 1911 proved a particularly busy one for Dr. Moscati. In July, he was chosen as the Naples University Chair in Chemical Physiology and he began lecturing on laboratory research as it applied to clinical medicine. Professor Piazza notes that:

> There was no development in medicine that he [Joseph] did not know thoroughly because there was not the slightest detail of research with which he was not familiar. He followed in the journals of various countries the new developments in science. As he had lived for many years in scientific institutes

and in the wards of the Hospital for Incurables, dedicated to the study of science and invalids, everyone was astonished at this young man of only thirty-six who in so short a time was reaching the head of the whole medical world of southern Italy.

Having attained these successes and advancements, Dr. Moscati considered for a time whether to marry. After many vigils and fervent prayer, about the year 1912 or 1913 he consecrated himself to a life of celibacy. Having made this decision, he thought that he was called to the religious life as a member of the Company of Jesus. However, the Jesuit Fathers themselves discouraged him, since they felt the will of God for him was to remain in the world in the practice of the medical profession.

At the start of World War I, in 1914, Joseph suffered the loss of his mother. The following year, when Italy declared war against Austria, he volunteered for military service, receiving the rank of major. While caring for the wounded Italian soldiers he gave them the most prompt and scrupulous treatment, but his consolation lay not only in seeing the soldiers profiting from his medical assistance, but also in seeing them become good and devout Catholics.

The saving of souls by caring for the body was Dr. Moscati's policy. His deep conviction was that the health of the body depends upon the soul remaining in the state of grace. Everyone noticed the spiritual care he took of all those whom he approached, and he could gain by a few whispered words in the ears of his patients what relatives and friends could not bring about through lengthy arguments. For example, a patient dying of stomach cancer absolutely refused to listen to any suggestion that he receive the sacraments. The man's sister turned to Joseph for help, and he approached the dying man to speak a few words. The dying man listened attentively, and then, to the astonishment of his family, he asked for the sacraments and received them with devotion.

Many incidents are told of sinners returning to the sacraments through the influence of this good doctor, and many are the times that he refused payment for his services. Once at Amalfi, after having examined all the patients who were presented to him, he refused payment from all of them. To those who asked why, he replied, "These are working folk. What have we that has not been given us by Our Lord? Woe to us if we do not make good use of God's gifts."

Once Joseph was called to visit a railway worker who lived in a squalid lodging. The saintly doctor carefully examined the man and then explained to his relatives the serious nature of the ailment. He prescribed remedies, and he encouraged everyone to have confidence that the man would be cured. He then advised them to call the parish priest at once, "Because," he said, "one must attend to the salvation of the soul as well as the health of the body." While this was taking place, the patient's friends were donating their hard-earned money for the prescription and the doctor's fee. When Dr. Moscati saw what they were doing, he too contributed toward the prescription and staunchly refused any payment for his services. The workmen are said to have been so surprised by the doctor's generosity and kindness that they fell at his feet and attempted to kiss his hands, but it is reported, "he escaped and left the hovel hastily."

Many times, in an effort to help the poor he treated free of charge, Joseph would leave money, though he did so secretly to avoid embarrassing them. One poor woman found fifty lire folded in her prescription; another found five hundred lire under her pillow; and another poor person was cared for in the hospital at the doctor's expense. Dr. Moscati's favorite patients were the poor, the homeless, religious, and priests, and from them he would never accept a fee.

Joseph was always ready to quiet frightened patients, and to provide spiritual advice and consolation. To a nun who said that she did not want to die of suffocation, Dr. Moscati replied: "A religious should never talk thus, for even an ordinary Christian must be ready to die that death which God wills for him." To another religious who complained of a rather rigid diet, the doctor said, "God makes us suffer here in order to reward us in the heavenly Kingdom; by resigning ourselves to dietary restrictions, and suffering, we shall have greater merit in the eyes of the Almighty."

There were times when the doctor seemed to have been divinely inspired. Once, after carefully examining a priest, Joseph sat down at his desk to write a prescription, but then wrote nothing. Instead, he picked up a copy of *The Imitation of Christ* and read. "In thy cell thou shalt find that which thou mightest lose outside. The cell, when continually dwelt in, becomes sweet, and when it is ill-cared for engenders afflictions." The priest understood the message and made the necessary adjustments in his manner of living.

Father Cibarelli witnessed the doctor's advanced spirituality in what appeared to have been Joseph's divinely inspired treatment of his patients. Concerning a visit to a poor female patient, Father Cibarelli wrote: "He made the palpations and tapings with great concentration, his eyes half-closed and his head on one side as if he were not visiting a patient, but listening to voices from above." Another colleague, Dr. Marzo, wrote, "It seemed at times that his diagnostic foresight, permeated with inward knowledge, was inspired by supernatural beings." Another friend, Professor Landolfi, added, "His diagnoses sometimes appeared to border on the miraculous, and occasionally it seemed that angels came to the aid of one who was so near to them."

Joseph not only cared for the sick but also helped students at the University of Naples. There he became the center of attraction for scholars who were amazed by his bewildering mastery of the sciences, his imposing moral uprightness, and his rare spiritual greatness. Students, colleagues, and young graduates greatly admired him, while the doctor, for his part, enjoyed his contact with them. His greatest happiness was when his pupils accompanied him to Mass, stayed to pray with him, and afterward went home with him. One of his pupils wrote, "In contact with him we were overcome by the irresistible fascination of his goodness, and not only did we drink of the inexhaustible fountain of his doctrine, but we were drunk with the sweet perfume of gentleness and goodness which emanated from his pure candid soul."

Someone asked Joseph how he managed to cope with such a busy and demanding schedule, and the saint replied in the words of St. Paul, "I can do all things in him who strengthens me." The doctor always maintained that it was the daily reception of Jesus in the sacrament of the Holy Eucharist that sustained him in his daily work. At the foot of the altar, he would remain motionless, as if in ecstasy, kneeling on the stone floor while contemplating the Most Blessed Sacrament.

The doctor's second source of strength was his deep and heartfelt devotion to Mary, especially under the title of the Immaculate Conception. Members of his family tell that he always carried a rosary in his pocket and that before making a serious decision he would take the rosary in his hand and kiss it. It is said that never a day passed that he did not remain at the foot of Our Lady's altar in the attitude of a loving and devoted son.

His devotion to the Eucharist and to Our Lady resulted, as a natural consequence, in the most outstanding virtues, one of which was purity, a virtue that he maintained by vigilance and continual mortification. Dr. Moscati limited his hours of sleep, observed all the fasts and abstinences imposed by the church, avoided amusements and worldly friendships, and denied himself the comforts and advantages which his social and economic position would have permitted him.

Dr. Moscati, in his devotion to charity, refused to speak of others' defects or faults. He declined, with delicate care, to hide the mistakes of his colleagues, and he made heroic efforts to overlook the jealousy, envy, and animosity that were sometimes directed against him. The doctor also practiced profound humility and was frequently seen performing the most menial services for his poor patients.

Many times the saintly doctor predicted that his life would not be a lengthy one. On April 12, 1927, he rose at his usual time for meditation and went to St. Clare's Church where he served Mass and received Holy Communion. He returned home and advised his sister, with whom he lived, to arrange for a priest to hear the confession of a colleague, a lapsed Catholic, who was a patient in the hospital. The doctor is said then to have visited a poor, sick woman in her home, and to have made his usual rounds in the hospital. He returned to his home where he began examining the many patients who were waiting for him. At three o'clock, he felt ill. He stopped work and retired to his room. Dr. Moscati sat in his chair, crossed his arms, and died a peaceful death. He was forty-six years old.

The news of Dr. Moscati's death spread quickly, arousing grief and deep regrets. Many students, colleagues, the poor, religious, and outstanding members of the government visited his body. Among the first visitors was Cardinal Ascalesi, who said to those present: "The doctor belonged to the church. It was not those whose bodies he had cured, but those whose souls he had saved who were waiting to greet him when he left this earth."

Joseph's funeral was an imposing and moving ceremony during which his colleagues made speeches, which were full of regret, grief, admiration, and the highest praise for the virtues of the departed. The local paper, *Il Mattino,* reported, "Rarely indeed has Naples witnessed such an impressive spectacle of infinite sadness." The doctor's sister once wrote, "They speak of me as the sister of the saint," while Professor Morisani closed his letter of condolence to Dr. Moscati's brother in this manner: ". . . every family which had the good fortune to know your brother, today remembers and venerates him as a saint."

The doctor's interest in the care of the sick continues from heaven, as indicated by the cures that have continued to take place through his intercession. A biographer of the saint reported:

> During his lifetime, Dr. Moscati's physical presence at the bedside of his patients gave them comfort and an interior consolation and peace. After his death, sufferers have frequently obtained graces and cures through him, usually seeing him beside them with a power for good which God communicates in the world of the blessed, a thousand times more effective than during his lifetime. Many moving episodes, which have no human explanation, confirm this.

The Sacred Congregation for the Causes of Saints approved two miracles obtained in 1973 through Dr. Joseph Moscati's intercession. On November 16, 1975, Pope Paul VI, who cited the doctor's career as an example of harmony between science and faith, solemnly beatified Joseph. Pope Paul VI fixed November 16 as Blessed Joseph Moscati's feast day. At the doctor's canonization on October 25, 1987, many people from Naples were among the crowd of 890,000 who attended the Mass that was concelebrated by twenty-five bishops and two cardinals.

The body of St. Joseph Moscati is kept in an artistically decorated sarcophagus under the main altar of the Church of the Gesu Nuovo in Naples.

Venerable Joseph Toniolo
1845 – 1918
Professor, Father of Seven
Italy

This Venerable's whole life was spent in the fields of education and social activism. Joseph was born in Treviso, Italy and had an uneventful childhood and adolescence. He entered college at Padua and excelled in his studies, earning a degree in law. He remained at the college as an assistant, but eventually took a position at the university in Venice where he taught political economy. Eventually he moved to Pisa where he became a professor, a position he held for the rest of his life.

When he was thirty-three, Joseph married Schiratti Maria with whom he had seven sons. Theirs was a family rich in tenderness and prayer, a family that lived in the peace and love of God. To his sons, "he behaved indeed like a clergyman of the house." To them he was also a teacher, an educator, and was most concerned with each so that they found in him a true father.

Two years after he married, Joseph became interested in the work of the conferences and became part of Catholic Action. Joseph was involved in the formation of the Popular Union, a group of Italian Catholics who conformed to the ideals of the pontificate of Leo XIII. Joseph would later become a leader of the Italian Social Catholics and one of the greatest social witnesses of his time as the great apostle of the encyclical *Rerum Novarum*.

Rerum Novarum ("On the Conditions of the Working Man"), written in 1891, marked the beginning of the Church's response to the Industrial Revolution. A document of social ethics, *Rerum Novarum* was the basis for Joseph's personal sociological stand, which upheld ethics and the Christian spirit in the laws of the economy. Joseph proposed a response to rising Marxist and liberal thought in Italy through the creation of guilds of masters and workers, which would be organized and recognized by the state. His proposal is said to have answered both the Marxists and the liberals.

Joseph was involved in many charitable and social organizations, including the Catholic Union for Social Studies (1889), the International Review of Social Sciences (1893), the Italian Catholic Society for Scientific Studies (1899), as well as others. He was also involved in the early days of the founding of the Catholic University of the Sacred Heart. The university was finally established two years after his death.

In his writings, Joseph advanced numerous proposals of action: various festivals, the limitation of working hours, the defense of small ownership, the guardianship of the jobs of women and small boys. His writings were so numerous they were collected in a volume entitled *Opera Omnia*, which is loosely translated as "Work Together." Joseph advocated definitive action by Catholics in the social field and encouraged the Catholic Union for Social Studies in Italy. He also influenced the organization of a Christian democracy.

Joseph died on October 7, 1918 in Pisa, at the age of seventy-three. It has been said of him that he did not belong to this or that parish, but to the entire Catholic Italy.

To honor Joseph, the Catholic University of the Sacred Heart established the Institute Giuseppe Toniolo, which received a letter from Pope John Paul II on the eightieth anniversary of its founding. In the letter dated June 24, 2000, the pope recognized the aim of the institute by writing: "My venerated predecessors showed their deep esteem always for the institute whose duty is to guarantee that the university of Italian Catholics is always faithful to its objective . . . the scientific research illuminated by faith and the preparation of qualified Christian professions who work in full harmony with the magisterium of the church."

Joseph Toniolo was declared Venerable by the church in 1971.

Venerable Ladislaus Batthyany-Strattmann
1879 – 1931
Eye Surgeon, Father of Fourteen
Hungary/Austria

Of all the laymen included in this book, Ladislaus was undoubtedly the wealthiest. Moreover, he used his wealth wisely in the care and education of family members and in the care of countless sick and needy.

Ladislaus was born into a very wealthy and noble Hungarian family. There were thirteen brothers and sisters, though several died before reaching adulthood. Ladislaus' father abandoned the family, and Ladislaus and an older brother were placed in the care of the Contessa Antonia Korniss, a Lutheran. Ladislaus' mother died soon after, reportedly from a broken heart.

Ladislaus' father seemed determined to keep Ladislaus and his older brother at a distance. He sent the boys to a Jesuit school in Vienna, where they would stay for four years. The brothers went on to a Jesuit college in Kalocsa, where the older brother became ill and died. Ladislaus studied agriculture for six months before enlisting in the military. He served as a lieutenant for one year and was discharged. He returned to school, this time to study chemistry, astronomy, and philosophy. As many college students do, he became confused about right and wrong, about priorities, responsibilities, and morality. He became involved with a young woman and fathered a child, a daughter.

The consequences of his actions helped Ladislaus realize his sin. He repented, and returned to the sacraments and the practice of virtue. Determined to set a correct course for his life, he set his sights on, and eventually obtained, a license to practice medicine.

When his father died, Ladislaus inherited the responsibility of administering his family's estate and the care of all family members, a commitment he honored with seriousness and great care.

At the age of thirty, Ladislaus married Countess Maria Teresa Coreth, a lady-in-waiting at the Vienna court. Their union produced fourteen children. The marriage was a happy one and their family life was exemplary, with early morning Mass and Holy Communion sanctifying the day and the family recitation of the Rosary blessing their sleep. The children were affectionate with their father, and strictly, and lovingly, obeyed his corrections and instructions.

Ladislaus wanted to transmit his love of virtue and the Church to his children, and did so after Mass. He led them in meditation, and each day gave the children a specific religious task to perform. As a Franciscan tertiary, he practiced the teachings of St. Francis of Assisi and the saint's love of the Holy Eucharist. His devotion inspired many to a greater love of the Mass and Eucharistic Adoration.

Both Ladislaus and his wife felt a special call to practice charity. They funded the construction of a modern, thirty-bed hospital in the town of Kopcseny, which was later expanded to seventy beds. All the expenses in the construction of the hospital, the cost of medical supplies and the salaries of employees were paid entirely by Ladislaus and his wife. He once said that, "By helping those who suffer, I can play the role of Simon of Cyrene who carried Christ's cross."

The patients in this hospital were exclusively the poor who were treated as though they were royalty. Ladislaus' care of his patients extended to the payment of all their expenses, and he assisted the elderly and saw to their dignified retirement.

After World War I, Ladislaus built a second hospital in a wing of his family's castle. He began to specialize in ophthalmology, and became so well known for his work that the state arranged for the departure of a special train at dawn to accommodate the numerous poor patients who went to him for help. Observers say that before the most difficult eye surgeries Ladislaus would recollect himself in prayer in the chapel before the Holy Eucharist. He once wrote in his journal. "The days we cannot receive Holy Communion are not really complete days." He is known to have served Mass with great recollection and wrote, "One can pray with special devotion when serving at Mass," and, "To follow the Mass with the Missal makes it more intimate."

In time, the responsibilities of his family's estate forced him to change his residence to Kormend, Hungary, but before leaving he entrusted the hospital to the region of Burgenland and in his new residence he prepared a new hospital with twenty-five beds.

He was so greatly respected that the Hungarian bishops elected him president of the *Kozponi Sajtovallalat*, the Catholic press. Another honor was bestowed on him when Pope Pius XI conferred on him the Order of the Golden Spur and named him to the permanent committee of International Eucharistic Congresses.

In November 1929, Ladislaus underwent cancer surgery. He suffered for two years more, dying in January 1931. The Cardinal Archbishop of Vienna personally presided at the funeral and at the burial in the family crypt at Gussing, in Austria. The study into the virtues of this holy man began in 1944 and progressed steadily until he was declared Venerable in 1997.

Servant of God Leo Dupont
1797 – 1876
Attorney, Promoter of the Holy Face Devotion
France

Leo was born into a family of great wealth and position. His mother was an exemplary Christian and his father, Nicholas, was heir to a sizable fortune. France, under the rule of Napoleon Bonaparte, was a turbulent place, and Nicholas decided to move his family to the French Island of Martinique where they might live in safety and peace. When Nicholas died, his widow returned to France with her two boys, Leo and Theobald, and in time remarried, becoming Madame Arnaud.

At the age of nineteen Leo Dupont is described as a very attractive young man, eager to begin his higher studies. His mother thought it best for him to study law so that after his graduation he could gain some honorable post in the government of Martinique where the Duponts owned vast sugar plantations. Leo agreed, and with what would be about $10,000 by today's rates for his expenses, he started school in Paris.

Leo registered at the university and then turned his attention to more worldly concerns. He secured a fashionable apartment and expanded his already considerable wardrobe. He visited the finest tailors and clothed himself in the latest French fashions. His appearance and his polished manners attracted much attention.

Leo fit right in with Paris' aristocratic society. He was invited to a succession of soirees and balls where he danced so gracefully that "the finest French young womanhood, noticing him, concealed their admiration with difficulty." The parents of many young women sought him out, hoping to gain him as a son-in-law. Young, wealthy, and brilliant,

Leo was not interested in acquiring a wife; he had his mind set on becoming acquainted with the world. For two years, Leo enjoyed the pleasure of Parisian social life.

Then Leo met a Mr. Bordier, who instructed a group of street cleaners and chimney sweeps in Christian doctrine in preparation for their reception of the sacraments. Leo was intrigued that a well-dressed gentleman would spend his time with a group of poor street urchins. Leo discovered that Mr. Bordier belonged to the Congregation of Mary, a society that took an earnest interest in combating the evils of the French Revolution that still plagued Paris. After meeting Mr. Bordier, Leo consulted a friend, Father Frayssinous, who would later become Leo's spiritual director. Under Father Frayssinous' direction, Leo, who had always attended Sunday Mass and said the prayers suggested by his mother, turned toward living a more fervent spiritual life.

In addition to Mr. Bordier, Leo also met St. Madeleine Sophie Barat, who ran a boarding school in Paris. Leo began to show outstanding generosity to charities, and at St. Madeleine Sophie's school, Leo paid the tuition for two girls whose families were experiencing financial reverses.

After five years of study, Leo Dupont received his law degree. He began to consider marriage, and at the age of twenty-seven he fell deeply in love with Caroline Audiffredi, a pious, demure young lady who accepted his proposal of marriage. The ceremony was celebrated on May 9, 1927 with a solemn High Mass. There followed years of contentment at their home in Des Follets, a beautiful estate where the house, surrounded by gardens, faced the sea, and hills afforded a view of incomparable beauty. One day, while attending Mass, Leo began wondering what he was doing for God. He remembered that a Sulpician priest once told him he thought God had a special work for Leo to do in the world.

In 1932, the Duponts' daughter Mary Caroline Henriette was born. The couple had been married five years, and their daughter's birth was a great joy. Madame Dupont, who had had a premonition that she would die young, did not recover from the pregnancy and birth. Less than one year later she died from an undiagnosed illness. Before her death Caroline had one request of Leo: that he would have their daughter educated by the Ursulines at Tours, a school where she had been greatly impressed with her teacher, Mother Lignac. Leo Dupont promised, and Caroline died leaving behind a heart-broken husband and a ten-month-old baby.

Leo Dupont and his mother, now twice-widowed, moved to Tours. They settled in a large house near the Ursuline boarding school where he promised his dying wife that Henriette would be educated. Leo made the acquaintance of the parishioners of the Cathedral of Tours and served as administrator of the church property. He also joined the Society of St. Vincent de Paul and began teaching poor students to read and write, and helped with catechism lessons. Still busy with his law practice, Leo Dupont found time to visit various churches and shrines and contributed to their needs.

At his spiritual director's prompting, Leo began the daily recitation of the breviary and grew deeper in the spiritual life. About this time, he became devoted to St. Teresa of Ávila, the reformer of the Carmelite Order. He read her *Autobiography* and was impressed with the passage regarding penance: "I declare that I commenced to comprehend the things pertaining to salvation only after I determined to disregard the demands of my body. . . ." After reading this, Leo began the practice of penance and the regular use of a whip on his body. Also about this time, Leo visited the celebrated Scripture scholar Dom Gueranger at the Abbey of Solesmes, who was regarded as the deepest spiritual thinker of his day. Leo derived great spiritual benefit from this meeting.

To combat writers who were spreading propaganda against the Holy Eucharist, Leo wrote a book, *Faith Revived and Piety Reanimated Through the Eucharist*. One of the first copies was given to the Carmelites of Tours who were the frequent recipients of his generosity and for whom Leo handled most of their business affairs. During one of his visits, the prioress, Mother Mary of the Incarnation, told Leo of an extraordinary new postulant, Sister Marie Pierre of the Holy Family. Sister Marie Pierre was a nun of rare spiritual favors who received visions of Our Lord that developed into The Holy Face Devotion. Our Lord gave certain prayers to this nun, which were to make reparation for those who blasphemed and for those anti-religious persons known as communists. These prayers, Our Lord told her, would atone for the sins against the first Three Commandments of God. One of the prayers, known as the Golden Arrow is: "May the most holy, most sacred, most adorable, most incomprehensible and ineffable name of God be praised, blessed, loved, adored and glorified in heaven and on earth, by all the creatures of God, and by the Sacred Heart of Our Lord and Savior Jesus Christ in the most Holy Sacrament of the Altar." Our Lord had asked that the prayer be distributed by means of leaflets. During other visions, Our Lord asked for the formation of an association "to honor the Name of My Father." Our Lord once told Sister Pierre, "If you did but know the glory a soul acquires in saying only once in the spirit of reparation for blasphemy: *Mirabile Nomen Dei*, "Admirable is the Name of God." This prayer was often repeated by Leo Dupont.

The bishop hesitated to approve the devotion, though he did give his Imprimatur to a pamphlet of prayers composed by Leo with the assistance of certain priests. Leo assumed all the expenses and was the chief distributor of the pamphlet. Our Lord then began to give promises to the little nun for those who practiced the devotion, among them being, "In proportion to your care in repairing the injuries My Face receives from blasphemers, will I take care of yours which has been disfigured by sin . . . that all who by words, prayers or writings defend My cause in this Work of Reparation for blasphemy will be defended by Me before My Father. . . ."

Leo's daughter Henriette, now fifteen, was enjoying life with her father and grandmother, when a contagious fever spread through Tours. Henriette and other boarders at the Ursuline boarding school were sent home. The following morning Henriette showed definite symptoms of the malignant fever. Fervent prayers were offered, but she grew steadily worse. The Lord asked of Leo the sacrifice of his daughter. With her death, Leo lost all interest with the demands of society and the world. He put aside his fashionably-colored clothing and began wearing black, which he wore for the rest of his life. From Henriette's death on, Leo lived entirely for God.

The large dowry Leo had reserved for Henriette was given to chari-table causes, among them convents, churches, orphanages, and the Little Sisters of the Poor. These contributions and others he had made dur-ing his thirteen years at Tours reduced his fortune until he was no longer the rich man he had once been. He had no regrets — his for-tune was turned into gold for eternity.

Sister Marie Pierre, the little Carmelite visionary, died on July 8, 1848. Leo assumed the task of promoting the devotion to the Holy Face. The archbishop, disagreed, and he gathered all the documents written by the nun, formally sealed them, and locked them in the diocesan archives.

A miracle intervened. In Rome, the pope had ordered special prayers, including a three-day exposition of the True Wood of the Cross and the relic of Veronica's Veil. On the third day of the exhibition, the faithful noticed a remarkable change on the Veil of Veronica. The ac-count of the miracle was recorded as follows:

> Through another veil of silk which covers the true Relic of Veronica's Veil, and absolutely prevents the features from being distinguished, the Divine Face appeared distinctly, as if living, and was illumined by a soft light; the features assumed a death-like hue, and the eyes, deep-sunken, wore an expression of great pain. The Canons immediately notified the clergy of the ba-silica and people quickly assembled. Many wept; all were im-pressed with a reverential awe. An apostolic notary was summoned; a certificate was drawn attesting the fact. . . .

Soon after, copies of the Image of the Holy Face were printed and touched to the True Veil. These were distributed worldwide, and Leo came to possess two. He framed both of them, giving one to the Noc-turnal Adoration Society, which he himself had founded, and the other he hung in his parlor. To show special devotion, he had an oil lamp burning constantly before the image.

One day Miss Estelle, an acquaintance, called on Leo in reference to a business matter. At the conclusion of their business, Leo noticed the elderly lady rubbing her eyes with a kerchief. Miss Estelle explained that for sometime her eyes had been "paining me fearfully. I can get no relief." Leo suggested that they say a prayer before the Holy Image. When they finished their prayer, Leo dipped his finger in the oil from the lamp, explaining that oil from a lamp that burned before an image of Mary in Rome often cured all sorts of infirmities. He then touched the lady's eyelids with the oil from his lamp. Suddenly she exclaimed joyfully that the pain had left. Soon after, a young man came to Leo's residence on an errand. When Leo noticed the man limped, Leo suggested that they pray before the image. Leo then anointed the man's leg with the oil. The young man stood up and began jumping with joy. He had been instantaneously cured. In a short time, twenty persons had been cured by means of the oil from the lamp. By the end of the year, Leo Dupont had lost track of the countless cures effected through the oil and the recitation of the Litany of the Holy Face that had been composed by Sister Marie Pierre. Three years after the first cure, Leo Dupont conservatively estimated that 60,000 little vials of oil had been given away. Requests came from distant parts of Europe and America, and many, not knowing his name, addressed their requests simply to "The Holy Man of Tours."

Because so many had asked for copies of the Holy Image, Leo had 25,000 lithographs made and distributed all at his expense. As to the miracles of healing, certificates signed by reputable physicians attested to the miraculous cures effected through the power of the holy oil and Devotion to the Holy Face.

Leo's house on Rue St. Etienne was soon flooded with visitors who visited the "Holy Room" to pray before the Image. He once wrote: "Day by day the crowds increase. Sometimes on Saturdays more than three hundred persons come to my parlor. . . . The proof that grace is acting upon souls may be seen from the fact that all understand that the Novena of Prayers and Anointings with oil conclude with Confession and Communion."

Archbishop Morlot, who had refused to approve the devotion, was aware of the many cures, and yet he steadfastly refused to change his mind. He did, however, send two people for a possible cure. Even when these also were cured, the archbishop maintained his silence.

On days when his parlor was less crowded, Leo Dupont developed arrangements for a better and more efficient method of helping the poor. In remembrance of the eleventh century St. Martin of Tours who had divided his cloak and given half of it to a poor man, Leo, who very much resembled the saint, formed the St. Martin's Clothing Society. Clothing donated for the poor was repaired, cleaned, and distributed by volunteers. In the first four months, the society distributed three hundred garments and received legacies from many of the wealthy who were anxious to join in this assistance to the poor.

Leo's devotion to St. Martin of Tours led him to search for the area where the saint's church once stood, having been torn down years earlier by revolutionaries. When the exact location was confirmed, Leo Dupont at once set about building a church on the exact spot, perhaps not a magnificent basilica like the one that stood originally, but a smaller church as magnificent as his reduced account could afford. With the discovery of the saint's tomb, the chapel was built.

Now advancing in years, Leo became a victim of the gout and spent much time in bed. The stream of people visiting his home continued, but because he could no longer do so, a servant was hired to distribute vials of oil and holy cards with the prayers to the Holy Face. Leo was permitted to make this distribution because his was a private ministry. After the death of Archbishop Morlot, Bishop Guibert took his place. Even though miracles had continued to be worked for seventeen years, the new bishop refused permission for the Devotion. By now, Leo was confined almost entirely to his bed. Among other ailments, he was struck with a paralysis, but with a crippled hand, he continued his correspondence on behalf of the Devotion. When a priest offered to occasionally offer Mass in his sick room, Leo refused, saying he was not worthy of such a privilege. He was, however, consoled by the regular reception of the Holy Eucharist.

Bishop Guibert was reassigned but his replacement, Bishop Fruchaud, also refused permission for the Devotion. Bishop Fruchaud was replaced by Archbishop Colet, who had all the documents relative to the Devotion removed from the archives. After carefully examining them, Archbishop Colet gave full permission for the life and revelation of Sister Marie Pierre to be published and the Devotion encouraged. After thirty years of prayer and efforts, Leo saw his desire fulfilled. When news of the archbishop's approval reached his ears, the poor invalid exclaimed, "Blessed be the Name of God."

A few days later, realizing that his end was near, Leo Dupont made final arrangements with a cousin, and with his devoted servants in attendance, he died on March 18, 1876. He was seventy-nine. Although buried in the cemetery beside his beloved daughter and his mother, many who attended the funeral prophesized that someday his remains would be removed to a church. This still might be a possibility since his Cause for beatification is pending.

According to his last requests, Leo Dupont's house on Rue St. Etienne was to be sold to settle his estate, but the archdiocese bought it, remodeled it, and turned it into an oratory. Archbishop Colet himself dedicated the building and approved an order of priests known as The Priests of the Holy Face to administer the chapel. Only a few months after Leo Dupont's death, the order was canonically erected on December 8, 1876. Father Peter Janvier, who had been a long-time friend of Leo Dupont, was installed as director. In addition to his duties Father Peter wrote two biographies, one of Leo Dupont, the other of Sister Marie Pierre and the Devotion to the Holy Face. These were widely distributed and have been translated into many languages.

The Devotion to the Holy Face was given full approval by Pope Leo XIII. The Confraternity was transformed into an Archconfraternity with special indulgences for its members in addition to all the promises made by Our Lord to all who practice and promote devotion to the Holy Face.

Leo Dupont's Cause was introduced in 1939. With the deserving canonical title of "Servant of God," Leo Dupont, the "Holy Man of Tours," awaits beatification.

Venerable Louis Necchi Villa
1876 – 1930
Professor of Biology, Neurosis Sufferer
Italy

Louis Necchi Villa is the only layman in this book whose parents were divorced. His father, Luigi, was a captain in the infantry and was often absent from home, which caused difficulties for his wife. The couple divorced when Louis was five, and his mother, unable to face supporting and raising her children alone, remarried. Louis' stepfather was Federico Villa, a sculptor. Earlier in their relationship, Louis' mother and stepfather were indifferent to religion; however, the sculptor returned to the faith shortly before his death. The divorce of his parents, the subsequent upheaval in the family, and the introduction of his stepfather into his life may well have been the source of the neurosis from which Louis would suffer.

Despite the turmoil in his life, Louis received his First Communion at the age of twelve, and the following year enrolled in Parini High School. One of his classmates was Edward Gemelli, the future Padre Agostino, with whom Louis had a lifelong friendship. The religious atmosphere of the Parini school contrasted sharply with the religious indifference at home, and later Louis would speak of the contribution the school made toward his conversion in 1893 at age seventeen.

After high school, Louis enrolled at the College Leo XIII where he was assisted by the famous Jesuit Guido Marriuaai, who was Louis' spiritual director for the next thirty years. Under the influence of Father Guido, philosopher and theologian, Louis gained a solid philosophical and theological base and an interest in the scientific and social problems that would become the foundation of his life.

Louis enrolled in the school of medicine at Pavia. He joined the group known as St. Severino Boezio, and was soon elected president. In a scholastic environment hostile to religion, Louis became involved in debates on social problems in which he championed the ideas of the social Christian according to pontifical teachings. He spoke of absolute fidelity to the teachings of the encyclical *Rerun Novarum,* and he worked for the social progress of city workers and farmers.

In 1902, Louis graduated with a degree in medicine. He briefly joined the military where he worked in the military hospital of St. Ambrogio. When a friend entered the seminary, Louis wondered if he was also called to the priesthood. To determine his calling, Louis took a course of spiritual exercises and concluded that he was called to the state of matrimony and the secular apostolate.

In 1904, Louis went to Berlin for a period of medical practice and laboratory research. Though busy in his work, Louis somehow found time to develop apostolic activities for Italian emigrants. He was asked to teach anatomy at the Catholic University of Friburg in Switzerland, but the young doctor refused this position so he could continue to have direct contact with the sick. In addition to his medical activities, Louis also found time to court Victoria Della Silva, whom he married in Milan on April 26, 1905. Their union was blessed with three children, Camilla, Gian Carlo, and Antonio.

In 1908, Archbishop Cardinal Ferrari of Milan invited Louis to join the diocesan committee of the Catholic Works. The doctor soon became president of the group, and he remained in that position for most of his life. That same year the secularists were trying to abolish the teaching of religion in the primary schools. The doctor, in his position as town adviser, successfully argued for the continued teaching of church doctrines. He was soon chosen a delegate of the Popular Union, then vice-president, then president. He left the presidency of the Popular Union, which was the nucleus of the Italian Catholic Party, but continued as advisor as he also did with the Catholic Works in Milan. There were other organizations to which he applied his talents, all in the interest of social welfare and aid to the poor and distressed.

During the World War I Louis was recalled to duty, despite his age and some visual difficulties. For eighteen months, he worked at the front in a field hospital. After his discharge, he returned to Milan and once again became involved in diocesan matters. He also began to do research in the mental aspect of psychology and biology, devoting himself to the care of the sick with nervous problems and children with abnormal traits. Having himself experienced the same mental disorder since childhood, he was a natural for work in the field. Neurosis is described as arising from no organic lesion or change and involves symptoms such as insecurity, anxiety, depression, and various fears. Louis organized a department in the Institute St. Vincent for the education of the children and remained the department's director for ten years. He continued his studies in this field and wrote on the subject of neurosis for various publications.

Louis helped establish a journal of philosophy as well as other papers and organizations. His social and medical activities and the many articles he wrote for various journals are numerous. He was helpful in the foundation of the Catholic University of the Sacred Heart, and he accepted the position of professor in the department of biology and a chair on the faculty of philosophy.

In the autumn of 1929, the doctor underwent several surgical procedures. The first operation revealed a malignant tumor, from which he suffered miserably, but which he concealed behind a constant smile. Death claimed the holy doctor on January 10, 1930, at the age of fifty-four.

News of Louis' death aroused a great emotion in the Catholic and secular world. Many articles appeared in the Italian and foreign press, and before long, biographies on Louis' life appeared in several languages. His body was first buried in the family crypt, but was later transferred to the crypt in the chapel of the Catholic University. On his tombstone, in addition to his name and pertinent dates, is found simply, "Franciscan Tertiary."

One of the doctor's biographies states: "The life of this man, tormented by doubt and by neurosis, shows that this does not contrast with holiness. The weight of the psychic conditioning, of which the Venerable sometimes experienced, under the action of the Holy Spirit can be approved and lived as a means of sanctification. Louis Necchi Villa knew how to love, to work and to produce benefits for the society in which he lived with inexhaustible fertility."

Louis' Cause was initiated three years after his death by Cardinal Schuster, and was eventually introduced in 1951. He was elevated to the position of Venerable in 1971.

Blessed Luigi Beltrame Quattrocchi

1880-1951
Attorney, Husband, Father
Italy

On October 21, 2001, Pope John Paul II made history again by proclaiming Luigi Beltrame Quattrocchi and his wife Maria — together — the first Blessed spouses of the Church. Previously, spouses had been proclaimed separately, usually for heroic witness, and never for the fact that they were a husband or a wife. With their beatification, Pope John Paul II has declared Luigi and Maria models for all Christians spouses and parents.

Luigi Beltrame was born January 12, 1880 in Catania, Italy, and grew up in Urbino. Luigi's uncle, his mother's brother, and his wife were childless, and somehow they persuaded Luigi's parents to let them raise Luigi as their own. His parents agreed, and Luigi Beltrame became Luigi Beltrame Quattrocchi. Luigi kept his ties with his parents and his siblings, while he lived at his aunt and uncle's home.

As a young man, Luigi enrolled in the University of Rome where he studied jurisprudence. After he obtained his law degree, Luigi found a position with the Inland Revenue Department, and throughout his life would work as an attorney and civil servant. Though considered honest, unselfish, and virtuous, Luigi did not have a strong faith. Maria Corsini would help him develop one.

Luigi met Maria in 1899. Maria was of the noble Corsini family of Florence, and her family's social and cultural activities had a tremendous influence on Maria's life. She was well educated, loved music, and was both a professor and a writer. She was also involved in many Christian organizations, including Women's Catholic Action. The couple began a courtship that was documented in their love letters, which expressed their love for each other and their religious sentiments.

On November 25, 1905, Luigi married Maria in the Basilica of St. Mary Major in Rome. Within the next four years, three healthy children were born: Filippo in 1906, Stefania in 1908, and in 1909, Cesare. At the end of 1913, Maria was again expecting, but this pregnancy was different. Maria's doctors diagnosed placenta previa, a life-threatening condition for both mother and child. The doctors, concerned for Maria's survival, advised her to save her own life by having an abortion. Luigi and Maria refused, and placed their trust in the Lord's Providence. In a conversation after her parents beatification, daughter Enrichetta said:

> Neither my mother nor my father thought in the least of following the doctor's advice. Their faith in God was greater than any advice, and their obeying the will of God, total and full of trust. They expressed their "yes" together, seeking strength in the cross. Mother spent the remaining period resting, at the end of the eighth month delivery was brought on, and so, on April 6th, 1914, I was born. From the time I found out about the events surrounding my birth, I have felt a sense of immense gratitude towards God and towards my parents.

The crisis of the pregnancy and birth served to draw the spouses even closer together. Their son Cesare remembers his parent's ever-increasing spiritual growth, noting something of a race between them: "She [Maria] began in the ' pole position' as she already lived an intense faith experience, while he was certainly 'a good man, just and honest but not very practicing.' "

In time, Luigi grew closer to God. The couple began attending daily morning Mass and in the evenings they prayed the Rosary together. They also kept the family holy hour in honor of the Sacred Heart of Jesus on the eve of the first Friday of the month, and they participated in the night vigil prayers and weekend retreats organized by the Monastery of St. Paul-Outside-the-Walls. The couple wanted their children to love those things that cannot be seen, saying that they wanted their children to appreciate life "from the roof up."

The Quattrocchi children report that their parents did not argue in front of them; instead, the couple chose to settle their differences of opinion through conversation, which they held away from young ears. According to Cardinal José Saraiva Martins, Prefect of the Congregation for the Causes of Saints, Luigi and Maria worked to make "a true domestic church of their family, which was open to life, to prayer, to the social apostolate, to solidarity with the poor, and to friendship."

During the Second World War, Luigi and Maria's apartment in Via Depretis, near St. Mary Major, was a shelter for Jews and other refugees. The couple was known in Church circles for their help to political dissidents under fascism, and they joined a number of Church-run charitable and social organizations. Their house was always open to their numerous friends and those who knocked at their door asking for food. The couple maintained a sense of peace for their family through these often-violent days in daily reception of the Eucharist and in prayers.

Luigi became an ardent supporter of the Scout Movement in Italy. Filippo recalls that his father was among the first to adhere to the Scouts and that he and his brother were some of the first participants. "Love for nature accompanied by field study and the teachings of Christian pedagogy acquired in that period have always remained carved in our soul."

Also carved in the souls of the Quattrocchi children were their parents' lives of faith and witness. Filippo and Cesare, both entered seminaries and became priests; Stefania entered the cloistered convent of the Benedictines of Milan and became a nun. Enrichetta, the daughter who almost wasn't, remained with her parents.

Luigi and Maria were a couple who loved and respected each other through the ups and downs of married family life. At their beatification, Pope John Paul II characterized the deep spirituality of Luigi and Maria, saying: "The blessed couple lived an ordinary life in an extraordinary way. Among the joys and anxieties of a normal family, they knew how to live an extraordinarily rich spiritual life."

In November 1951, Luigi died of a heart attack in their home on Via Depretis. Maria survived another fourteen years, dedicating her life to prayer and her work with several Catholic charities. On August 26, 1965, she died in Enrichetta's arms at their house in the mountains, at Serravalle. In 1993, their daughter, Stefania, Sister Maria Cecilia, joined her parents in death.

The Cause for Beatification for Maria and Luigi Beltrame Quattrocchi was opened on November 25, 1994 with the couple raised to the honor of the altars on October 21, 2001. On October 28, 2001, the relics of Luigi and Maria were transferred to their crypt in the Shrine of Divino Amore (Divine Love) at Rome.

Servant of God Luigi Rocchi

1932 – 1979
Muscular Dystrophy Invalid
Italy

For a man who was immobile for twenty-eight years, Luigi Rocchi displayed a great love of people through his correspondence, his cheerfulness in spite of pain, and his loving dependence on the mercy of God and the grace of his heavenly Mother.

Luigi was born at Tolentino, the city made famous by St. Nicholas. Luigi was a healthy and happy child born into a family of workers, but in 1951, at the age of nineteen, he began to experience the early signs of muscular dystrophy. His condition became progressively worse until, by the age of twenty-eight, his hands and feet were paralyzed, and he was completely immobile.

From the early days of his sickness, his cheerfulness and optimistic attitude attracted many people to him, and the number grew so that he was either receiving visitors or answering their letters. What attracted so many to Luigi was his gift of communicating the joy of living and his love of God and nature. For those suffering in mind or spirit, he shared his hope in the Lord and gave comfort to souls by way of his countless letters. For a time he could write the letters, but when his hands became paralyzed, he beat the keys of a typewriter with a stick he held in his mouth. It is said that he wrote as many as twenty-two letters a day. Many have been preserved and have been reprinted in various publications.

For Luigi it was a great sacrifice that he was unable to help the Lord in other ways since he would have liked to assist poor men, the suffering ones, and the oppressed in the Third World. They were the people Luigi called "living crucifixes." But he suffered a great deal as they did, and accepted his condition in imitation of the crucified Jesus and never complained.

Luigi was able to make two pilgrimages, one to Lourdes, where he prayed for all his suffering friends, and one to Loreto, where he visited the holy house of his heavenly Mother. Accompanying him on these journeys was his beloved mother who was his attentive and caring nurse. She admits that in the beginning her nursing duties were very difficult, but because of Luigi's cheerfulness and prayerful attitude, she found her chores much more agreeable and less tiring.

All who met Luigi were struck by his great joy and love of everyone. When asked about his gaiety, he replied: "What is the secret of my joy? I am thirsty for God. So much thirst for God."

Monsignor Capovilla, the secretary of Pope John XIII, knew Luigi very well and once wrote that Luigi seemed destined to radiate his ideals well beyond the confines of his city: "He has been appreciated and his house has become one great school of spirituality. . . ."

The archbishop of Macerata and Ravenna, Monsignor Ersilio Tonini, wrote about Luigi:

> I have known him very well and I have been immediately spellbound by him. Two aspects particularly struck me, Luigi's serenity and his desire not to be pitied. Luigi had a great gift, a liberty of spirit — a liberty of the mind. I have never seen anyone as happy as he. But there is another characteristic, the need to

share his happiness, to encourage in others a deep relationship with God, for them to find happiness in pain . . . I can say that Luigi was one of the most beautiful souls I have ever met in my life. . . .

Luigi died in Tolentino on March 26, 1979 at the age of forty-seven. Since his death, through many books and other materials, Luigi has become well known to countless people throughout the world who did not have the privilege of knowing him in life.

The bishop of Tolentino, in the diocese of Macerata, initiated the Cause of beatification on October 17, 1992.

Venerable Luis Magana Servin
1902 – 1928
Tanner, Martyr
Mexico

The oldest of the three children of Raymundo Magana Zuniga and Mari Concepcion Servin Gomez, Luis was a responsible and well-behaved child of a tranquil nature who enjoyed playing with friends, and especially liked baseball. He was blessed to be a member of a pious family who inspired him in the way of Christian living and provided him with a good Catholic education.

Even as a child, Luis rose early and attended Mass with his father. His day followed a regular routine: after Mass, he attended school and in the afternoon helped his father with his work in the tannery. In the tannery, he was regarded as his father's "right hand man," helping him with dedication and cheerfulness. The day ended with the family's recitation of the Rosary.

When Luis was old enough to assume more responsibilities, he observed the counsel of Monsignor Jose Mora y del Rio, the bishop of Mexico City, who said: "Treat your workers with love and they will never leave you." Luis put social justice into practice by doing as the bishop advised. He was kind and treated his workers with Christian dignity. Luis was generous with them and with the poor, and in return, they respected and admired him, holding him in the highest regard.

As a young man, Luis joined the Association of Saint Mary of Guadalupe, a group that united artisan workers. Also, he became interested in the social issues of the day, studying the encyclical *Rerum*

Novarum of Pope Leo XIII that was published in 1891. Luis helped introduce to his city the Catholic Association of Mexican Youth (ACJM), a resistance group that worked during the years 1926-1929 to free the country from the repressive dictates of the Mexican government that was persecuting the Catholic faithful. During one of the ACJM meetings, Luis met the great defender of religious freedom, Anacleto Gonzalez Flores, whose biography also is included in this book.

Luis was in the group that founded the Nocturnal Adoration Society in Arandas in 1922. During his time of adoration, Luis gained the strength and enthusiasm for the defense of the Church. He was also involved in the activities of his parish, especially in helping to organize youth groups to help the poor. Luis was devoted to the Blessed Virgin, especially under the title of Our Lady of Guadalupe. When there was an unsuccessful attempt to destroy the image in Mexico City with dynamite, Luis was among those in Arandas who performed special acts of reparation.

Luis was a prosperous young man who already owned a house when he met his future wife, Elvira, who was an orphan. In 1926, when he was twenty-four and she eighteen, they were married. Their marriage was a very happy one. Their son Gilberto was born in 1927, but sadly, Luis did not live to see the birth of his daughter Luisa. She was born five months after the martyrdom of her holy parent.

Luis' town of Arrandas, a primarily rural area, became a town of great resistant to the repressive government. During the persecution, priests exercised their ministry in secret while wearing disguises. Many men joined in the fighting while the women and children served as messengers among the groups of resistance fighters. Luis was a pacifist who did not enlist as one of the fighters, but he pledged to help spiritually and materially wherever such help was needed. In spite of the danger, he organized the distribution of arms, food, and other necessities to the fighters.

Eventually the news of the murder of Father Luis Batis and three young members of the ACJM reached Arrandas. People were horrified to learn that the martyrs' bodies had been hung from trees at the south of town near the bank of the river. The military authorities did this to frighten the people of Arrandas, and then demanded that the farmers bring their harvests to a designated place to prevent their being used by the resisters. Many of the farmers left their land without harvesting the crops and went into hiding. Luis' family graciously lodged many of them. The government demanded that the municipal president of Arrandas provide a list of all who were suspected of aiding the resisters. Luis' name appeared on the list. He may have also been reported to the government by an informer who knew of his work with the ACJM.

When federal soldiers came to his house on February 9, 1928, to arrest him, Luis was not at home. The soldiers took Luis' younger brother, Delfino, telling the family that if Luis turned himself in that same day, they would release the boy.

When Luis returned home to find his parents and his wife in tears, he calmed them, and told them he would speak with General Martinez, who would release the boy. "The most they can do to me," he said, "Would be to take me to Guadalajara where they are taking everyone." However, the family knew the danger involved.

Luis then bathed and dress in a new suit. He ate a leisurely lunch then knelt in front of his parents for their blessing. He kissed his little son and left the family and his pregnant wife. When neighbors saw him leaving they warned Luis not to go, believing he would be shot. Luis opened his arms and looking heavenward replied, "What happiness! Within an hour I will be in the arms of God."

Upon entering the military office, Luis identified himself as the one they were looking for and requested that they release the boy as they had promised. General Martinez analyzed the young man before him and gave orders for the boy's release, adding, "We are going to see if in truth you are as valiant as you seem." Then he ordered that Luis be taken to the church and shot immediately.

With an escort of eight soldiers, the firing squad, and with Pancho Muerte who had also been arrested, Luis crossed the town plaza and entered the atrium of the church. Luis refused the traditional blindfold and asked to make a statement. Two witnesses who were hiding gave testimony as to what was said. Luis bravely spoke:

> I am neither a Cristero or a rebel. But if you accuse me of being a Christian, that I am. You soldiers who are going to shoot me, I want to tell you that from this moment I pardon you and I promise you that on arriving in the presence of God you are the first ones for whom I will intercede. *Viva Cristo Rey. Viva Santa Maria de Guadalupe.*

The noise of the firing squad sounded. Luis' family was fully aware that the gunshots meant the execution of their martyr.

Luis now awaits beatification together with seven other resisters who defended the Catholic faith during an unfortunate time in Mexico's history. With the Decree of Valor being proclaimed on May 21, 1999, Luis Magana Servin is now distinguished with the title of Venerable.

Venerable Luis Padilla Gomez
1899 – 1927
Writer, Martyr
Mexico

The early religious training that Luis Gomez received from his parents, Dionisio Padilla and Mercedes Gomez de Padilla, and the lessons taught in the Jesuit-run San Joseph Institute when he was young, led Luis to consider a religious vocation. Though he entered the Conciliar Seminary of Guadalajara, in a few years, feeling he did not have a true vocation, he left.

While in the seminary Luis wrote in a diary he called "Misticas," which revealed his love and devotion to the Sacred Heart and the Immaculate Heart of Mary. After leaving the seminary, he destroyed this diary, but he began another that he called "Remembrances and Impressions." In this work, he tells of his great love of all things religious. After making the spiritual exercises in the city of Leon, he wrote in his diary, "My motto: God with me and for me. How I want to live without fear of life. Now I want to die with great hope in the future life." Prophetic words from a man who would die at age twenty-eight.

After leaving the seminary, Luis dedicated himself to an apostolate as a catechist. He became active in social matters, joining the Catholic Association of Mexican Youth (ACJM) when it was founded in Guadalajara. He soon became the archdiocesan president of the group. The ACJM was founded during a critical time in Mexico's history, when the anticlerical government of President Plutarco Elias Calles was persecuting the Church and trying to abolish it altogether. Luis also worked with the Popular Union founded by the Servant of God Anacleto Gonzalez Flores (whose biography is included in this book). Both the ACJM and the Popular Union opposed the Mexican president, and soon began an armed opposition to the laws enacted against the Church.

During this turbulent time, Luis again felt the call to the priesthood, but his entrance into a seminary was impossible since they and all the churches in Mexico had been closed. Priests were being imprisoned, church properties were being seized, and many people were killed simply for being Catholic.

With the Catholic Church underground, Luis, too, wondered if he might be martyred, and mentioned this in his diary in 1925. He wrote, "I will not scrimp on giving my blood to God." When the day came and he was arrested, he wrote: "I pardon them. I humbly pardon them thinking of you, Lord. . . . It is so good, so sweet to pardon . . . Lord, when they turn against me to torment me or treat me with cruelty, I will bless the wounds they inflict on me, thinking of You."

On the morning of April 1, 1927, Luis was arrested by the secret police at his home. He was taken to the Colorado jail where he met Anacleto and two brothers named Vargas (their biographies are included in this book). Luis was beaten and insulted before being sentenced to execution.

The four men bravely faced death. Standing with their arms in the form of a cross and shouting *Viva Christo Rey*, "Long Live Christ the King!" they were released from this life and entered paradise as martyrs to the faith.

Hundreds came to Luis's home to venerate the holy martyr before the burial. In 1981, his mortal remains were transferred to the Church of San Jose in Analco. Luis now awaits beatification. A decree recognizing his valor was issued by the Vatican on May 21, 1999.

Servant of God Manuel Lozano Garrido
1920 – 1971
Journalist
Spain

Manuel Garrido spent twenty-eight years in a wheelchair, but that was not his only affliction. Manuel was also blind for the last ten years of his life.

Manuel was born healthy on August 9, 1920 in Linares, Jaen, in the region of Andalusia, Spain. For a career he choose journalism, and he wrote for the religious media, including the newspaper *Ya* and the Associated Press.

When Manuel was twenty-two he contracted spondylitis, a condition that inflames the vertebrae. From then on he endured pain and the rapid deformity of his back, which would eventually necessitate his use of a wheelchair. Despite the pain, Manuel continued to write articles for magazines and newspapers that centered on evangelization. For his journalistic accomplishments, in 1969, the Spanish Bishops' Conference awarded him their most prestigious honor, the Bravo Award.

218

Manuel never let his deformity hinder his work, nor did he permit blindness to interfere with his zeal to use the media for the good of souls and the Church. Despite his blindness he continued to write intense articles, and he dictated nine books to his sister Lucy and friends. Among these books are: *The Stars are Seen at Night,* and *The Naked Tree.* The same publishing house that printed his books also published his biography, *Joy in Suffering,* which was written by the postulator of his Cause, Reverend Rafael Higueras.

In his last will Manuel reveals the sweetness and goodness of his heart: "Friends, we will not see one another for sometime; I anticipate my meeting with the Father; I thank you for being with me at my death, as you were by my side when I was in my wheelchair. I am yours and I renew my appointment with joy. Look after Lucy (his sister), and remember that everything is a grace."

Manuel died on November 3, 1971 at the age of fifty-one. The investigation for the Cause of his beatification began soon after, and according to the postulator of his Cause, all the documentation and testimonies that have been collected prove that Manuel Lozano Garrido led a virtuous and exemplary life. Already the Cause has been graced with the first miracle of healing, which five doctors have confirmed and declared to be inexplicable. The details of this cure will be added to all the documents that will be presented to the pope for the acceptance.

Saint Manuel Morales
1898 – 1926
Organization Worker, Martyr
Mexico

During the ceremony conducted by Pope John Paul II on May 21, 2000, twenty-five Mexican martyrs were canonized. Of this number, twenty-two were members of religious orders and three were layman: Manuel Morales, David Roldan, and Salvador Lara. (David and Salvador are treated elsewhere in this volume.)

These martyrdoms took place during a stressful time in Mexican history. The new Mexican Constitution of 1917 included laws meant to suppress the Catholic Church. The enforcement of the laws took place arbitrarily during the years, but during 1926-1929, they were enforced with a vengeance. Churches were confiscated, religious ceremonies were forbidden, the clergy wore disguises and went into hiding, while priests, nuns, and laypeople were either imprisoned or executed. Religious services continued in secret, with family homes becoming sanctuaries for the Blessed Sacrament.

In an attempt to have the repressive laws repealed, various groups were organized whose sole aim was to address the matter by peaceful and legitimate means. A large group known as the National League for the Defense of Religious Liberty (LNDLR) was founded in Chalchihuites with Manuel Morales serving as president.

Manuel was the only married man of the three who were martyred and canonized. He had been a former seminarian, but left the seminary to help support his impoverished family. He eventually married and had three sons. Manuel was known as an exemplary husband and father who was pious and faithful to his religious obligations. He was dedicated to helping in the ministries of his parish, and was especially devoted to the Blessed Eucharist. In an effort to help the Church during the persecution, in addition to serving as president of the National League, Manuel served as secretary of the circle of Catholic Workers and was a member of Catholic Action whose members render all sorts of charitable services to the poor and the sick.

As president of the National League, Manuel called a meeting on July 29 and said at the time, "The League will be peaceful, without mixing in political affairs. Our project is to plead with the government to repeal the constitutional articles that oppress religious liberty." Unfortunately, the secret police were told of the meeting. A large contingent of soldiers surrounded the place and entered, calling out the names of the leaders who were harshly treated and arrested. Manuel, David Roldan, the vice-president, and Salvador Lara, the secretary, were taken to the municipal headquarters and placed in a cell with their friend, Father Luis Batiz.

The prisoners were kept in the damp prison cell for more than two weeks. On August 15, 1926, the four men were put in two cars and taken to the town of Zacatecas. In the mountains near Puerto Santa Teresa, the cars stopped and the prisoners were removed. The government representatives apparently thought that if the leaders of the National League would deny their principles, the people might also follow them and the rebellion would be suppressed. For this reason, the prisoners were told that if they recognized President Calles' anti-religious laws they would be set free. The four steadfastly refused.

Manuel Morales and Father Batiz were moved forward, but Father Batiz pleaded with the guards to let Manuel go free since he had children to support. Manuel quickly announced, "I die, but God does not die. He will take care of my wife and my sons." Then in a loud voice he shouted the cry of the rebellion, "Long live Christ the King and the Virgin of Guadalupe!" Both he and the priest were then shot. Manuel was twenty-eight.

After repeating the same words in a loud voice, David Roldan and Salvador Lara were also executed. These three laymen were canonized on May 21, 2000.

Blessed Marcel Callo

1921 – 1945
Printer, Martyr
France

Devotion to the Mother of God began early for Marcel Callo: he was baptized on the feast of the Immaculate Conception, December 8, 1921, in the Church of Notre Dame de Bonne Nouvelle at Rennes, France.

Marcel was born into a family of nine children. Though his father worked for the city's street and bridge department, the responsibilities of raising nine children made it difficult for Marcel's parents to provide all that was necessary for them.

As a child, Marcel was described as having been a leader, always happy, frank, and open. Marcel was something of a perfectionist and he liked to organize, express, and defend his ideas. He liked order, and though he understood that he was not always correct, he struggled to make concessions.

Since he was one of the older children, Marcel was expected to help in the care and management of the household. He willingly helped his mother wash the dishes, straighten the house, and wash and dress his younger brothers and sisters. He did his chores with care and in good spirits.

Marcel completed his primary studies at St. Anne School at Rennes and was soon apprenticed to a printer. He was thirteen. He was proud to support himself and to help financially with the needs of his family. Most of the young people gave their salaries to their mothers, and Marcel was no exception. In turn, his mother gave him what was needed for his expenses. He loved his trade and was proud to work with his hands. He once wrote that, "Work assures us of the necessities of our existence and is for us a source of merit for the other life."

During his apprenticeship, Marcel disliked his fellow workers telling improper stories and using vulgar language. Marcel found more like-minded companions in an organization known as the JOC, *Jeunesse Ouvriere Chretienne* (Young Christian Workers). Founded under the inspiration of Pere Cardijn and Pere Guerin, the JOC provided instruction in the Catholic faith, good fellowship, and wholesome activities. Marcel's friends in the JOC later described him as, "Dynamic, very cheerful . . . he knew how to laugh and how to make people laugh. He was an excellent friend." Another companion said, "Marcel possessed a joyful character, always happy and always very Christian." Another reported, "I always thought he had a good sense of humor. He was alive, dynamic, and had the stuff of a leader." These friends also revealed that Marcel liked to wrestle and play football, ping-pong, cards, and bridge.

In 1941, when Marcel was twenty, he met and fell in love with Marguerite Derniaux. Marcel treated her with respect, as befitting someone in the JOC. As he once said: "I am not one to amuse myself with the heart of a lady, since my love is pure and noble. If I have waited until I was twenty years old to go out with a young lady, it is because I knew that I wanted to find real love. One must master his heart before he can give it to the one that is chosen for him by Christ."

It was almost a year later, in August 1942, that Marcel declared his love, and another four months passed before he "suffered the embarrassment" of their first kiss. As his fiancée later wrote, "That day I was celebrating the completion of the training for my work. After Mass he kissed me for the first time. He had wanted to delay this gesture in order to thank God that we knew each other."

Four months later, the young couple imposed on themselves another rule for the spiritual life. This included the recitation of the same prayers, the frequent assistance at Mass, and the reception of the Holy Eucharist.

Marcel's orderly life of work and prayer was interrupted on March 8, 1943 when World War II reached the city of Rennes — with bombs. The train station was destroyed, along with many of the homes and shops on the streets around it. Since Marcel worked close by, he and other workers went about helping those who were injured. When Marcel came to the place where his sister Madeleine worked, he dug through the debris of the building until he found her body. He fought the pain of his sorrow as he told his parents and his family the terrible news.

Soon after the bombing, Marcel was ordered to report to the S.T.O., *Service du Travail Obligatoire* (Service of Obligatory Work) in Germany. While the Germans occupied France, young men were forced to report for work in Germany. Failure to do so would result in the arrest of a man's family. Marcel delayed telling his family as long as he could because of the recent death of his sister. An aunt in whom Marcel confided his secret told him that she knew he would greatly benefit his friends in Germany. To this Marcel responded, "Yes, Aunt, I will do everything possible to do well because you know that it is not as a worker that I leave, but as a missionary."

Marcel made the five-day trip to Zella-Mehlis, Germany, only eleven days after his sister's death. His family now endured two losses, since there was doubt in their minds that Marcel would ever return. At Zella-Mehlis, Marcel reported to a factory that made rockets, which he learned would be used against the French people. Although forced to work and quartered in barracks, he and the other workers were not considered prisoners, they were given the freedom to come and go, and to participate in various activities.

While he was in Germany, Marcel missed the first Mass of his newly ordained brother and the first Holy Communion of his little sister. Probably because of homesickness, Marcel suffered from discouragement, and for three months he fought a terrible depression. During this time Marcel wrote home that there was no Catholic church in Zella-Mehlis, but he found a room where Mass was offered on Sundays. This, he said, was a great comfort to him. When he wrote to his family he described his feelings, and his need for consolation, and reported that, "Finally Christ reacted. He made me to understand that the depression was not good. I had to keep busy with my friends and then joy and relief would come back to me."

Marcel had told his aunt that he was leaving home as a missionary, and true to his word, he began to work to restore good morale and hope among his deported friends. He organized a team of his Christian workers to play bridge, cards, sports, and other activities. He also organized a theatrical group that performed small plays. He wrote home: "I believe I am still in Rennes in full activity. I give much and I receive much in return. When I do good things for others I am satisfied."

With a holy deliberation, Marcel continued to organize these activities, despite his own discomforts. He suffered from painful boils, headaches, and infected teeth, which he said often, transformed his head into a balloon. He endured all while working more than eleven hours a day.

For his French comrades, Marcel was able to arrange for a solemn Mass to be celebrated in their language. In a letter home, he wrote:

We had our first French Mass this morning. The result is that I am happy . . . it was a successful beginning. What enthusiasm! We sang with one voice and we chanted the Credo. For us it was magnificent. . . . At the end I addressed a few words, then we prayed for all the ones we left in France and for all our friends working in Germany. All the people were very pleased. . . . They came to congratulate us and asked for a French Mass every month. I am very happy to arrive at that result.

The German officials eventually became aware of Marcel's religious activities. This prompted Marcel's arrest on April 19, 1944. While Marcel was being taken away, Joel Poutrel, one of Marcel's friends, demanded a reason for the arrest. The agent of the Gestapo responded, *"Monsieur est beaucoup trop catholique"* (Monsieur is too much of a Catholic.) Marcel appealed to his friend, "Please write to my parents and to my fiancée that I am arrested for Catholic action."

Marcel admitted during his interrogation that he was engaged in Catholic activities and that he knew this was forbidden in Germany. He was taken to the prison in Gotha, where he continued his life of prayer and his concern for his companions. It is believed that Marcel received his last Holy Communion during his stay at Gotha. Consecrated Hosts were secretly brought into the prison and were confided to a JOC friend, Henri Choteau, who kept them in a box for distribution. In a small journal that Marcel kept in prison he wrote on the feast of Our Lady of Mount Carmel, "16 July . . . Communion . . . immense joy."

After he was officially accused of participating in Catholic activities among his French friends, Marcel was moved to the prison at Mathausen on October 24. He was to suffer there for five months. In spite of sickness, he inquired about the needs of his companions, and encouraged them by saying, "It is in prayer that we find our strength."

Marcel now suffered from general weakness, fever, swelling, bronchitis, malnutrition, and dysentery. Reportedly, he never complained, and he "expired softly like a lamb." He died on the feast of St. Joseph, his namesake, March 19, 1945, exactly two years from the day he left France for Germany.

When Marcel left France, his fiancée told him, "You will be a martyr." Marcel Callo had replied, "I will never be good enough for that." The Catholic Church thought otherwise — Pope John Paul II beatified Marcel on October 4, 1987.

Blessed Marino Blanes Giner
1888 – 1936
Bank employee, City Council Member, Father of Nine
Spain

Marino Blanes Giner was born in the city of Alcoy in the diocese of Valencia on September 17, 1888. His parents, Jaime and Josefa Giner, educated their son in a Catholic atmosphere and saw to his first reception of the sacraments. His was a normal childhood in all respects, with regular attendance at Mass and the reception of the sacraments.

At the age of twenty-five Marino married Julia Jorda Lloret and formed a blessed Christian home for the nine children who would join them. He was a devoted husband and father, seeking the convenience and happiness of each member of the family and being careful to educate his children in all that pertained to the Catholic faith. In the document that was submitted for his Cause of beatification it is said that Marino was "a man of deep faith who participated in the Mass and received Communion daily. . . . that he was devoted to the Mother of God and the Rosary which he prayed with the family and that as catechist and social apostle, he led an intense life of piety . . . that he exercised an organized apostolate not only in Alcoy but in the archdiocese . . . and that he demonstrated that it is possible for the faithful to achieve sanctity in any state of life. . . ."

Marino tried to spread an evangelical spirit in the workplace, especially in his position as an employee of the Spanish Bank of Credit and as a member of the city council of Alcoy. To supplement his income, his mother gave him the funds to start a business of tanning leather for shoes, but in time, the business entered bankruptcy, as did his mother's small restaurant. Marino might not have been successful in business, but he was enormously successful in other ways.

A deeply religious man, Marino was moved by the Holy Spirit to organize apostolates, being himself a member of several lay associations. He was a Franciscan tertiary and a member of the Association of Christian Doctrine. He was a member of many other associations including the Congregation of St. Vincent de Paul, the Apostolate of the Virgin of the Abandoned, and was president of his parish's Nocturnal Adoration Society. He also founded the Catholic Instruction Center and collaborated with the parish priest in teaching catechism, having gone on many Sundays to farmhouses where he taught catechism not only in Alcoy, but also those in surrounding villages. He was also charitable when his economic situation and the needs of his family permitted it. On Sundays, he helped the nuns in the Hospital Oliver in the personal needs of the patients.

When the situation in Spain became unsettled during the years 1931 to 1936 with the formation of the Republic and the persecution of Catholics, everyone was warned of the hostility that would be aimed at those who were engaged in the apostolates. Marino continued all his activities, especially that of teaching the faith. His activities might have gone unnoticed had it not been for Marino's assignment of securing the integrity of the two Catholic churches, that of San Mauro and St. Francis.

One night, after returning from mailing a letter, he passed the church of St. Francis and noticed twelve bottles of gasoline in the shadow by the front door. Greatly alarmed, Marino called the police, who removed everything. This attempt at the destruction of the church did not stop the persecutors since matters became worse in Alcoy on July 18, 1936 with fires in many churches. Images and religious objects were burned and many Catholics were imprisoned. Realizing that he was in great danger, he placed his trust in divine Providence. When his wife insisted that he go into hiding, Marino replied, "I have done nothing wrong. I don't have a reason to hide."

Eventually two militiamen arrived at his home and took Marino, his neighbor, and a brother-in-law to court where one of the militiamen identified Marino as the one who found the gasoline in front of the church. Later that night Marino was transferred to the municipal jail while the others returned home. After about two months Marino was transferred to the prison Esclavas where he demonstrated a true Christian spirit and trust in God.

His wife said, "I visited him several times and I always found him calm and optimistic." Marino's daughter said, "We took him food and we always found him brave in spite of his knowing he would eventually be killed. . . . I found out that he and the others recited the Rosary every night."

In the jail were people of all social classes. A fellow prisoner said that Marino "was distinguished for his liking and treatment of the humblest and more abandoned. . . . He was always smiling, affable, full of the love of Christian fraternity for all. . . . This made me see the degree of sanctity and faith of Mr. Blanes."

During his seven weeks of imprisonment, Marino had only one request: to meet with his sister Paquita so that he could ask her to help his wife and children. Whether this request was granted is unknown. On September 7, Marino was taken out of the prison and martyred. A certificate in the civil registry of Alcoy documented this, but his family was not notified. On September 8, when Marino's brother went to take him food, he was told, "Last night we gave him freedom." Marino's wife then sent her son for the same purpose. The jailers told him, "They have taken him to Alicante and we no longer know anything about him."

The parish priest of San Mauro and St. Francis once related that there were interred in the cemetery the remains of three martyrs of the parish, Amalia Abbot, Florence Carols, and Maria Jorda, women of Catholic Action, and the "memory" of Marino Blanes Giner, a man of Catholic action. This martyr of the faith was beatified on March 11, 2001.

Servant of God Mario Ferdinandi
1916 – 1946
Attorney, Judge
Italy

Mario Ferdinandi, and his sister Teresa, are the second non-martyred brother and sister to be beatified (Jacinta and Francisco were the first). Mario and Teresa are awaiting beatification, their Causes were accepted during the same year, 1979.

Born to Marino and Maria Ferrotti, Mario received an excellent primary, secondary and high school education. While his sister was pursuing sanctification in the area of teaching, Mario seems always to have been involved in studying and preparing for his final profession. At the age of seventeen, he enrolled in a college in Rome to study jurisprudence and graduated in 1937. Fresh from his studies, Mario applied for a job with the government. Thinking he might not obtain a position, he also applied for the position of magistrate. Both offered him employment. He accepted the position of assistant deputy commissioner of safety and security and he stayed in this position until 1939 when he became eligible for military service. Mario was assigned to the 52nd Infantry Regiment, called "the Alps," as a second lieutenant and was sent to the western front. In 1941, his military career ended when he was discharged due to illness.

In 1942, Mario completed his studies of the court system and was nominated as magistrate of Norcia, where he served for two years. He was then transferred to the courts of Perugia, where he served as a judge in the penal section. He was only twenty-nine years old. Mario served only one year as a judge. He died in Perugia in 1946 at the age of thirty.

Mario's life was not only spent in study and work, but also in seeking his sanctification. He was a young affiliate in the Catholic Action movement and was a member of the Conference of St. Vincent. In the city of Todi, Mario was the president of an organization known as "Pier Giorgio Frassati" (whose biography appears elsewhere in this book), and was the secretary of the social activities of the group. As an authentic Catholic, he cultivated three ardent loves: the Eucharist, the Madonna, and the pope.

Soon after Mario's death, the bishop of Todi forwarded to the Congregation for the Causes of the Saints all the necessary documentation regarding the petition for Mario's beatification.

Mario and his sister, Teresa, are both entombed in the church of the Madonna of Campione.

Venerable Matthew Talbot

1856 – 1925
Laborer
Ireland

For anyone with a compulsive problem, this Venerable is the one to look to for encouragement. He overcame two overbearing urges: alcohol and smoking.

Life began for Matt Talbot on May 2, 1856 in the small seaside village of Clontarf, which is located two miles from Dublin, Ireland. He was the second of twelve children born to Charles Talbot and Elizabeth Bagnall. Charles was a dock laborer, a man of uncommonly small stature and somewhat aggressive bearing. Little is known of Elizabeth except that she was described, almost unkindly, as being rather "plain-looking."

At the age of eleven, Matthew was enrolled at the Christian Brothers School. At this time in Ireland, children found jobs at an early age and compulsory school attendance was rarely observed. The Christian Brothers labored to help the children of poor families who were able to spend only a short time in school. Matt Talbot was to be a short-timer, and he was placed in a "special" class where he learned the basics of reading and writing. He was also taught his prayers and the truths of the faith in preparation for his reception of the sacraments.

After only one year of instruction, Matt left school in the summer of 1868 and began working in Dublin as a messenger boy for a wine merchant. Though not yet a teenager, he soon began to sample his employer's product. His sister, Mrs. Mary Andrews, reported in 1931 that while Matt worked at this job:

> He learned to take alcoholic drink to excess. Our father saw this, gave him a severe thrashing and found a new situation for him as a messenger boy in the Port and Docks Board Office. But Matt continued to drink, notwithstanding all my father did to cure him. Matt left his job after three years so as not to bring disgrace on his father who was also employed by the Port and Docks Board. Matt then became a bricklayer's laborer, but continued his drinking habits, though he always worked very hard, all his wages went to drink — he even pawned his boots to buy drink. He often missed his Easter duty in those years, but was always careful about Sunday Mass . . . he had no women or girl friends and there was never anything against his moral character.

Unfortunately, Matt's father, Charles, was himself an alcoholic. According to Pat Doyle, a close friend of the family, "Matt and all of them (Matt's brothers) had the liking for drink from the father." The only exception was John, the eldest.

One of Matt's sisters, Susan Fylan, gives us other details of her brother's activities:

> He told me himself that he sold his boots and shirt to get drink, and he used to get drink on credit, often having his wages spent in advance. He was quiet most of the time when drunk, but used to curse and swear; he used to come home and lie down; drunkenness was his only vice; he was hot-tempered and when

drunk used to have rows and fights, but ordinarily he was quiet and was not cross with us at home. I heard him say (after his conversion) that even when drinking he was devout in his mind to the Blessed Virgin and used to say an odd Hail Mary, and he attributed his conversion to this.

Matt remained a good and steady workman in spite of his heavy drinking. While employed as a hodman for a bricklayer, he accomplished more in half-an-hour than the other workers managed in an hour. The master builder customarily placed Matt in front to make the rest of the men keep up with him. For this reason Matt became known as "the best hodman in Dublin."

Since his income was insufficient to maintain his excessive drinking habit, Matt sometimes supplemented his wages by collecting and selling empty bottles. When his thirst persisted, he often stood outside Carolan's Pub and collected tips for holding horses.

In 1948, Matt's niece Annie Johnson said that Matt and his brothers had such a craving for whiskey they stole a violin from a fiddler and sold it for drink. From his early teens until his late twenties, Matt was an alcoholic who carelessly lost his self-respect, refused to listen to the appeals of his mother, and drank not only his earnings, but also any money he and his companions could come by honestly or otherwise.

Matt's sister Mary Andrews related the events that preceded Matt's conversion. Matt, it seems, had missed work for several days because of his drunken condition. He was without money and was waiting at the corner of William Street and North Strand for his friends. Since they were leaving work with their wages, Matt expected them to invite him for a drink. When all of them passed by without the expected offer, Matt was given a great deal to think about and turned home. Matt's sisters tell that upon entering the house, his mother said, "You're home early, Matt, and you are sober!" Matt replied, "Yes Mother, I am." After dinner he remained in the house, which was most unusual, and finally remarked to mother, "I'm going to take the pledge." She smiled and said, "Go, in God's name, but don't take it unless you are going to keep it." As he was going out, his mother said, "May God give you strength to keep it."

Matt made his confession at Clonliffe College, and took the pledge not to drink for three months. The following morning, a Sunday, Matt received the Holy Eucharist for the first time in years. Afterwards, he was a changed man. He worked regularly, avoided his former companions, and spent more time in church. The inclination to return to his former habits stayed with him, and he struggled to keep the pledge. When the three months expired, he renewed the pledge for life. Matt's conversion is said to have occurred in the year 1884, when he was about twenty-eight years old.

Matt was a changed man. Reportedly, "His workmates were astonished when they heard of Matt taking the pledge; and they were still more astonished when he kept it."

The energy and determination that Matt devoted to his labors were the same traits that he brought to the service of God. Still working as a hodman, fetching mortar and bricks for the trained workers, he spent every free moment in prayer. He was never heard to swear again. His sister Mary Andrews said that after his day's work, Matt was seldom off his knees. He observed fasts and slept on a broad plank with a solid lump of wood for a pillow. He attended Mass daily, and on October 18, 1891, Matt joined the Franciscan Third Order. Since he no longer squandered his income on alcohol, he gave freely to his mother, the poor, and religious organizations, especially the missions. When his brothers continued to drink despite Matt's efforts to reform them, he left home.

Matt went weekly to confession in Clonliffe and was engaged for a long time in paying back the debts he had accumulated during his drinking years. He even spent years searching through the poorhouses of Dublin for the fiddler whose violin he had stolen, so that he could reimburse him for the price of the instrument. When this effort was unsuccessful, he invested the money in Masses for the welfare of the fiddler's soul.

During the early years of his conversion, Matt collected books on religious topics. Remembering that his early education was meager,

Matt must have labored to read these books, at least until he gained some proficiency. His selection of books clearly indicated that he was under the direction of some zealous and unusually perceptive priest who was, himself, a man of great spirituality and deep prayer. All of these books, which bear many of Matt's notes, are carefully kept today in the archbishop's house in Dublin. Among these books is a pocket-sized copy of the New Testament, which is thought to have been carried by Matt for a long time. As a result of reading various biographies, Matt developed a great devotion to St. Teresa of Ávila, St. Thérèse of Lisieux, and St. Catherine of Siena.

Matt's friend John O'Callaghan received one of these books in which Matt had written on the fly-leaf these thoughtful words: "Three things I cannot escape: the eye of God, the voice of conscience, the stroke of death. In company guard your tongue. In your family guard your temper. When alone guard your thoughts." In another book Matt wrote: "In prayer we speak to God, in spiritual reading and sermons God speaks to us."

When the new Matt had firmly replaced the old, he is described as a man always in a good humor and friendly with everyone. His usual greeting was "God be with you," and he was frequently heard singing hymns. His room was free of luxuries and was quite bare except for his plank bed, a chair, a table, a crucifix, and some holy pictures. Throughout his life, Matt wore only old clothes that had been given to him. According to Raphael O'Callaghan, who knew Matt well, "There was nothing striking or impressive in Matt Talbot's appearance. To meet him on his daily rounds he was a very commonplace type of working-man, poorly clad, but clean. He was somewhat below middle height, of slight and wiry build. He walked rapidly, with long strides and a loose, swinging gait. His bearing indicated recollection, rather than preoccupation."

Despite Matt's short stature and his well-worn attire, it is known that about the year 1892 he attracted the attention of a pious Catholic girl who worked as a cook for a Protestant clergyman. Seeing his regular habits and his respect-filled treatment of women, she decided to make his acquaintance and finally suggested marriage. Matt considered the proposal, but declined the offer after completing a novena for guidance. He later told a confidant "the Blessed Virgin told me not to marry."

Matt's spirituality deepened while his pious practices likewise increased. The late Sean T. O'Ceallaigh, a former President of Ireland, once testified that as an altar boy, he came to know Matt Talbot personally.

> I came to know him during the time I served Mass at St. Joseph's Church. I knew him from 1890 to 1897 and I spoke to him occasionally. Sometimes I used to open the door for the 7 a.m. Mass and on such occasions I used to see him waiting on the steps of the church before the door was opened. . . . We altar boys called him Mr. Talbot. Sometimes the boys referred to him as 'Holy Joe'. In the morning he used to wait, kneeling on the steps of the church, praying, with rosary beads in his hand. He usually received Holy Communion . . . I also saw him in church at the evening devotions and I saw him making the Stations of the Cross after these devotions. . . . He used to pray very fervently and seemed to have a great esteem for prayer. . . . He often prayed with outstretched arms, with his eyes raised to the crucifix, and seemed oblivious of everyone . . . I would say that he was the nearest I could imagine to one in ecstasy. It was before Our Blessed Lady's altar that he was always to be found; he showed special devotion to her. . . . On Sundays he heard several Masses.

Matt's free time from work was devoted to prayer and recollection, but he was still very much interested in the welfare of those he met. Mr. O'Ceallaigh adds: "He often spoke to myself and some of the other boys. He would ask us if we said the Rosary and if we were fond of doing so. He recommended us to say it. He often asked us a question in catechism and gave us good advice. . . . He was friendly and kind to us, and we were not afraid to approach him; on the contrary, we used to go to him frequently and talk with him. He was very affable."

Matt gave away his pipe and tobacco after his conversion and never smoked again. Added to his ever-present craving for alcohol, Matt suffered the penance of additionally depriving himself of nicotine. Mr. O'Callaghan reveals that Matt once confided to him that it cost him more to give up tobacco than to give up alcohol. John Robbins, who knew Matt for about thirty years, said, "Matt made what I considered a heroic sacrifice in giving up smoking, for he had been a very heavy smoker, using seven ounces of tobacco in the week. When he decided to give it up he went to his confessor in Clonliffe to take a pledge against it."

A number of years after his conversion, Matt began working as a laborer for timber merchants, T&C Martin. The change seems to have been made solely because his working hours enabled him to attend the 6:15 a.m. Mass, and provided more time before work for his prayers and devotions.

At the lumberyard Matt was known as being a most conscientious workman who would not waste a moment of his time. His fellow workmen noticed that during his free time and lunch period, he either read a devotional book or prayed in a secluded area of the lumberyard to avoid notice. His noontime meals were so frugal as to draw the attention of many who wondered how he could perform his strenuous work on such little nourishment. Matt avoided all ostentation, and he was always in good humor. He was much respected as being a holy man and his fellow workers liked him, even though he reprimanded them for using foul language.

After his hard-drinking brothers had moved elsewhere, and after his father's death in March 1899, Matt returned home to care for his mother. Undoubtedly Elizabeth was greatly pleased in her old age to be in the company of her devout son, and to be able to benefit from the help given by a daughter who also lived at home.

In addition to his many penances, Matt's mother was soon aware that he undertook frequent fasts beyond those observed for Advent,

Lent, Ember Days, and certain vigils. He ate sparingly at other times and slept only four hours a night, devoting his waking hours to prayer. He is known to have been under the guidance of a spiritual director who knew of these penances and apparently approved of them. Yet, another penance, and one that was also undertaken with the consent of his spiritual director, consisted in the wearing of chains under his clothing. These were so arranged about his body that a constriction and discomfort existed at every movement, yet no one was aware of his difficulty or even suspected that he was performing this unusual form of penance.

Matt belonged to several religious organizations which he financially supported and whose meetings he faithfully attended. Among these groups were the Men's Sodality of the Immaculate Conception, the Pioneer Total Abstinence Association of the Sacred Heart, the Apostleship of Prayer, the Living Rosary, and the Confraternity of St. Michael the Archangel. For thirty-five years, until his death, Matt was a faithful member of the Franciscan Third Order.

In 1913 when labor called for a large strike in Dublin, Matt Talbot went on strike with his fellow workers. There was no bitterness in this action, and he was never asked to picket or attend meetings. He believed, as did other laborers, that a workingman deserved a fair wage. Matt was greatly pleased that those who undeniably had been underpaid received a decent wage as a result of the strike action, and he was likewise pleased that his own earnings were increased since he could contribute more to charity and the missions.

Matt's mother died in 1915. One of her granddaughters told how kind and devoted Matt was to his mother, and how she often woke at night to see her son kneeling by his bedside, praying. Matt suffered from kidney and heart ailments during the last years of his life. In 1923, two years before his death, Matt was admitted twice to the Mater Misericordiae Hospital. While he was under the care of the Sisters of Mercy, they considered his condition so grave on the first occasion that he was administered Last Rites. After his release from the hospital, his condition was one of great discomfort, and he suffered difficulty breathing. During Matt's second visit to the hospital, one of the sisters remarked that he spent every moment he could in the chapel. One of Matt's roommates has given other details, stating that he saw Matt: ". . . praying during the night with arms outstretched and holding his rosary in his hand. He used to lead the recitation of the Rosary in the ward. He was very grateful for anything done for him; his disease could cause considerable suffering when he got the attacks, but Matt did not complain and he ate whatever he got. As far as I can recall, Matt spent all his free time visiting the Blessed Sacrament."

During the last months of his life, Matt confided that he suffered a great deal from pain in his heart and that he frequently experienced great weakness. Before Matt's second discharge from the hospital, his doctor warned him of the possibility that he might die suddenly of heart disease, but somehow his condition improved so that he was able to return to light duty at work. It is known that he continued to work, and that he did so the day before his death.

On Trinity Sunday, June 7, 1925, at 9:45 a.m., while Matt Talbot was walking to Mass, he paused and then fell to the ground. A number of people rushed to him, while one of them ran to summon a priest. When the priest arrived, it was obvious that Matt Talbot, the reformed alcoholic, was dead. While the twenty people who were present knelt beside the body, Father Walsh recited prayers for the dying.

Matt Talbot was sixty-nine years old at the time of his death; forty-one of those years had been spent in penance and prayer.

When Matt's body was being prepared for burial, the penitential chains were discovered, and removed. One of the chains had been placed below one knee, immediately below the kneecap, in such a way that it must have caused pain when he knelt. The attendants reported that the chains were not imbedded in the flesh, but that they had apparently been worn for a long time, as grooves had been worn into the skin. Once removed, the chains were placed beside the body in the casket.

Matt died on a Sunday but his burial in Glasnevin Cemetery did not take place until the following Thursday. The humble casket was accompanied by many of the poor who had previously benefited from his generosity.

Matt Talbot's reputation for holiness soon became widespread, and speculation abounded that he would eventually be awarded the honors of the altar. In 1931, six years after his death, the first inquiry into his life and virtues began. Six years later, a papal decree was signed which introduced his Cause. Another inquiry took place in 1948. During these two inquiries, sixty-eight people who had known Matt Talbot gave depositions concerning his former alcoholic dependency, his courageous reform, and his virtuous and penitential life of forty-one years.

Matt Talbot's remains were exhumed in 1952 as part of the procedure toward his beatification. One of those present at this ceremony was the former altar boy, Sean T. O' Ceallaigh, President of Ireland. In February 1962, the remains of Matt Talbot were removed to the Church of Our Lady of Lourdes on Gloucester Street, the parish church Matt attended for many years. The tomb has a glass panel, which reveals the coffin. It bears a plaque inscribed, "The Servant of God, Matthew Talbot, 1856-1925."

Another plaque is situated on a wall on Granby Lane and reads, "The mark opposite this plaque indicates the spot where the Servant of God, Matt Talbot, collapsed and died on Trinity Sunday, June 7, 1925. His cause of beatification and canonization was introduced in Rome May 3, 1947. Erected by the Dublin Matt Talbot Committee Nov. 5, 1972."

A simple cross, chiseled into the sidewalk on Granby Lane, indicates the spot where Matt Talbot died.

Venerable Miguel Gomez Loza
1888 – 1928
Attorney
Mexico

Miguel was born in Paredones (now El Refugio), a suburb of Tepatitlan, Jalisco on August 11, 1888 to Petronilo Loza and Victoriana Gomez. When Miguel was only two years old, his father died, leaving behind a grieving widow and two sons. Miguel displayed a talent for leadership early in life. While still young, he served as an acolyte, a sacristan, and a catechist, and he held the respect of his peers. Miguel even gathered signatures on a petition to change the name of his hometown from Paredones to El Refugio in honor of the Blessed Virgin.

At the age of twenty-two Miguel took part in the Catholic National Party, serving as representative at the voting booths in El Refugio. During one election, when he heard that the opposing party was planning an electoral fraud, he organized a group to carry the voting urns to the city of Tepatitlan to ensure a fair counting of the votes.

Miguel moved to Guadalajara and entered the seminary, but realized in a short time that he did not have a vocation to the priesthood. Instead, he enrolled as a lay member of the Institute of the Sacred Heart of Jesus. While in Guadalajara, he met the Catholic resistance leader Anacleto Gonzalez Flores (whose biography is included in this book). Anacleto was the chief of the resistance that opposed the repressive dictates of the Mexican government during the persecutions of 1926-1929, when many died for the faith. Miguel and Anacleto were candidates from Tepatitlan at the convention of the Catholic National Party, and with Anacleto, Miguel established a number of cooperative ventures, including the student group La Girondia.

Miguel's interest in the government and social issues lead him to enter the University of Morelos, where he studied law in an effort to help the Church.

In 1914, the government rolled through Guadalajara, seizing church properties, expelling priests, and closing private schools and universities. Miguel returned to El Refugio, where he stayed until 1915, when he was able to resume his studies. The closing of the university did not deter his social work — Miguel became a member of the Catholic Association of Mexican Youth (ACJM) and founded various groups of workers. Also, he established the Catholic Confederation of Work, a national congress of Catholic workers that unified industry workers, commercial employees, and agricultural laborers.

According to his spiritual director, Father Vicente Maria Camacho, Miguel was jailed no less than fifty-eight times for organizing protests against the government. At times, he was tortured and beaten, and a number of times was at the point of being shot for his resistance and his faith. Reportedly, each time he was arrested he remained serene and composed, leading his fellow prisoners in prayer and singing. As a sign of his devotion to Mary, the Virgin of Refuge, he always wore a pin depicting her image on his shirt directly over his heart. He wore the pin until the day of his death.

In 1922, at the age of thirty-four, Miguel graduated with a degree in law. That same year he married Maria Guadalupe Sanchez Barragan. Sometime during the day of their marriage, a friend jokingly told Miguel that he should buy a lunch kit for his wife so she could bring him food during his many incarcerations.

When the government started a more intense persecution of Catholics in 1924, Miguel became one of the leading organizers of the Union Popular in Guadalajara. The main purpose of the Union was to unite Catholics to protest the arbitrary actions of a government determined to erase all hint of the Catholic Church. Because of his brave actions in defending Mexican Catholicism, Pope Pius XI presented Miguel with the Cross Pro Ecclesia et Pontifice.

In 1925, in protest of President Calles' laws against the Church, the Union Popular declared an economic boycott, which failed. In July the churches were closed, Mass was said in secret, and priests went into hiding.

The Union Popular decided it was time to take up arms. Miguel did not — his mission was to travel from one resistance camp to the other, motivating the combatants, and to solicit the ecclesiastical authorities to provide chaplains for the spiritual needs of the troops.

After the death of Anacleto on April 1, 1927, Miguel was named the chief of the rebellion and governor of the district of Jalisco. On March 21, 1928, Miguel was staying at El Lindero, a ranch near Atotonilco, when he was discovered during an inspection by federal troops. When Miguel was recognized, he was promptly killed. His body was later taken to Guadalajara where thousands gathered for his funeral. His remains were later taken to the sanctuary of Our Lady of Guadalupe in Guadalajara where they joined those of his friend and fellow martyr, Anacleto Gonzalez Flores.

Miguel's Cause for beatification was introduced with those of Anacleto Gonzalez Flores and six others. The Decree of Valor for all of them was declared on May 21, 1999.

Blessed Nikolaus Gross
1898 – 1945
Miner, Union Official, Writer, Father of Seven
Germany

Like many of the men in his family before him, Nikolaus Gross became a miner in the village of Niederwenigern, the city of his birth. He attended school for seven years before going down into the pit, but afterward the young miner continued his education by reading on his own and by attending evening classes. He apparently had a quick mind and studied hard because he promptly rose in the ranks until he became a man of distinction whom many admired.

While still in the mines, at age nineteen, Nikolaus registered in the Christian Miners' Labor Union, and at twenty, he became a member of the Zentrum Christian Party. By the age of twenty-two he was secretary for the young miners, and began to work on the *Westdeutschen-Arbeiter-Zeitung*, the newspaper of the Catholic Workers' Movement. Two years later, he was its director.

On May 24, 1923, at the age of twenty-five, the hardworking young man married Elisabeth Koch from his home town of Niederwenigern. They were to become the parents of seven children, five boys and two girls, all of whom benefited from the good example and pious practices of their parents.

Nikolaus eventually assumed the editorship of the *West German Worker* newspaper, but as soon as the danger of National Socialism became evident, the paper decided against this political movement. After the National Socialists seized power, the paper became one of its sharpest critics. Finally, in 1938, the newspaper was forbidden to continue production, though Nikolaus continued to produce an underground edition. He continued writing articles, pamphlets, and brochures in defense of the Church and particularly for the Catholic workers.

Nikolaus' brochures spread throughout Germany, giving assistance to the people in their struggles and hardships under the ruthless regime. Booklets such as "Victory of Life," "Our Dear Wife," "In the Light of the Eternal Lamp" treated religious topics. Another popular brochure, "In the Spring of Life," was a discussion between father and son. Twenty titles were published in 1938, and a countless number of reprints, but many more were published much later by Nikolaus' son, Bernhard Gross, in January 1992.

During the Second World War Nikolaus joined the anti-Nazi resistance movement as a nonviolent opponent of the regime and worked for the revolt against Hitler. Nikolaus once wrote: "We Catholic workers strongly and clearly reject National Socialism, not only for political and economic reasons, but also, decidedly, because of our religious and cultural position." What was important to Nikolaus was to witness and transmit the Catholic faith.

In 1943 he wrote: "The majority of great enterprises result from daily fulfillment of one's duty in small, everyday things. What is valuable in the doing is our special love for the poor and sick."

From his headquarters in Cologne, Nikolaus kept his readers informed about the harmful effects of Nazi propaganda and helped prepare the people for the July 20, 1944 assassination attempt on the life of Adolf Hitler. The resistance group was naturally blamed as one of those who planned the assassination. As a well-known leader of the movement, Nikolaus was arrested on August 12, 1944 together with members of his group. It is said that his parting from his wife and seven children was heart wrenching, but he accepted this trial as God's will and never regretted his actions against the repressive regime or his work for the Church and its members. He once said, "If we do not act now, how are we to exist before our children?"

In one of his manuscripts that was confiscated by the Gestapo, Nikolaus had written: "If we are asked to do something that goes against God or the faith, not only can we not do so, but we must refuse to obey." Nikolaus was granted a trial in the court of justice and was condemned to death because of his resistance against the Nazi regime. He remained in jail until January 23, 1945, when he was hanged in the Berlin-Plotzensee prison. His body was incinerated and his ashes scattered.

Pope John Paul II has beatified Nikolaus Gross.

Venerable Peter ToRot

1912 – 1945
Catechist
New Guinea

This extraordinary Catholic was born and lived all his life in or near the village of Rakunai, on the Island of New Britain that is part of the modern Papua New Guinea located northeast of Australia.

Peter's father, Angelo ToPuia, was a respected "luluai" or chief of his native village of Rakunai and was one of the first to be baptized in 1898. He and his wife laTumul lived happily and had six children; the last two died during childhood. These good parents taught their children to show great respect and reverence for the village leaders and elders and to be kind and generous to their neighbors. The children were taught their morning offerings and evening prayers, which Peter recited with particular reverence. Peter was a typical boy who occasionally was involved in pranks for which he readily and honestly confessed his involvement, never defending himself against his father's correction. He was a happy youngster and demonstrated a willingness to improve.

Peter is known to have seldom missed school, and every morning he arrived early to serve Mass. His schoolmates later testified that Peter ToRot was always the first student to answer questions asked by the teacher and is known to have been a diligent student. His teachers corrected him occasionally, because of his behavior, but he never spoke words of complaint or anger since he was always grateful for advice and correction. He is also known to have received the sacraments of Penance and Holy Communion before the usual age.

Peter was a natural leader, sincere and honest. In class, he worked hard as he also did in the family's fruit and vegetable garden when he returned home from school. He was always willing to help his parents and is said to have never refused a chore recommended by them.

Since Peter was devout and loved church activities, the parish priest, Father Laufer, suggested that Peter, at the age of eighteen, seemed very suitable for the priesthood. After thoughtful consideration, Peter's father thought his son was more suited to the life of a catechist. Since Peter's heartfelt desire was to serve the church, he happily agreed to attend St. Paul's Catechist College in Taliligap about five miles from his native village. There he learned, in addition to the Catholic faith, English, reading, writing, arithmetic, oratory, music, and singing.

Handsome and energetic, Peter immersed himself in all school activities, in games, recreation, at daily Mass, and in prayer sessions. Peter realized wholeheartedly that this was his vocation — to serve God in the teaching ministry, to sacrifice oneself for love of his neighbor, and to work with all one's heart for the good of the church. His sacrifices were noted, especially when working in his private garden, which every student had and which each student was to maintain for a portion of their food. This work took place in the afternoon, and in spite of the hot sun, while his friends waited in the shade, Peter continued his work. We are told that he did not miss a working period during his entire stay at the school.

Peter was also a prayerful student, often visiting the Blessed Sacrament, reciting his Rosary and engaging in mental prayer. He chose the Blessed Mother as his special patron and prayed for her help in overcoming temptations and difficulties. He frequently went to confession and attended Mass every day. At this time, it was noted that his virtues included obedience, humility, charity, loyalty, and diligence. It was also remarked that he had a peace-loving nature.

After more than two years of studies, Peter was ready to begin his ministry. Under the supervision of Father Laufer, Peter taught the subjects he had in school. He loved teaching, but sometimes his devotion was put to the test, especially when Father Laufer asked him to teach students after school was over. Peter never objected and willingly obeyed.

In the evenings, Peter found time to visit the village people, especially those who were sick. He prayed with them and encouraged them in the faith. Peter's only times of annoyance were when Catholic villagers, without good reason, did not attend Sunday Mass. Tata, the new village leader of Rakunai, once remarked, "Peter's example moved the hearts of many men and women to follow his true Christian way of life."

Three years after starting his catechetical work, he married Paula laVarpit, a Catholic who had been one of his pupils. Paula, like her husband, was devout and happily supported her husband in his work. But the marriage, for the first few months, was not ideal. Paula admits that they argued occasionally, but she confessed, "I was the cause because of my disobedience and laziness in doing certain things."

Only once did Peter exert his authority in a physical manner when he gave Paula a "solid beating." Paula explained that this took place "because I refused to weave mats from coconut leaves for our kitchen." A beating in such a case was the usual response from a husband for flagrant disobedience. However, unlike other husbands, Peter is said to have later asked his wife's forgiveness, a thing unheard of in the village. For her part, Paula is said to have been proud of the fact that Peter had to beat her only once during their marriage.

Peter loved his wife and respected her. He listened to her complaints and helped her in every way. The two of them prayed together in the morning before they started work and at night before they slept. They were the parents of two children, the third was born after Peter's death and soon died. Peter is known to have helped his wife with the care of the children and to have greatly respected the sacrament of matrimony.

All was peaceful until the Japanese invaded the island in 1942. The territory was occupied by force with the enemy garrison remaining for more than three years. During that time, the people suffered many trials, in addition to being forced from their homes. During this time, Peter demonstrated his loyalty to Christ, his deep faith, and personal courage.

Religious persecution began when all foreign missionaries were put in prison or expelled. Father Laufer was ordered to leave, but not before he called Peter and solemnly commissioned him to look after the people of God. The catechist promised to do his best. Religious practices were then curtailed and not long after they were totally prohibited. With the loss of Father Laufer, Peter assumed many of the priest's duties: baptizing, performing marriages (then permitted in this missionary field), caring for the sick, giving religious instructions, and burying the dead.

The Japanese objected to large gatherings of people and deliberately demolished the parish church in 1943. Peter then built a smaller one and again organized prayer meetings at night but with smaller gatherings of people to avoid provoking the Japanese.

Remembering the great commandment: "You must love God with your whole heart, mind and soul, and your neighbor as yourself," Peter continued all his duties in spite of the difficulties and dangers he faced. He once said, "If I die, it will be for God's sake alone."

Somehow, Peter found time to visit other villages and his brother catechists to encourage them in their difficult ministry. He also visited priests who were confined to prison to bring them food. When he heard that the Japanese were starving some Indonesian soldiers who were prisoners, Peter prepared some chickens and brought them to the prison. His love of neighbor included everyone.

Eventually the Japanese enforced a total ban on religious activities. The resourceful Peter, determined to continue his work, saw to the digging of an underground prayer room on his own property. Here he continued to give religion classes, to conduct prayer meetings, and witness marriages.

Because the enemy thought the people were praying for the war to be prolonged with the ultimate defeat of the Japanese, they were determined to destroy the faith by legalizing polygamy, which was prohibited by the Church. To accomplish this the Japanese called all the leaders of the area together for a meeting. Polygamy was explained and encouraged. Many of the leaders were swayed and decided to take a second wife. When Peter heard of this, he was determined to defend the faith, to fight this pagan decision and defend Christ's sacrament of marriage, even if it meant losing his life.

The Japanese were cunning in introducing the taking of a second wife. If the chiefs were inclined to do so against the Church, others would weaken and act accordingly with other religious teachings and practices gradually diminishing in importance.

Because Peter continued his religious activities and spoke against polygamy, he was called to court on a number of occasions. One time he was arrested for a few months and then released. Nevertheless, the dedicated Peter resumed his catechetical work. Arrested a second time and released, Peter again ministered to the people. Because polygamy was causing considerable disturbances among the villagers, Peter again did what he could to discourage the practice. His activities, particularly the Sunday services, were reported to the authorities by a spy, which resulted in his third and final imprisonment in early 1945. When questioned if he conducted Sunday services, Peter admitted fearlessly that he did. For this act of defiance, he was hit numerous times on the head, chest, and throat.

While in prison Peter was given the job of cooking for the prisoners, which included his two brothers who were released after a month's detention. His inconsolable mother and wife visited, but Peter calmed them by saying, "Stop crying. Pray. I am here in a good cause. I am quite happy about it since I am here on account of my faith." To a fellow prisoner he remarked: "It is better for them to kill me as a catechist because I am a defender of the Church."

Again, his mother and his wife Paula with their two children visited him bringing him food as before, together with the rosary and the catechetical crucifix he had requested. Paula argued that if he renounced his catechetical work and promised to live an ordinary life, he might be released. To this Peter replied, "It is fitting that I die for the Name of God the Father, the Son and the Holy Spirit, and for the sake of my people." He punctuated the statement by making a devout Sign of the Cross. To reassure his mother that he was being properly cared for, he told her that a doctor had orders from the Japanese to visit him and to give him medicine. She wondered about this since he was not ill.

The morning of his death, Peter was visited by the local chief, Anton Tata, who spoke of his fears for Peter since he had pleaded with the Japanese officers for Peter's release, but was refused. Peter calmed the chief's fears and displayed admirable courage before exclaiming, "Do not worry. I am a catechist and I am only doing my duty."

Despite the efforts of the Japanese to hide Peter's martyrdom, one prisoner did manage to witness the event from a neighboring hillside. From there, he could see what took place through the window in the lighted room where Peter had been led to the doctor. The witness, Arap To Binabak, later testified to what he witnessed.

Although the Japanese claimed that Peter's death resulted from natural causes, a minor illness, evidence would prove otherwise.

When Peter's uncle Tarue went to visit Peter, he was shocked to find Peter dead. The body was lying face up, but leaning slightly to one side. One hand was under his head, while one of his legs was bent under the other. A piece of red ribbon was bound around his head and pieces of cotton were seen in the ears and nostrils. Peter's throat bore a big blister and a swelling, indicting strangulation. The throat was also flattened since the Japanese had laid a piece of timber across the throat with a weight upon it. All evidence pointed to torture, especially when the uncle was preparing the body for burial. From Peter's mouth, ears, and nose flowed a white substance resembling candle wax. It was apparent that the cotton had been used to prevent the fluid's release. "It smelt like an awful stinking medicine" noted Peter's brother. Moreover, there was an injection mark of a needle on his left arm. Peter had suffered torture and was martyred willfully by the Japanese.

When the death of Peter ToRot was made known to the villagers of Rakunai, they were convinced that he had been killed because of his faith and his faithful performance of his duties as a catechist. Peter was buried in the village cemetery, near the Rakunai parish church. On the stone cross above his grave are engraved these words in the Tolai language, "Peter ToRot, a martyr for the faith." The catechetical school that now trains young catechists on the island is known as the Peter ToRot College.

The Apostolic Decree recognizing the martyrdom of Peter ToRot was signed by the Prefect of the Congregation of the Causes of Saints in the presence of Pope John Paul II on April 2, 1993. The martyr is now known as Venerable Peter ToRot.

Blessed Pier Giorgio Frassati
1901 – 1925
"The man of the eight beatitudes"
Italy

Everyone who knew Pier Giorgio Frassati agreed that he was an extraordinary young man. Handsome, athletic, a lover of nature and the arts, socially and financially secure, a man engaged in the social and political life, Pier Giorgio was, most of all, a devout Catholic deeply committed to prayer and to helping the poor.

He was born in Turin, Italy on April 6, 1901, and was baptized the same day at his home because of his frail health. His father, Alfredo, was the founder and owner of the influential liberal newspaper, *La Stampa*, and served for a time as Italy's ambassador to Berlin. Pier Giorgio's mother, Adelaide, was a gifted artist who is identified by some as having been temperamental. The only other member of the immediate family was a sister, Luciana, who was born in 1902.

The Frassati's family life was described as "religiously superficial." Alfredo was agnostic, though he never spoke against the Church or religion in the presence of his family. Adelaid is said to have practiced her faith only as a duty. To their credit, Pier Giorgio's parents provided their children with a Catholic education, saw to the children's morning and evening prayers, and required they attend Mass on Sunday and take catechism lessons. Pier Giorgio's first great spiritual influence was his grandmother, a devout Catholic.

In his early years, Pier Giorgio was a typical boy. A letter written by five-year-old Pier Giorgio to his father said as much: "I will pray to the Child Jesus for you so that you are happy." Pier Giorgio then added: "I promise that I won' t *hit* Luciana anymore." Just a few years later, having outgrown the occasional physical activity against his sister, and having matured somewhat, he wrote in another letter: "I will not *argue* with Luciana anymore." And, like many a boy who lagged behind in his studies for whatever reason, Pier Giorgio was not permitted to advance from the second to the third grade.

While still in grammar school, Pier Giorgio attended the Jesuit Fathers Social Institute, where he began to advance rapidly in the spiritual life. He participated in daily Mass and Holy Communion, a practice that did not meet his parents' approval. Because of their social position, they were afraid he would become a fanatic or perhaps some day even a priest. They had planned for him to follow his father at *La Stampa* and to inherit his father's seat in the senate, or like his father, to become an ambassador. Pier Giorgio's parents denied him permission to participate, but Pier Giorgio pleaded and won. He was to tell his spiritual director, Father Pietro Lombardi, S.J.: "I have won; Mama has given me permission to receive Holy Communion every day."

Each morning as he arrived at school, Pier Giorgio went directly to the chapel to participate in the Mass, frequently serving as altar boy. As he grew older, when he planned his hiking and mountain climbing trips, he would still attend daily Mass, or he would arrange for a priest to join his group to celebrate Mass on the mountain.

While attending the Jesuit Fathers Social Institute, Pier Giorgio learned about a movement known as the Apostleship of Prayer, which recommended the daily offering of prayers, actions, joys, and sufferings of each day in union with the sacrifice of the Mass through the Immaculate Heart of Mary. At the age of thirteen Pier Giorgio enrolled in the movement, and he carefully preserved his registration card and the monthly leaflets in a scrapbook. He continued to live the spirituality of the Sacred Heart throughout his lifetime.

Pier Giorgio's love of the Blessed Mother blossomed when he joined the Marian Society. He consecrated himself to the Madonna and entrusted his purity to her, which he maintained during his years at the university. The recitation of the Rosary seems to have been a treasured devotion even when he was a child. During Pier Giorgio's boyhood, his father once found him kneeling by his bed, fast asleep with a rosary in his hand. The father lost no time in complaining about this to Monsignor Roccati who replied, "Senator, would you prefer that he fall asleep with a trashy romance novel in hand? Let him continue in this dear habit and you will not have to worry!"

Pier Giorgio was rarely seen without a rosary in his hand and he did not hide it when others were nearby. Many times those who witnessed this act of devotion marveled at seeing a handsome young man passing the rosary beads through his fingers, and often, at his invitation, they joined in the recitation.

This pious young man demonstrated his love of the Madonna by frequently visiting the Black Madonna at the sanctuary at Oropa. He seems to have been surrounded by the miraculous since he also frequently visited the miraculous image of Our Lady known as the Madonna of Consolation in Turin, and he prayed before the shrine containing the Holy Shroud, the burial cloth of Our Lord. It is also noted that he made his first confession in the Church of Corpus Domini, which was the site of a Eucharistic miracle.

Pier Giorgio made an annual spiritual retreat at the Jesuit retreat house in Turin where he found great peace and spiritual consolation. He was also an active member in the Confraternity of the Most Holy Sacrament and the Confraternity of the Holy Rosary.

As to his vocation in life, Pier Giorgio had planned to work among the poor miners in America, and began studying mining engineering at Polytechnic University to prepare. At the same time, his father wanted him to join the staff of his newspaper, *La Stampa*. Somehow, Pier Giorgio was able to both study and work.

In Italy during Pier Giorgio's life (and beyond), a social-communist movement existed which slandered religion through the occasional abuse of the clergy and the profaning of churches. To combat this, religious demonstrations, like Eucharistic congresses and processions, were held. These demonstrations only provoked the middle class and the communists to unite against the Catholic forces. To counter the efforts of these groups, two Catholic movements were formed, the Circle of Catholic Action and the Federation of Italian University Students. Pier Giorgio became very active in both movements and attended the meetings and congresses. During one large meeting at Rome when 50,000 Catholic youths were attacked by the royal guards, Pier Giorgio, who was carrying the flag, defended his fellow protesters with his fists and with the flagpole. He also went to the aid of a priest who was attacked. Unfortunately, Pier Giorgio was overpowered and taken to the police station with a number of others. Since his father was then serving as ambassador to Berlin, Pier Giorgio, as a diplomat's son, was set to be released without further action, but Pier Giorgio insisted that all the others should be released with him, which they were. The incident was mentioned in the next day's newspaper, but he minimized everything by saying, "I have done a little thing well, simply my duty." It is said that on his journey home from Rome to Turin, he prayed the Rosary on the train.

Pier Giorgio was definitely a man of principles, convinced that only Christianity with its social doctrine, its ideas of brotherhood, social justice, and charity for all would bring peace both socially and politically. He supported rural banks, agricultural reforms, and workers' participation in the management of companies. He was strongly anti-fascist and deeply resented the communists. He merged his political ideas with his religious ideas and promoted them in print and with fliers. He distributed and publicized a variety of weekly and daily Catholic newspapers to help Christian society and the faith.

As Fascism gained strength in Italy, both Pier Giorgio and his father struggled against it. Finally, Alfredo Frassati was compelled to close the newspaper because of his antifascism and later, when Benito Mussolini came to power, resigned his position as ambassador. About this time, Pier Giorgio became a Dominican tertiary, choosing the name of Girolamo in honor of Savonarola.

About this time, Pier Giorgio also expressed his love for Miss Laura Hidalgo, with whom he hoped to marry and raise a family. However, his parents were suffering through severe marital difficulties, and their struggles had a profound effect on their son. Pier Giorgio renounced his dream of marriage, writing to a friend: "Why create one family in order to destroy another?" He added, "I urge you to pray that the Lord gives me the Christian strength to serenely overcome this and that he gives to her every earthly happiness and the strength for us both to arrive at the end for which we have been created." He was then twenty-three years of age and demonstrated in this sacrifice a great deal of spiritual fortitude.

In a talk he gave for the Circle of Catholic Action, Pier Giorgio seemed to remember his sacrifice when he remarked: "Prayer is the supplication that we raise to the throne of God. It is the most effective means for obtaining the graces from God which we need, especially the strength of perseverance . . . and in recommending fervent prayer I number all the practices of piety . . . before all, the Eucharist . . . eat of the Bread of Angels and there you will find the strength to fight the interior struggles."

It should be noted that Pier Giorgio was not a solemn, sanctimonious young man, but one full of spirit who loved joking and fun and radiated a joy that attracted many to him. His sincere love of people influenced many to change their lives and become more spiritually oriented. Many loved being in his company, either while mountain climbing or by simply enjoying his humor and pleasantness at the university.

Pier Giorgio gave his attention to his friends, but also to the poor and sick. He first came to know about the St. Vincent de Paul Society while attending the Jesuit school in his youth. Throughout his life, especially during his early manhood, he gave of himself to the poor and the sick in many ways: by visiting them, by purchasing medicines, even by helping them by carrying firewood. His countless forms of assistance were offered with humility and hidden from the attention of others.

A German news reporter who observed Pier Giorgio at the Italian Embassy wrote: "One night in Berlin, with the temperature at twelve degrees below zero, Pier Giorgio gave his overcoat to a poor old man shivering in the cold. His father, the ambassador, scolded him, and he replied simply, "But you see, Papa, it was cold."

Pier Giorgio likely contracted the sickness from which he died through his frequent contacts with the sick and the poor in the slums. He contracted fulminating poliomyelitis, and less than a week later, on July 24, 1925, at the age of twenty-four, he died. In just a few days, he would have received his university degree; instead, on July 6, his funeral Mass was offered by Monsignor Roccati in the parish church in Turin. Mingling with the people of finance, politics, and culture who attended the funeral were the poor, the disinherited, and the suffering who had benefited from Pier Giorgio's kindnesses.

Pier Giorgio's countless acts of charity would have gone unnoticed and unknown had it not been for the great number of the poor who deeply lamented his passing and gave accounts of his assistance. So many and varied were these accountings that Pier Giorgio's sister, Luciana, collected hundreds of these testimonies in a book entitled, *The Charity of Pier Giorgio*. While his acts of charity were rarely mentioned by him, he did make a reference to them when he wrote to a friend, "Jesus comes every day to visit me sacramentally in the Eucharist; I return the visit by going to find him among the poor." Even his sister, Luciana, did not know the full extent of his charitable deeds. When asked: "How did it affect you to live with a saint?" She answered: "We did not realize! Only the death revealed it!"

Others recognized Pier Giorgio's virtues. The day after his death a reporter wrote, "The funeral was the first testimony, the first consecration of the grand soul of Pier Giorgio Frassati; it could be said: here begins his process of canonization." This declaration seems to have been prophetic, as the introduction of the Cause of beatification was opened several years after Pier Giorgio's death. The Decree of Heroic Virtues promulgated on October 23, 1987 revealed: "His charity was not only realized through good works but by remaining aware of the necessities and responsibilities of an existence inserted in the world and working in society."

The beatification ceremony took place on May 20, 1990 in St. Peter's Square with Pope John Paul II declaring to the youth who had assembled: "Prayer and the practice of the sacraments gave substance and tone to his manifold apostolate and to his whole existence. Enlivened by the Spirit of God, he was transformed in a marvelous adventure. Everything became an offering and a gift, even his illness, even his death. This is his message as he continues to speak to all and particularly to the youth of our time." The pope called him, "The man of the eight beatitudes."

Because of his participation in various confraternities, Pope John Paul II, on June 8, 1990, named him the Patron of all Italian Confraternities.

During the Jubilee Year of 2000, the body of Blessed Giorgio was brought from the Cathedral of Turin where it had been enshrined to Rome. Kept temporarily in the Church of San Lorenzo in Lucina, it was venerated by the faithful, especially youth, as its presence in Rome coincided with World Youth Day. During this time, Vatican Radio interviewed Blessed Pier Giorgio's niece, Wanda Gawronska. Asked about his inner strength, his niece responded, "Most certainly from the Eucharist, from daily communion with Jesus. Moreover, he had a profound devotion to the Virgin."

A stained glass window depicting Blessed Pier Giorgio was installed in the Newman Centre of the University of Toronto on November 1, 1999, the feast of All Saints. Attending the ceremony was Blessed Pier Giorgio's niece Wanda who said of her uncle, "God gave Pier Giorgio all the external attributes that could have led him to make the wrong choices: a wealthy family, very good looks, manhood, health, being the only heir of a powerful family. But Pier Giorgio listened to the invitation of Christ: 'Come and follow me.' He anticipated by at least fifty years the Church's understanding and new direction on the role of the laity."

During the beatification ceremony, Pope John Paul remarked that Blessed Pier Giorgio Frassati was ". . . a perfect model of daily sanctity within everyone's reach."

Venerable Pierre Toussaint

1766 – 1853
Slave, Hair Dresser
Haiti/United States

Pierre was born on the L'Artibonite plantation on the island of St. Dominique (now known as Haiti), which was owned by Monsieur Jean Jacques Berard, one of few masters who saw to it that all his slaves were baptized Catholic. Pierre Toussaint lived in a loving family on the island and knew from his earliest years that his family had been brought in chains from Africa to St. Dominique, which was under French rule, to work in the sugar, coffee, and tobacco fields. These products, together with exotic fruits, were sent to France, and made the French settlers on the islands very wealthy. But the wealth was gained through the blood and sweat of the slaves who were often rewarded for their labors by repeated beatings, burnings, maimed limbs, and whip-streaked backs.

The plantation of Monsieur Berard was different. He was a man of honor, and he believed that all men should be accorded dignity, regardless of their condition in life. Berard was also one of the few plantation owners who did not abuse his slaves, for which he was greatly respected and experienced little or no trouble among those who worked for him.

Berard kept slave families together, saw to their baptism, and permitted them to practice their faith. For this reason, Pierre and his family attended St. Marc church on the island, and Pierre showed a love of all things religious at a very early age. Pierre's family included: his father, who was Berard's most trusted field hand; his mother Ursule, who was Madame Berard's personal servant; two sisters, Marie-Louise and Rosalie, who worked in the house; and a brother, who helped his father in the fields. Pierre worked in the house with his grandmother, Zenobie, who was the most respected among the slaves and the favorite of the Berard family. She taught Pierre to read and write, a skill unknown to the other slaves. Zenobie also taught Pierre all that was expected of a house servant: the fine art of serving at the table, the most respectful manner of conducting himself, and the proper way to greet visitors at the door. But Berard gave Pierre an added assignment — the care of his extensive library. Pierre was permitted access to the library and he studied about the world beyond his island home. When Pierre was given a fiddle, he proved to be a gifted musician and taught himself to play popular songs. His skillful playing entertained the Berard's guests for whom Pierre was proud to play.

Pierre's was a happy and contented life. For the slaves on the other plantations, ill treatment by overseers and planters stirred plans of revenge and escape. Night after night, many of them gathered in the woods where drums beat warnings and disgruntled slaves aired their grievances and hatred. The island was uneasy, and fears of a slave uprising grew.

Because of the uncertain situation, Berard made plans to temporarily take his wife and her two sisters to New York until the trouble he expected had been resolved. Berard also took Pierre, his sister Rosalie, and their Aunt Marie with him. The Toussaint family was unhappy when they were told of the arrangements, but then it was to be only a temporary move. Pierre's grandmother continued to teach him English, and he learned the various coins of the United States. He looked forward to the trip, and with the plantation in capable hands, the Berards and their slaves boarded a ship for the three-week voyage to New York.

The Berard family took a home at 105 Reade Street in New York. Soon after they were settled, Berard informed Pierre that he had arranged for him to learn a trade, and that he had already made plans for Pierre to be apprenticed to Mr. Merchant, the coiffeur. Mr. Merchant, it seems, had been impressed with Pierre's manners and intelligence and agreed to teach him the fine art of dressing and styling ladies' hair. Pierre learned his trade quickly. Tall, dignified, and polite, he soon became a favorite among the aristocratic ladies he served. They were also pleased with his massive hairstyles of tiered curls, poufs, and twists so popular for those who entertained or attended soirees and balls.

Pierre had interests other than hairdressing. When he first settled in New York, he began attending Mass at St. Peter's church on Barclay Street. He attended this church each morning before keeping his styling appointments, and he visited the Blessed Sacrament in this church each evening before going home. The pastor, Father William O' Brien and his assistant, Father Matthew O'Brien, to whom he unburdened his fears for the safety of his family on the island, often consoled Pierre.

When months passed without a word from the plantation, Berard decided to return home alone. Even before his master left for the plantation, Pierre had made a frequent habit of visiting the wharves where newly arrived steamers brought news of violence from the islands. Word came of slaves killing their abusive masters and driving their families from vast estates. Sometime after Berard left, he wrote his wife of the slave revolt and told her that it would be sometime before the family could return. Shortly after another letter arrived for Madame Berard: while at their island home, her husband died suddenly of pleurisy.

A short time later Madame Berard handed Pierre a bag containing her jewels and instructed him that he should sell them at once. The family was destitute. Monsieur Berard had only brought with him an amount of money he thought would last during their temporary stay in New York, and his investments had failed, too. Money was desperately needed. Pierre did not sell the jewels, but returned them with a sum of money he had saved from the money he had earned as a hairdresser. Pierre then began to pay the rent and buy the food and other necessities for Madame Berard, her sisters, and the house slaves. The promise of repayment when fortunes improved was understood, but no money was ever repaid. Pierre was always mindful of the many courtesies and interests shown by Madame Berard while he was a slave on the island, and in gratitude for her small favors then, he often brought her flowers and sweets, hoping to alleviate the grief she was experiencing over her husband's death.

About this time, Pierre began taking home young slave boys whose impoverished refugee owners had abandoned them. He made the acquaintance of a beautiful slave Juliette Noel, and when her distraught mother told Pierre another family intended to buy Juliette, Pierre purchased Juliette's freedom. Pierre made Juliette's mother promise that his charity would never be revealed. Sometime later Pierre also saved enough to purchase the freedom of his sister Rosalie, who let it be known that she resented her brother's support of Madame Berard, who refused to grant him the gift of freedom.

When the period of mourning expired for Madame Berard, she began to have visits from Monsieur Gabriel Nicolas who had been wealthy on the island, but was now reduced to earning his living by playing his violin at dinner parties and in orchestra pits of New York theaters. Gabriel Nicolas confided in Pierre, who encouraged his visits. Eventually, Madame Berard consented to marry Gabriel.

In addition to continuing his support of the household, and helping the poor who sought his financial aid, Pierre was approached by Father Matthew O'Brien to help raise funds for the new St. Patrick's Cathedral to be built at Prince and Mulberry. The good priest knew of the esteem with which Pierre was held by New York society, and he realized that a request from Pierre would scarcely be denied. With pleasure, the ladies promised to attend the fundraising activities.

Madame Berard-Nicolas' health began to fail. On her deathbed, with the help of an attorney, she composed the document that made

Pierre, the slave, a free man. He could now "enjoy liberty like any other freedman." The document was dated July 2, 1807.

Two weddings now took place: Pierre's sister Rosalie married Jean Noel, and Pierre married Juliette Noel, whom he had admired for so long. Rosalie moved to other quarters with her husband, but Pierre and his new bride settled on the third floor of the house whose rent he had paid for many years. The first floor had sitting rooms, a parlor, and a kitchen. Gabriel Nicolas, the widower, and some of the servants occupied the second floor, and the abandoned refugee boys settled in the basement. These boys were given assignments: helping in Pierre's hairdressing shop, running errands, and performing other services as needed.

Pierre was a happy and contented married man, but he was very concerned for the situation with his sister Rosalie. Her husband was jealous and difficult, and he abandoned his wife when their child Euphemia was born. Rosalie became ill with tuberculosis, and died, leaving her baby Euphemia to be brought up in her brother's household. Euphemia was given all the love and care that could be lavished on a child.

Pierre was even happier. His wife was a cheerful and happy homemaker and Euphemia was the joy of his life. Still exhibiting the dignity that had become his trademark, he was always in demand as a hairdresser, and many a society matron sought his advice. Many contributed to the charities he supported. One of these society matrons, who knew Pierre sheltered black children in his home, approached him about starting an orphanage for white orphans. With the help of Reverend John Powers, an orphanage was opened. When this orphanage became too small, another was built that accommodated 150 children.

In addition to helping with the orphanage, Pierre was also contributing and obtaining moneys for the repair of St. Peter's Church. He continued to help raise funds for St. Patrick's Cathedral and the school for black children at St. Vincent's. He helped dozens of slaves obtain their freedom, and he contributed to the support of many a refugee from the island. During the frequent epidemics, Pierre went into quarantined areas to assist the sick. When asked how he could manage so much, he pointed to all that can be accomplished with the help of God.

Euphemia, the sweet, beloved joy of his life, was a bright child and learned from her uncle Pierre how to read and write. She contracted a cold, which lead to the discovery that she had tuberculosis. Doctors were called, but the already thin child wasted away and, to the grief of her uncle, died at the age of fifteen. Pierre went often to church to pray for her and knelt, as was his custom, before the crucifix at St. Peter's. He often repeated, "I will take it as God sends it." After Euphemia's death, Pierre was never the same. For a time he even closed his shop.

In time, Pierre resumed his work in both his shop and in the homes of fashionable ladies. As always, he attended morning Mass. One of his wife's relatives tells of stopping by church and seeing Pierre deep in prayer. So deep and so long were Pierre's prayers that the relative left, returning much later to find Pierre still on his knees in the church.

Pierre was scrupulously careful in keeping records of all incoming funds and outgoing payments so that those who did not know him better could not question his honesty. His gifts to the poor continued, and each first Monday of the month he gave to Sister Cecilia at the orphanage the money he had collected to keep the orphanage open. Sometimes he was asked by the sisters to find a home for an orphan where the young person might earn a living. After the placements, Pierre did not forget the children; he continued to turn a watchful eye toward them. Often he would bring orphan boys home where they were clothed, fed, and trained.

At seventy-one, Pierre was still collecting funds for the orphanage, assisting Father Powers in raising funds to rebuild St. Peter's, and responding to calls for assistance from Bishop Du Bois. He was also training boys to assist him or to work in the homes of his patrons. All of these visits were made on foot, as black people were not permitted to ride in most trams. Pierre walked wherever he had to go. His most humiliating experience took place when he, his wife Juliette, and an elderly friend went to the cathedral to attend a special service. They were met at the door by a young usher who informed them there were no pews set aside for black people. Pierre simply shook his head, crossed himself, and led the women away. The event became public knowledge with feelings of resentment experienced by all, including his white patrons who offered profound apologies.

When news of a horrific earthquake on Haiti reached New York, Pierre's home became a clearinghouse for information on the disaster. Haitian immigrants knew where to find consolation — at the doorstep of Pierre Toussaint. The house at 105 Reade Street was well known.

Pierre finally decided that instead of paying rent at 105 Reade Street, they would buy a smaller house, which they did at 144 Franklin Street in the same neighborhood. Not long after they moved into their new home, Juliette was told she had cancer. With his beloved wife confined to bed, Pierre was often found kneeling outside the bedroom on a prie-dieu, praying before the crucifix he treasured. When Juliette died, Pierre reacted to her death much as he did when Euphemia died: with great sorrow and with great compassion. He began a round of visits to the ill and infirm, and he continued to bring homeless boys to the house where he provided food, clothing, and job training.

Pierre's health began to decline, and on June 30, 1853, at the age of eighty-seven, Pierre went to his eternal reward. He left no relatives, but for his funeral the new St. Peter's Church was crowded with people who had benefited from his charities. Prominent white people who had come to know and love this former slave wept for him, and they attended the High Mass that was in all respects fit for a prince of the church. Newspapers took notice and ran not only obituaries, but also articles detailing Pierre's life. Mentioned in these reports was the fact that for sixty years Pierre had attended Mass at six o' clock each morning, without pause, until his health failed. Pierre was laid to rest beside his niece Euphemia and his wife Juliette in the old St. Patrick's Church cemetery.

At the time of Pierre's death, newspapers gave glowing testimonies: "Pierre was respected and beloved by widely different classes of the city. He moved among them in a way peculiarly his own. He possessed a sense of the appropriate, a self respect, and a uniformity of demeanor which amounted to genius." Father Quinn, who preached his funeral eulogy remarked: "All would be grateful for having known Pierre. . . . There are few left among the clergy superior to him in zeal and devotion to the Church and for the glory of God; among laymen, not one."

Miracles were soon reported as a result of prayerful petitions to Pierre Toussaint. In 1965, the Pierre Toussaint Guild was founded and in 1968, Terence Cardinal Cook alerted Rome to the sanctity and charities of Pierre. In 1989, John Cardinal O' Connor presided at the first session of the diocesan inquiry relating to the sanctity of the former slave, the first step toward the introduction of his Cause for beatification.

Through the years, Pierre's simple tombstone was partially effaced by the elements until only part of his name was still visible. In 1990, his remains were exhumed and positively identified by archaeologists, forensic scientists, and anthropologists. His remains were then placed in the old St. Patrick's Church.

Much of what is known of Pierre is due to the Schuyler family. A prominent Dutch family, the Schuylers knew Pierre well, and two of the Schuyler brothers were appointed as executors of Pierre's will. George Lee Schuyler has preserved Pierre's papers and letters.

Pope John Paul II bestowed the title Venerable on Pierre Toussaint in December 1996. This holy, charitable man now awaits beatification.

Servant of God Renato Masini
1901 – 1931
Doctor, Professor
Italy

Renato Masini was born in La Spezia, Italy, the fifth child of Decio and Oliva Masini. While he was still an infant, the family moved to Lucca. Renato studied medicine at the University of Pisa, and after graduation choose to join the staff of the university instead of a hospital.

Renato enrolled in Catholic Action, and for years was a promoter of the organization: he frequently lectured about the Blessed Mother's Immaculate Conception. He became a member of the Congregation Mariana in the parish of St. Maria Nera for which he also served as president. Also, he worked in the Catholic Society of the Holy Face and the Society of Pope Pius XI.

For a time, Renato considered becoming a priest. He began the study of philosophy and theology as well as the writings of St. Thomas Aquinas, but realized during his studies that he was not called to the ministry. Instead, he once again focused on an apostolate to the poor and sick.

He joined the Society of St. Frances of Paola as a layman in 1925, and helped found the St. Martino Cathedral parish of Lucca. At this time he also joined the Society of St. Vincent de Paul, and for four years served as its president, leaving in 1929 for reasons of health.

Renato Masini suffered atrociously until his death on May 5, 1931 at the age of thirty-one. Monsignor John Barsotti, a priest of the cathedral, was the first to promote the Cause of beatification, which was accepted in 1944.

Venerable Salvador Huerta Gutierrez
1880 – 1927
Mechanic, Explosives Technician, Father of Twelve
Mexico

Salvador came from an extraordinary family whose heroism and dedication to the church cost four of them their lives and earned them the glorious title of martyr. Salvador is the brother of Ezequiel Huerta Gutierrez and the uncle of Manuel and Jose Gonzalez, all of whom have had their Causes of beatification accepted by the Congregation for the Causes of the Saints. All gave their lives in defense of the church during the terrible persecution leveled at the Catholic citizens of Mexico from 1917 when a new constitution was accepted, but especially during the years of the martyrs, 1926-1929.

From childhood, Salvador was thoughtful, cheerful, and loving. He seems to have been a close companion to his brother Ezequiel, a gifted tenor and singer, and attended operas with him. When he finished his studies, he decided against a college education. He felt attracted to mechanical work, and accepted a position in a shop operated by Germans where he learned a great deal. After becoming proficient at his trade, he moved to Zacatecas and worked for a time as an explosives technician in the mines. He was a careful and responsible worker. Still, there were a few accidents, one of which almost cost him his life. Salvador always claimed afterward that his escape was a miracle and that God had apparently reserved another form of death for him.

Salvador moved to Aquascalientes and worked in a place where train locomotives were made and repaired. This position allowed him to make frequent visits to his family. On one of these visits, he met Adelina Jimenez, a girl of twelve and an orphan who lived with an uncle. Salvador waited a few years and then declared his intentions. Some difficulty arose because of the eight-year difference in their ages and the gloomy prediction that Salvador would not be able to provide for her in the style to which she had become accustomed. Salvador eventually won her heart and her hand. They had a loving relationship, and lived in a pious and contented situation. Eventually they became the parents of twelve children. Later they moved to Guadalajara to be closer to Salvador's parents. Soon Adelina began to experience liver problems, which grieved her loving husband.

Their children remember that Salvador was firm but very caring and always sacrificed himself for the benefit of the family. Since they never lacked for anything, they thought themselves to be rich. On Sundays, after attending Mass, they journeyed to Lake Chapala for family recreation. Salvador taught them piety more from his example than with his words. Frequent receptions of the sacraments of confession and Holy Communion, as well as visits to the church and various spiritual exercises were taught by his example. He was a dedicated member of the Nocturnal Adoration Society and always stopped by the Church of Calvary for a visit while on his way to work each day. At meals his usual blessing ended with this plea: "Divine Providence, I ask in each instant and moment that we may never lack a house, clothes, work or sustenance."

Salvador was now working in his own shop where he repaired cars with such success that he was called the "Magician of Cars." He was so highly respected for his work that his shop thrived to such an extent that eight workers were hired to help him. Salvador taught them mechanical skill as well as inspiring them to the things of God.

Salvador's brother, Ezequiel came to visit him on April 1, 1927, to discuss the horrible execution of their friend Anacleto Gonzales Flores who was the leader of the Cristero Movement, which fought against the Mexican government and its repressive laws against the church. The next day Salvador was at work when the secret police came and ordered him to fix a car at the headquarters of the police. Salvador suggested that they bring the car to his shop where he had all his tools. They refused, saying it was necessary for him to do as he was told. Without losing his composure and realizing the danger awaiting him, Salvador quietly assembled a bag of tools and began walking to his destiny.

While in the office of the police chief he was questioned about his two priest brothers, about the Cristero movement, and the hiding place of the archbishop. Since his only response was silence, he was tortured and then thrown in a damp prison cell with his brother Ezequiel. Agents searched his house and found incriminating objects such as rosaries, religious articles, and a revolver. On the butt of the gun were inscribed these words, "And the word was made flesh and lives among us," words used by the Cristeros.

That night the two brothers suffered from their injuries and the bitter cold. While it was still dark, two guards entered and ordered them to follow. The two arose and entered the cart to be taken to the cemetery of Mezquitan. When they were against the wall, Ezequiel turned to his brother and said, "We pardon them, right?" Then, while his beautiful voice rose in song to the glory to God, he was killed. Salvador then turned to his dead brother and said, "Brother, you are already a martyr." He then took hold of a candle and held it in front of his chest telling his executioners, "I put this light on my chest so you won't fail to hit my heart. I am ready to die for Christ," which he did.

Salvador and Ezequiel Guttierrez are awaiting beatification. The last action taken on Salvador's Cause was made when the Decree of Valor was accepted on May 21, 1999.

Martyrs of the Spanish Persecution
1936-1939

The persecution against the church in Spain is said to have been the most extensive religious persecution known to history since the time of the Roman Empire, a persecution greater than that of the French Revolution.

When the persecution ended, the number of martyrs exceeded 10,000. The exact number will never be known, but the estimate is 13 were bishops; 4,184 diocesan priests and seminarians; 2,365 men religious and 283 religious women; and 42 lay men and women. Pope John Paul II beatified 233 of these martyrs on March 11, 2001.

The trouble began when the Second Spanish Republic was proclaimed on April 14, 1931. Almost immediately anticlericalism began with fires started in churches in Madrid, Valencia, Malaga, and other cities. Since the government did not act to prevent such vandalism and did not attempt to bring the perpetrators to justice, it was accused of complicity. When sectarian laws increased day by day, the Jesuits were suppressed and expelled.

When the Popular Front was victorious in the first half of 1936 — a movement comprised of socialists, communists, and other radical groups — conditions became more grievous with more churches set on fire. Crosses and symbols of the church were destroyed, parish priests were driven away or imprisoned, and processions were forbidden among many other restrictions.

The persecution became more terrifying with greater violence on July 18, 1936. From then until April 1, 1939, Spain became the land of martyrs. These are from all sectors of the church since they include priests, religious, and laity who represent thirty-seven dioceses. Of the 233 who were beatified, the laypeople include: twenty-two women and twenty men who represent the then flourishing Spanish Catholic Action — people of all ages and professions who continued their apostolates in spite of threats and the fear of arrest and death.

Here then are brief biographies of the laymen martyred. All 233 martyrs of the Spanish Persecution are the first Blesseds of the third millenium.

Blessed Arturo Ros Montalt (1901-1936) was married and the father of six children. He was a jute worker who belonged to several Catholic associations. He was considered a gift to the people and had an intrepid apostolic spirit.

Blessed Carlos Diaz Gandia (Garcia) (1907-1936) was married and the father of an eight-month-old girl. He had a deep spirituality that was nourished by the Holy Eucharist.

Blessed Carlos Lopez Vidal (1894-1936) was married without children. He was the second sacristan of the Colegiata of Gandia and was martyred in the stone quarry of that city. He was dedicated to the Church and gave assistance to those in need. He never hid his religious fervor in the face of imprisonment and death.

Blessed Francis de Paula Castello y Aleu (1914-1936). His biography is given elsewhere in this volume, beginning on page 109.

Blessed Ismael Escrihuela Esteve (1902-1936) was married and the father of three children. He was an agriculturist by profession and belonged to a very religious family. He was very active as a member of Catholic Action and was dedicated to parish work.

Blessed Jose Maria Corbin Ferrer (1914-1936) was an unmarried college student. He is the youngest of the martyrs who inspired his companions to live virtuously with the testimony of his life. He was twenty-two when he died.

Blessed Jose Maria Zabal Blasco (1898-1936) was married and the father of three children. He was employed at the north station of Valencia. He was a man of deep faith who was engaged in the social apostolate with joy and an authentic Christian spirit.

Blessed Jose Medes Ferris (1885-1936) was married without children. He was martyred together with his three religious brothers. A farmer and an active member of many Catholic associations, he is regarded as an authentic social apostle who gave testimony of his faith.

Blessed Jose Perpina Nacher (1911-1936) was married and worked as a telegraph operator. He was also a lawyer who was charitable to the poor and practiced an intense apostolic activity.

Blessed Jose Ramon Ferragud Girbes (1887-1936) was married and the father of eight children. He was an agriculturist by trade and belonged to Catholic Action and to Nocturnal Adoration as well as other associations of the parish. He was a catechist and a founder of the Catholic Labor Union.

Blessed Juan Bautista Faubel (Cano) (1889-1936) was married and the father of three children. He worked in the field of pyrotechnics (fireworks). He was a man of deep faith and a daily communicant. He belonged to several associations, was charitable with the poor and sick and bravely defended the Church.

Blessed Juan Gonga Martinez (d. 1936) was unmarried and worked as a clerk in an office. He could not be a priest for reasons of health, and because of this, he lived as a secular giving testimony to the spiritual life. He was a dedicated worker in his parish.

Blessed Marino Blanes Giner (d. 1936) was married and the father of nine children. His biography is given elsewhere in this volume, beginning on page 228.

Blessed Manuel Torro Garcia (d. 1936) was married without children. He worked as a surveyor, lived an intensely Christian life in the apostolate, and never hid his other occupation as a Catholic medical instructor when there was intense danger. He was thirty-four at the time of his death.

Blessed Pablo Melendez Gonzalo (d. 1936) was a journalist and the lawyer for Valencia's archbishop. He was married and the father of ten children. He was assassinated together with his son **Alberto**. He served as president of the Catholic Action of Valencia and worked under the auspices of the archbishop in associations and movements. He was president of the lay organization Catholic Action and a founder of a Catholic political party.

Blessed Paschal Towers Lloret (d. 1936) was married and the father of four children. He worked in construction and was a great devotee of the Eucharist and the Virgin Mary. He dedicated himself to the social apostolate in various parochial associations.

Blessed Rafael Alonso Gutierrez (1890-1936) was married and the father of six children. He was an administrator of a post office and served as president of Catholic Action. He was found near death on the side of a road after being attacked by anarchists. When he was asked to identify his attackers, Rafael refused to name them and died soon afterward.

Blessed Salvador Damian Enguix Gares (1862-1936) was a widower with six children. He was a veterinarian by profession and belonged to several religious associations.

Blessed Vincente Galbis Girones (1910-1936) was a married lawyer and the father of a son. He was only twenty-six when he was martyred. From childhood, he was charitable, jovial and brave in the defense of the cause of God.

Toni Zweifel
1938 – 1989
Mechanical Engineer
Italy/Switzerland

Toni Zweifel was born in the historic city of Verona. His mother was Italian, and his father was a successful Swiss textile manufacturer. The family was financially secure. During the latter years of World War II (1943-44), Toni, his mother, and his sister Anna Rosa lived in Switzerland, returning at war's end. Toni attended primary, intermediate, and secondary schools in Verona, but moved to Zürich to study mechanical engineering at the Federal Technical Institute when he was nineteen. He studied there for five years.

A decisive point in the life of Toni Zweifel was his encounter with the organization known as Opus Dei. Toni was attracted to the atmosphere of the Fluntern Student Residence at the Federal Technical Institute, which was operated by members of Opus Dei, and he was permitted to move in before he finished his studies. When he realized that he could live a Christian vocation through his work, not in addition to or in spite of it, new horizons opened to Toni. He found Christ in everyday life, especially in his studies and in his professional work. Toni was convinced that he was called by God to this way of life and on March 19, 1962, he requested admission into Opus Dei. After his acceptance, Toni underwent a noticeable change. He became more cheerful; before, he had a rather serious demeanor. He was much more approachable, and his sense of humor shown through. Also, he became even less interested in material possessions, and he tried to avoid creating needs for himself other than those that were absolutely necessary. His spiritual life was growing ever deeper, and no matter how intense his work schedule, he always found time for prayer, for daily Mass, and for reading the Gospels and the classics of spiritual literature.

In July 1962, Toni began his first professional job with a firm in Zürich. Two years later, in 1964, Toni was performing scientific work at the Institute for Thermodynamics.

Always a devout Catholic, Toni discovered a closer relationship with God through his scientific and technical work. A dedicated, competent professional, he developed a number of patents that represented the cutting edge of technology for several decades, and he earned considerable respect and admiration from his colleagues.

In 1966 and for about six years thereafter, Toni served as the assistant director of the Fluntern Student Center. Additionally, he organized introductory courses for students entering the Technical Institute. In 1970, Toni was blessed to meet with St. Josemarie Escriva, the founder of Opus Dei, while both were attending a workshop in Rome.

After eight years of working for the Federal Technical Institute, Toni resigned a promising academic position to work entirely for the benefit of the underprivileged. He became the director of the newly founded Limmat Foundation whose efforts were directed at becoming a bridge between social developmental projects and financial supporters. From the beginning of the Limmat Foundation on March 13, 1972, and for the next seventeen years, until his death, Toni worked as the foundation's first director. Today, the Limmat Foundation supports hundreds of projects in more than thirty countries around the world.

Toni Zweifel

On February 19, 1986, forty-eight-year-old Toni was diagnosed with leukemia. He endured several weeks of chemotherapy, and for the next three years, Toni suffered through recurrences and repeated administrations of chemotherapy. Toni was a model patient. Understanding that he had almost no chance of surviving, he accepted the treatments and discomforts with composure and with the good humor of a person anchored in God. He realized he was given the opportunity to share in the cross of Christ, and he prepared himself for his eventual meeting with his God. He once pointed out to his visiting friends, "If leukemia was more painful than crucifixion, Jesus Christ would have died from leukemia." His friends and acquaintances always left his bedside enriched and strengthened in their faith and love of God.

During his last year of sickness, Toni prepared a successor to replace him as head of the Limmat Foundation. He left everything fully prepared so that others could begin where he had left off. Toni died on November 24, 1989. Strengthened with the sacraments of the Church, he eagerly anticipated his entrance into eternal life.

Toni was buried in Fluntern cemetery in Zürich. A postulator has been appointed and his Cause for canonization will soon be introduced.

Blessed Volodymyr Pryjma

1906 – 1941
Cantor, Martyr
Russia

In 1934, in the Ukraine, a government agency called the People's Commissriat of Internal Affairs (NKVD) began its dreadful work. The agency's mission: seek out Catholics, Russian nomads, Gypsies and other "undesirables" and incarcerate, exile, or eliminate them. The agency was under no obligation to obey standing civil laws and answered only to Joseph Stalin, the dictator who ordered mass arrests and murders through the NKVD.

Among the many Catholics martyred for their faith by this group was Volodymyr Pryjma, a Greek-Catholic Ukrainian who was born in the village of Stradch, Yavoriv District on July 17, 1906.

As a youth, Volodymyr was a pious young man whose main goal was to serve the Church. He possessed a fine singing voice, and in time became the cantor and choir director in the village church of Stradch. He also helped the priests of his parish in their secret ministries.

One day Volodymyr was traveling home with Father Nicholas Conrad, who had just come from hearing the confession of a poor sick woman who had requested the sacrament. Volodymyr and the priest were walking through the forest near their village when agents of the NKVD set upon them. They were taken to prison, where both Volodymyr and the priest were mercilessly tortured and murdered. In 1946, within five years of their deaths, the Communist government formally abolished the Greek Catholic Church.

The NKVD still exists. A recent statement found on the NKVD web site gives this dubious claim: "The People's Commissariat of Internal Affairs is responsible for ensuring peace, law, and order within the boundaries of the state. The People's Republic of the New Soviet Empire is a just and law-abiding society. Civil unrest and violent protest will not be tolerated!" Also added is this unsettling statement: "Under the jurisdiction of the NKVD you will find the KGB headquarters which is operated most efficiently. . . . If you have seen any suspicious activities report them to the chairman of the KGB immediately, it is most appreciated."

During a five-day visit to the Ukraine in June 2001, Pope John Paul II beatified twenty-eight Greek-Catholic Ukrainians in a ceremony witnessed by more than one million people. Among these martyrs was Volodymyr Pryjma, the only layman.

Appendix:
Occupations and
Difficulties of Life and Health

Agriculturist: Ismael Escrihuela Esteve, Jose Ramon Ferragud
   Girbes
Alcoholic: Matthew Talbot
Altar boy: Miguel Gomez Loza, Pier Giorgio Frassati
Ambassador: George La Pira
Amoebaean infection: Alphonsus Lambe
Architect: Aristide Leonori
Back problems: Manuel Lozano Garrido
Bank employee: Marino Blanes Giner
Bankrupt business: Antonio Petyx, Marino Blanes Giner
Basket seller: Ceferino Jimenez Malla
Blind: Manuel Lozano Garrido
Breathing difficulties: Matthew Talbot
Bronchitis: Marcel Callo
Cancer patient: Alphonsus Lambe, Carlos Manuel Rodriguez, Louis
   Necchi Villa
Cantor: Volodymyr Pryjma
Carmelite tertiary: Frank Duff
Catechist: Antonio Solari, Diban Ki-Zerbo, Attilio Giordani, Luis
   Padilla Gomez, Miguel Gomez Loza, Peter ToRot
Catholic Action: Albert Marvelli, Antonio Petyx, Attilio Giordani,
   David Roldan, Egidio Bullesi, George La Pira, Joseph Toniolo,

Joseph Lazzati, Manuel Morales, Mario Ferdinandi, Pablo Melendez Gonzalo, Pier Giorgio Frassati, Rafael Alonso Gutierrez, Renato Masini

Chemist: Francis de Paula Castello y Aleu

Choir director: Ezequiel Huerta Gutierrez

City Council member: Marino Blanes Giner, Albert Marvelli

Civil service employee: Frank Duff

Clerk in an office: Juan Gonga Martinez

Colitis: Carlos Manuel Rodriguez

College student: Jose Maria Corbin Ferrer

Construction worker: Paschal Towers Lloret

Convert: Diban Ki-Zerbo

Dancer: Alberto Capellan Zuazo

Dental problems: Marcel Callo

Digestive problems: Bartolo Longo

Dominican tertiary: Bartolo Longo, George La Pira, Pier Giorgio Frassati

Editor: Alcide De Gasperi, Joseph Lazzati, Nikolaus Gross

Engaged to marry: Marcel Callo

Engineer: Albert Marvelli, Aristide Leonori, George Ciesielski, Isidoro Zorzano, Jorge Vargas Gonzalez, Toni Zweifel

Eucharistic adoration promoter: Alberto Capellan Zuazo

Explosives technician: Juan Bautista Faubel (Cano), Salvador Huerta Gutierrez

Eye problems: Bartolo Longo, Ivan Merz

Eye surgeon: Ladislaus Batthyany-Strattmann

Fainting spells: Alphonsus Lambe

False accusations against: Aristide Leonori

Farmer: Alberto Capellan Zuazo, Franz Jägerstätter, Jose Medes Ferris

Forester: John Bradburne

Founders of lay organizations: Antonio Solari, Carlos Manuel Rodriguez, Filiberto Vrau, Frank Duff, Frederic Ozanam,

Giacomo Gaglione, Joseph Lazzati, Ladislaus Batthyany-Strattmann, Louis Necchi, Miguel Gomez Loza

Franciscan tertiaries: Aristide Leonori, Contardo Ferrini, Egidio Bullesi, George La Pira, John Bradburne, Luigi Beltrame Quattrocchi, Marino Blanes Giner, Matthew Talbot

Gypsy: Ceferino Jimenez Malla

Hair dresser: Pierre Toussaint

Headaches, severe: Marcel Callo

Heart disease: Matthew Talbot

Hodgkins disease: Isidoro Zorzano

Holy Face devotion promoter: Leo Dupont

Holy Name Society: Carlos Manuel Rodriguez

Horse trader: Ceferino Jimenez Malla

Hospital administrator: Artemides Zatti

Illegitimate: Franz Jägerstätter

Illegitimate (fathered child): Franz Jägerstätter, Ladislaus Batthyany-Strattmann

Infection, serious: Ivan Merz

Invalid: Luigi Rocchi

Inventor: George Ciesielski, Toni Zweifel

Journalist: Pablo Melendez Gonzalo

Judge: Mario Ferdinandi

Jute worker: Arturo Ros Montalt

Kidney problems: Matthew Talbot

Knights of Columbus member: Carlos Manuel Rodriguez

Laborer: Matthew Talbot

Lawyer: Bartolo Longo, Frederic Ozanam, George La Pira, Leo Dupont, Luigi Beltrame Quattrocchi, Mario Ferdinandi, Miguel Gomez Loza, Pablo Melendez Gonzalo, Vincente Galbis Girones

Legion of Mary member: Alphonsus Lambe, Frank Duff (founder)

Lepers, worked with: John Bradburne

Leukemia: Toni Zweifel

Malaria victim: John Bradburne

Martyrs: Anacleto Gonzalez Flores, Arturo Ros Montalt, Carlos Diaz
Gandia, Ceferino Jimenez Malla, David Roldan, Ezequiel Huerta
Gutierrez, Francis de Paula Castello y Aleu, Franz Jägerstätter,
Ismael Escrihuela Esteve, Jorge Vargas Gonzalez, Jose Maria Zabal
Blasco, Jose Ramon Ferragud Girbes, Juan Bautista Faubel (Cano),
Luis Magana Servin, Luis Padilla Gomez, Manuel Morales,
Marcel Callo, Marino Blanes Giner, Miguel Gomez Loza,
Nikolaus Gross, Pablo Melendez Gonzalo, Paschal Towers Lloret,
Peter ToRot, Rafael Alonso Gutierrez, Ramon Vargas Gonzalez,
Salvador Damian Enguix Gares, Salvador Huerta Gutierrez, Sal-
vador Lara, Vincente Galbis Girones, Volodymyr Pryjma

Mayor: George La Pira

Mechanic: Salvador Huerta Gutierrez

Medical doctors: Camillo Edward Feron, Edward Ortiz de
Landazuri, Joseph Moscati, Ladislaus Batthyany-Strattmann,
Louis Necchi Villa, Renato Masini

Medical instructor: Manuel Torro Garcia

Medical student: Ramon Vargas Gonzalez

Meningitis: Ivan Merz, Santos Franco Sanchez

Military member: Ladislaus Batthyany-Strattmann, Louis Necchi
Villa, Dino Zambra, Dominic Cesari, Francis de Paula Castello
y Aleu, Ivan Merz, John Bradburne (lieutenant), Joseph Lazzati,
Joseph Moscati, Mario Ferdinandi

Mine worker: David Roldan, Franz Jägerstätter, Nikolaus Gross

Mountaineer: Contardo Ferrini, Isidoro Zorzano, Pier Giorgio
Frassati

Muscular Dystrophy invalid: Luigi Rocchi

Musician: Carlos Manuel Rodriguez (piano), John Bradburne (various instruments), Pierre Toussaint (fiddle)

Neurosis sufferer: Louis Necchi Villa

Newspaper manager: Antonio Petyx

Nocturnal Adoration: Alberto Capellan Zuazo, Filiberto Vrau, Leo
Dupont, Luis Magana Servin, Marino Blanes Giner, Salvador
Huerta Gutierrez

Nurse: Artemides Zatti
Office worker: Alphonsus Lambe, Carlos Manuel Rodriguez
Opera performer: Ezequiel Huerta Gutierrez
Opus Dei member: Edward Ortiz de Landazuri, Isidoro Zorzano, Toni Zweifel
Paralyzed: Giacomo Gaglione
Pharmacist: Artemides Zatti
Piano player: Carlos Manuel Rodriguez
Poet: John Bradburne
Polio patient: Pier Giorgio Frassati
Pneumonia: Artemides Zatti
Politician: Alcide De Gasperi, Anacleto Gonzalez Flores, Joseph Lazzati
Post Office administrator: Rafael Alonso Gutierrez
Post Office employee: Dominic Cesari, Rafael Alonso Gutierrez
Prime minister: Alcide De Gasperi
Printer: Marcel Callo
Prisoners of war: Alcide De Gasperi, Anacleto Gonzalez Flores, Dominic Cesari, Joseph Lazzati, Miguel Gomez Loza
Professors: Camillo Edward Feron, Contardo Ferrini, Edward Ortiz de Landazuri, Frederic Ozanam, George Ciesielski, George La Pira, Ivan Merz, Joseph Moscati, Joseph Toniolo, Joseph Lazzati, Louis Necchi Villa, Renato Masini
Railroader: Attilio Giordani
Rosary promoter: Bartolo Longo, Matthew Talbot (Living Rosary)
Sacristan: Miguel Gomez Loza, Carlos Lopez Vidal
St. Vincent de Paul Society: Anacleto Gonzalez Flores, Antonio Petyx, Ceferino Jimenez Malla, Contardo Ferrini, Dino Zambra, Egidio Bullesi, Filiberto Vrau, Frank Duff, Frederic Ozanam, Ivan Merz, Leo Dupont, Marino Blanes Giner, Mario Ferdinandi, Pier Giorgio Frassati, Renato Masini
Sailor: Egidio Bullesi
Salesian cooperator: Albert Marvelli, Artemides Zatti
Scientist: Joseph Moscati

Secretary of State: George La Pira
Shepherd: Diban Ki-Zerbo
Ship designer: Egidio Bullesi
Singer: Ezequiel Huerta Gutierrez
Sinus problems: Ivan Merz
Slave, former: Diban Ki-Zerbo, Pierre Toussaint
Stepfather: Ceferino Jimenez Malla
Student: Dino Zambra, Pier Giorgio Frassati
Surgeon: Joseph Moscati
Surveyor: Manuel Torro Garcia
Tanner: Luis Magana Servin
Teacher: John Bradburne
Telegraph operator: Jose Perpina Nacher
Tobacco smoker: Matthew Talbot
Tortured excessively: Anacleto Gonzalez Flores
Tuberculosis patient: Egidio Bullesi
Ulcer patient: Alphonsus Lambe
Union official: Nikolaus Gross
United States visitors: Aristide Leonori, George La Pira
Vagabond: John Bradburne
Vatican II attendees: Frank Duff, Joseph Lazzati
Veterinarian: Salvador Damian Enguix Gares
Writer: Antonio Petyx, Carlos Manuel Rodriguez, Frederic
    Ozanam, Ivan Merz, Joseph Lazzati, Luis Padilla Gomez,
    Manuel Lozano Garrido, Nikolaus Gross

Sources

A Layman, A Man of Science, A Saint, Joseph Moscati, Professor of the University of Naples. Booklet, 1954.

Alcide De Gasperi. Papers.

A Puerto Rican Saint? Circulo Carlos M. Rodriguez, University Catholic Center. San Juan, Puerto Rico, 1995.

Accanto Alla Croce. Apostolato Della Riparazione. Bologna, Italy, 1962.

Attilio Giordani, Laico, Coniugato, Cooperatore Salesiano. Papers.

Bibliotheca Sanctorum. Citta' Nuova Editrice. Rome, Italy, 1987.

Borriello, L., E. Caruana, E., Del Genio, M.R., Suffi, N. *Dizionario Di Mistica.* Libreria Editrice Vaticana. Rome, Italy, no date.

Bradshaw, Robert. *Frank Duff, Founder of the Legion of Mary.* Montfort Publications. Bay Shore, New York, 1985.

Campesino Riojano Para Santo, Alberto Capellan Zuazo, 1984.

Clavey, Paul. *Pier Giorgio Frassati: From Dysfunction to Redemption.* Saints Corner, Article.

Congregatio de Causis Sanctorum, Ordinariatus Militaris Italiae, Betificationis et Canonizationis Servi Dei Salvii D'Acquisto. Positio Volume 1 Vita Documentata. Rome, Italy, *1996.*

Congregatio de Causis Sanctorum. Illerden. Canonizationis Servi Dei Francisci de Paola Castello et Aleu. Positio Super Martyrio. Rome, Italy, 1992.

Cruz, Joan Carroll. *Secular Saints*. Tan Books and Publishers. Rockford, Illinois, 1989.

Derum, James Patrick. *Apostle in a Top Hat, Frederick Ozanam*. Fidelity Publishing Company. St. Clair, Michigan, 1960.

De Giorgi, Salvatore. *Il Vangelo Dei Bambini*. Editrice. Rome, Italy, 1955.

Di Girolamo, S.J., Father Pasquale. *Blessed Pier Giorgio Frassati, From Prayer to the Apostolate*. Father Roger Arnsparger. Corbin, Kentucky, 1996.

Dolan, O.Carm., Albert H. *Matt Talbot, Alcoholic*. The Carmelite Press. Englewood, New Jersey, 1947.

Dove, S.J., Fr. John. *Strange Vagabond of God*. Poolbeg Press Limited. Dublin, Ireland, 1990.

Dr. Ingeniero Toni Zweifel. Vicepostulacion del Opus Dei en Suiza. Zurich, Switzerland, Boletin Informativo No. 1. 1996.

Duff, Frank. *Miracles on Tap*. Montfort Publications. Bay Shore, New York, 1961.

Elorz, Jose Miguel Pero-Sanz. *Isidoro Zorzano*. Ediciones Palabra. Madrid. Spain, 1994.

Favrais, Robert and Royer, Eugene. *Marcel Callo, jociste et martyr*. Actualites Notre Temps, 1987.

Firtel, Hilde. *Alfie Lambe, Legion Envoy*. The Mercier Press. Cork, Ireland, 1967.

Giuseppe Lazzati. Booklet.

Hanley, O.F.M., Boniface. *Ten Christians*. Ave Maria Press. Notre Dame, Indiana, 1975.

—. *Frank Duff, One of the Best*. Legion of Mary De Montfort House. Dublin, Ireland, no date.

Isidoro Zorzano, Servant of God. Office of Vice Postulation of Opus Dei in the United States. New York, New York.

Isidoro Zorzano, The Servant of God. Informative Bulletin #2. Office of Vice Postulation of Opus Dei in the Philippines. New Manila, Quezon City, The Philippines. August, 1997.

Jerzy (George) Ciesielski. Paper.

Sources

Joseph Moscati, Professor of the University of Naples, A lay-man, A man of science, A saint. Booklet, 1954.

Kennedy, Finola. *John Henry Newman and Frank Duff.* Praedicanda Publications. Dublin, Ireland, 1982.

L'Areco, Adolfo. *Costruttore Della Citta' Di Dio.* Editrice SDB. Rome, Italy, 1979.

Luigi Rocchi, Un Santo in Carrozzella. Comitato Promotore della Causa di Beatificazione. Tolentino, Italy, 1991.

Miglioranza, Franciscano Conventual, Fray Contardo. *Don Antonio Solari.* Padres Redentoristas. Buenos Aires, Argentina. 1995.

O'Flynn, C.M., Thomas. *Frank Duff as I knew Him.* Praedicanda Publications. Dublin, Ireland, 1981.

Padre Gesuiti. *St. Joseph Moscati, The holy doctor of Naples.* Chiesa Del Gesu Nuovo. Naples, Italy, no date.

Peter ToRot Catechist and Martyr. Archdiocese of Rabaul. Vunapope, ENBP, Papua New Guinea, 1993.

Purcell, Mary. *Matt Talbot and His Times.* Franciscan Herald Press. Chicago, Illinois, 1976.

Revert, Ramon Fita. *Marino Blanes Giner, Casado Empleado de Banca.* Publica la Delegacion Diocesana Para Las Causas De Los Santos de La Archidiocesis de Valencia. Valencia, Spain, 1999.

Rodrigo, OAR, Romualdo. *Gypsy Saint, Ceferino Jimenez Malla.* Comitato Internazionale per la Canonizzazione del Servo di Dio Ceferino Jimenez Malla. Rome, Italy, 1997.

Royal, Robert, *New Spanish Martyrs.* National Catholic Register. New Haven, Connecticut. April 16-22, 2000.

Saint Joseph Moscati, The Holy Doctor of Naples. Padri Gesuiti, Chiesa del Gesu Nuovo. Naples, Italy. no date.

Sanchez, Adolfo Olivera. *Rotos los Huesos, entera el alma. Pilina Cimadevilla, La sierva de Dios de diez anos.* Sociedad de Educacion Atenas. Madrid, Spain. no date.

Sanchez, Juan Antonio Narvaez. *El Doctor Ortiz De Landazuri.* Ediciones Palabra S.A. Madrid, Spain, 1997.

Sbriscia, S., Vannini, F., Bertelli, V.G., Moretti, R., Carriguiry, G., Calabrese, G., Giusti, S., Ciccone, L. *Il Vangelo Dei Bambini*. Editrice Ave. Rome, Italy, 1995.

Scallan, Dorothy, edited by Fr. Emeric B. Scallan, S.T.B., *The Holy Man of Tours*. TAN Books and Publishers, Inc. Rockford, Illinois, 1990.

Servant of God Giuseppe Lazzati. papers.

Tarry, Ellen. *Pierre Toussaint, Apostle of Old New York*. Pauline Books & Media. Boston, Massachusetts, 1991.

Toni Zweifel, Professional Work as a Christian Vocation. Vice-Postulation of the Prelature of Opus Dei in Switzerland. Zurich, Switzerland, August 1997.

Toni Zweifel, Una Vida Profesional al Servicio de Dios y de los Hombres. Ediciones Palabra. Madrid, Spain, 1997.

Una Vida Llena De Dios, Siervo De Dios Antonio Solari.

Un Santo in Carrozzella, Lettere del Servo di DioLuigi Rocchi. Comitato per la Causa di Beatificazione di Luigi Rocchi. Tolentino, Italy. 1995.

Zahn, Gordon. *In Solitary Witness: The Life and Death of Franz Jagerstatter*. Templegate Publishers. Springfield, Illinois.1964.

Index of Holy Men

Nikolaus Gross, Blessed, 247-249, 288, 290, 292
Ortiz de Landazuri, Servant of God Edward (see Edward Ortiz de Landazuri, Servant of God)
Ozanam, Blessed Frederic (see Frederic Ozanam, Blessed)
Pablo Melendez Gonzalo, Blessed, 280, 288-290
Padilla Gomez, Venerable Luis (see Luis Padilla Gomez, Venerable)
Paschal Towers Lloret, Blessed, 280, 288, 290
Perpina Nacher, Blessed Jose (see Jose Perpina Nacher, Blessed)
Peter ToRot, Venerable, 250-256, 287, 290
Petyx, Servant of God Antonio (see Antonio Petyx, Servant of God)
Pier Giorgio Frassati, Blessed, 233, 257-264, 287-288, 290-292
Pierre Toussaint, Venerable, 13, 265-272, 289-290, 292
Pryjma, Blessed Volodymyr (see Volodymyr Pryjma, Blessed)
Rafael Alonso Gutierrez, Blessed, 280, 288, 290-291
Ramon Vargas Gonzalez, Venerable, 170-172, 290
Renato Masini, Servant of God, 273, 288, 290-292
Rocchi, Servant of God Luigi (see Luigi Rocchi, Servant of God)
Rodriguez, Blessed Carlos Manuel (see Carlos Manuel Rodriguez, Blessed)
Roldan, Saint David (see David Roldan, Saint)
Ros Montalt, Blessed Arturo (see Arturo Ros Montalt, Blessed)
Salvador Damian Enguix Gares, Blessed, 280, 290, 292
Salvador Huerta Gutierrez, Venerable, 274-276, 288, 290-291
Salvador Lara, Saint 86-88, 220-222
Solari, Servant of God Antonio (see Antonio Solari, Servant of God)
Spanish Persecution, Martyrs of (see Martyrs of the Spanish Persecution)
Talbot, Venerable Matthew (see Matthew Talbot, Venerable)
Toni Zweifel, 281-283, 288-289, 291
Toniolo, Venerable Joseph (see Joseph Toniolo, Venerable)
ToRot, Venerable Peter (see Peter ToRot, Venerable)
Torro Garcia, Blessed Manuel (see Manuel Torro Garcia, Blessed)

OUR SUNDAY VISITOR
Your Source for Discovering the Riches of the Catholic Faith

Our Sunday Visitor has an extensive line of materials for young children, teens, and adults. Our books, Bibles, booklets, CD-ROMs, audios, and videos are available in bookstores worldwide.

To receive a FREE full-line catalog or for more information, call **Our Sunday Visitor** at **1-800-348-2440**. Or write, **Our Sunday Visitor** / 200 Noll Plaza / Huntington, IN 46750.

- -

Please send me: __A catalog
Please send me materials on:
__Apologetics and catechetics   __Reference works
__Prayer books   __Heritage and the saints
__The family   __The parish
Name_____
Address_____Apt._____
City_____State_____Zip_____
Telephone (   ) _____

A33BBABP

- -

Please send a friend: __A catalog
Please send a friend materials on:
__Apologetics and catechetics   __Reference works
__Prayer books   __Heritage and the saints
__The family   __The parish
Name_____
Address_____Apt._____
City_____State_____Zip_____
Telephone (   ) _____

A33BBABP

- -

OurSundayVisitor

200 Noll Plaza
Huntington, IN 46750
Toll free: **1-800-348-2440**
E-mail: osvbooks@osv.com
Website: www.osv.com